FRONTIER WAYS

Sketches of Life in the Old West

FRONTIER WAYS

Sketches of Life in the Old West

By Edward Everett Dale

Illustrations by Malcolm Thurgood

University of Texas Press · Austin

International Standard Book Number 0-292-72462-4
Library of Congress Catalog Card Number 59-9423
Copyright © 1959 by Edward Everett Dale
All rights reserved
Printed in the United States of America

First Paperback Printing, 1989

Requests for permission to reproduce material from this work
should be sent to Permissions, University of Texas Press,
Box 7819, Austin, Texas 78713-7819.

♾ The paper used in this publication meets the minimum
requirements of American National Standard for Information
Sciences—Permanence of Paper for Printed Library Materials,
ANSI Z39.48-1984.

To the memory of

FREDERICK JACKSON TURNER

my old friend and teacher

———

He brought me into pastures fresh and green
By waters still he led me by the hand,
And things, which I in youth had often seen
As meaningless, he made me understand.

———

Preface

WITH THE EXCEPTION of chapter eleven this book is made up of articles by the author selected from a much larger number which have appeared in various historical publications during a long period of years. Since comparatively few libraries have complete files of the journals or magazines in which they were originally published, they are in a sense buried and lost to most readers. It has therefore seemed worth while to assemble them in a single volume. While each essay is complete in itself all have a common theme which is the life of the pioneer settlers of the American West.

It is obvious that the book as a whole has been affected by the fact that each chapter was first written as an independent essay. This has meant that some repetitions have had to be eliminated, and other minor revisions made. It is hoped that the Foreword, the extracts from the author's unpublished verses, and the paragraphs introducing each chapter may serve as "connective tissue" to bind the chapters together in such fashion as to give a unified picture of pioneer life.

Some of the original articles were fully documented while others had few or no citations. For the sake of uniformity it has seemed best to omit all documentation. No bibliography is appended since any fairly comprehensive one would have to include many hundreds of titles and even then would be very incomplete.

The sources of information for the book as a whole are old letters, diaries, frontier newspapers, almanacs, pamphlets, books, and the oral testimony of living witnesses. In addition much has been obtained from the 132 typescript volumes called the *Indian-Pioneer Papers* to be found in the library of the University of Oklahoma. These consist of reminiscences of the early settlers of Oklahoma.

It must be confessed, however, that the author has leaned

heavily upon his own memories of observations and experiences during over a quarter of a century spent on the American frontier. These include memories of his boyhood life in a log cabin in the Texas Cross Timbers and in dugouts and sod houses on the western prairies of Oklahoma. Later he has been privileged to visit the most remote areas of all our western states and to spend much time among the people of the Ozark and Appalachian mountains where there still persist many features of a pattern of life which in most parts of America has long since vanished.

To the editors of the various journals in which the articles originally appeared the author wishes to express his sincere thanks and deep appreciation for permission to republish them in book form. These publications and the chapters taken from each are as follows: *West Texas Historical Association Year Book,* Chapter 1; *American Hereford Journal,* Chapter 2; *Nebraska History,* Chapters 3, 5, 7, and 9; *Journal of the Illinois State Historical Society,* Chapters 4 and 6; *Indiana Magazine of History,* Chapter 10; *Mississippi Valley Historical Review,* Chapter 8; *The Chronicles of Oklahoma,* Chapter 12.

My indebtedness to my former secretaries who typed these articles is gratefully acknowledged. Above all to my secretary, David L. Smith, who typed the entire manuscript, and to my wife, Rosalie, who assisted in its revision and has constantly given encouragement and help, I am deeply grateful.

Edward Everett Dale

Houston, Texas
May 10, 1959

Contents

x

Foreword

In 1893 when Frederick Jackson Turner first published his essay on "The Significance of the Frontier," he could hardly have realized the far-reaching influence it was to have on the teaching and writing of American history. For over thirty years after its publication Turner continued to teach at the University of Wisconsin and at Harvard. During these years he wrote a number of other essays on the same general theme, calling attention to the fact that the West furnished a fruitful field for study and research.

His former students quickly accepted the challenge thus offered to them and spread the ideas of Turner throughout the entire nation. As a result, most textbooks in American history written since that time have devoted considerable attention to the westward movement of our people and almost every important university in the United States now offers courses in Western history.

Within comparatively recent years a number of American historians have sharply criticized the writing and teaching of Turner and have advanced arguments, often "generating more heat than light," in an effort to prove that his entire viewpoint was wrong and many of his statements and conclusions wholly unjustified.

The author, who is a former student of Turner, has no intention of entering into any controversy with the critics of the so-called "Turner thesis." He does wish to point out, however, that even the most bitter of these will agree that for some two and a half centuries large numbers of American people did remove west to settle and develop unoccupied lands on the frontier. It must also be admitted that their new environment differed radically from that which they had known in the past. While this was true of the settlers on every frontier, it was especially so for those who left the wooded areas to establish new homes on the western prairies.

Obviously, these people brought with them not only their tools and household goods but much "intellectual baggage" acquired in the old homeland. Some of it doubtless included certain skills which, however valuable they may have formerly been, were useless in this different environment. On a prairie homestead the man adept in felling trees, splitting rails, and building a log house or stone chimney seldom had any opportunity to utilize such knowledge. If he had been foolish enough to bring with him his cross-cut saw, maul, wedges, and trowel he soon realized that they had been only ballast for his prairie schooner! Here he must learn to dig a dugout, construct a sod house, and build straw-covered sheds.

Skill in certain types of labor was only a small part of the intangible luggage brought to the West by the prairie settler. As a whole it embraced his entire cultural heritage to a greater or lesser degree, having some of its roots in Europe. It included manners, customs, and traditions with respect to food, speech, clothing, social behavior, recreation, cultural activities, and such institutions as the home, church, school, and local government. Above all it included habits of thought, mental attributes, traits, and characteristics.

Just as the prairie pioneer soon found that his knowledge of how to do certain tasks had become useless and that he must learn new techniques to meet new needs, so did he quickly discover that much of the whole pattern of his former life must be modified or entirely changed. Adjustments to a vitally different environment altered nearly every phase of his earlier way of life. New words and expressions crept into his speech, and new foods appeared on his table. His type of home, social life, recreation, medical practices, the church, school, and local government all differed from those to which he had been accustomed.

Such violent changes of lifeways could hardly fail to affect the man's mental processes; his manner of thought, ideas and ideals. These effects became more pronounced as the years went by and memories of life in his earlier home faded. Yet he worked hard to bring in more settlers and establish a stable society not too unlike that of the region of his birth. Long before this came, however, he was a different man. Years of pioneer life had made him so.

Moreover, his children born in the dugout or sod house grew to manhood or womanhood without knowing any other type of society than that of the prairie pioneers. As a result, the new traditions, customs, and characteristics acquired by the father were inherited by his offspring. This inheritance was a "state of mind" which persisted long after the conditions which produced it had passed away. Even today manifestations of this frontier heritage are readily discernible. A man born and reared on the West Texas plains may remove to an eastern city but he always carries with him a little of the West Texas plains in his heart.

Although the American Frontier has disappeared and its days and ways are only a memory, its flaming spirit still lives on. This is only too apparent to everyone who reaches for a magazine on the rack of a newsstand, attends a picture show, or watches television. Unfortunately perhaps, the writers of fiction and movie or television scripts feature almost entirely those vanguards of the frontier who preceded the actual settlers.

These included the explorers, hunters, trappers, Indian traders, gold seekers, buffalo hunters, ranchmen, and some others. None of them had any interest in the land itself but only in exploiting its natural resources of game, furs, precious metals, or native pasturage. Their operations also brought to the Far West such other picturesque characters as the stage drivers, railroad builders, bad men and women drawn by the lure of easy money, and the gunmen on the side of the law who sought to curb the activities of the thieves and outlaws.

With the exception of the ranchmen, and their cowboys, none of those engaged in any of the above vocations had any appreciable effect upon the lives and work of pioneer settlers who came west in covered wagons seeking for land upon which to establish homes. The ranchmen, themselves engaged in a pastoral form of husbandry, did have considerable influence, however, upon the society of the homeseekers who came to displace them. In consequence, two chapters on ranch life are included in this volume.

With the exception of these two chapters the entire volume is devoted to various aspects of the life of the pioneers who came to the West seeking for that most precious of all human material possessions, a home. Largely speaking, this home seeker is the forgotten man in the annals of the American West. The cowboy gallops madly across the screens of thousands of picture shows and millions of television sets. Many hundreds of books dealing with him, and such other colorful frontier characters as the trappers, miners, and western gunmen, have been published, but to the more prosaic life of the pioneer farmer very little attention has been given. Yet he was by far the most important factor in the conquest and development of our American empire.

His way of life has vanished and is largely forgotten by all but a comparatively few people. It is, however, a part of our social history and as such should be preserved and cherished. It was the pioneer settlers who won the West when the wooing was difficult and sometimes dangerous, and most of them now sleep in its soil. It is hoped that this book, written by one who was a pioneer on both the forest and prairie frontiers, may be of value and interest to a wide range of readers in its depiction of a pattern of life now gone forever.

FRONTIER WAYS

Sketches of Life in the Old West

I

I'm sitting tonight in my study
In the firelight's mellow glow
Checking in memory's tally book
The men that I used to know.
Men who boot to boot with me
Rode from the early dawn
Till the pale twilight gave place to night
In days that are long since gone.

I'm checking the names of Shorty,
Slim and Lucky and Joe
And Red who went with the Circle H
To ride in New Mexico.
Buck who was always quick with a gun
I guess is in prison still,
And Jim who wasn't quick enough
Is sleeping on old Boot Hill.

Scattered and gone are my comrades
Of days so long ago
Who never flinched or turned their backs
On any friend or foe.
Gone with the West that I knew and loved
For which I shall always yearn.
I wish this fireplace didn't smoke
And make my eyelids burn!

The Old Cowhand

I

The Romance of the Range

OF ALL THE SONS of that great mother of men, the American West, the cowboy has most nearly caught the fancy of our people. Writers of fiction and movie or television scripts have given, however, a false picture of the cowhand and his life. Ranching was a huge productive industry which vitally affected the economic life of the nation. Moreover, the men engaged in it greatly influenced the lives of the prairie settlers who came to displace them. For this reason the author, who rode the range for six or seven years, feels that this chapter should be included in a book dealing with the life of those people who journeyed west to establish homes on the frontier.

THE BUSINESS OF HERDING or livestock raising is one of the most ancient and honorable of all industries. The Bible is filled with allusions to pastoral life, and the strife of Cain and Abel has been characterized as the first example of warfare between range and grange.

Not only is herding one of the earliest pursuits of mankind, but there has ever clustered about the business and those engaged in it something of the glamour of romance, of daring deeds and high adventure. Badger Clark in his poem "From Town" has expressed this in picturesque fashion when he says:

> Since the days when Lot and Abram
> Split the Jordan range in halves
> Just to fix it so their punchers wouldn't fight.
> Since old Jacob skinned his dad-in-law of
>   six year's crop of calves

Then hit the trail for Canaan in the night,
There has been a taste for battle
'Mongst the men who follow cattle
And a love of doing things that's wild and strange,
And the warmth of Laban's words
When he missed his speckled herds
Still is useful in the language of the range.

Since that time many rival ranchmen have "split a range in
halves" to keep down strife among their punchers; more than
one enterprising young man has "skinned his dad-in-law" of a
liberal share of various crops of calves. The taste for battle has
manifested itself in many places, resulting in "wild and strange
doings," while not a few men who have missed a portion of their
"speckled herds" have resorted to language even more forceful
and picturesque than was included in the vocabulary of the
ancient Laban.

Men engaged in pastoral pursuits seem, moreover, to be peculiarly favored by Divine Providence. Mohammed was a herder
and a camel driver before he became the founder of the religion
of Islam. To a band of herdsmen of northern Spain appeared the
mighty light which led them to the body of St. James the Elder,
and caused the founding of the shrine of Santiago de Compo-
stela, while to shepherds watching their flocks by night came
the Angel of the Lord bringing "good tidings of great joy."

It is not in the Old World alone, however, that the herding
industry has been crowned by a halo of romance. The business
in America has not been lacking in that respect and the rise and
fall of the range-cattle industry on the western plains constitutes
one of the most remarkable epochs in all American history.

Ranching has existed in the United States as a frontier pursuit since very early times. Almost the first English settlers along
the Atlantic seaboard brought cattle with them, and as the better lands along the coast were taken up and planted to crops,
men owning a considerable number of animals removed farther
west in order to find pasture for their herds on the unoccupied
lands of the wilderness. Thus once agricultural settlement was

well started in its westward march across the continent, there was to be found along its outer edge a comparatively narrow rim or border of pastoral life. For a century and more it was there, slowly advancing as the area of cultivated lands advanced, a kind of twilight zone with the light of civilization behind it and the darkness of savagery before. The ranchmen could not push too far out into the wilderness because of the fierce tribes of Indians that inhabited it. On the other hand they could not linger too long on their original ranges or they would find themselves crowded and hemmed in by the men who depended upon cultivated crops for a livelihood. The American people had become "that great land animal." They pushed eagerly westward, occupied lands formerly devoted to grazing, cleared fields and planted crops, thus forcing the livestock growers again and again to move on to "new pastures."

Strange as this century-long westward march of an industry may appear, the final phase is even more startling and has no parallel in the economic history of any other nation in the world. Soon after the Civil War this comparatively narrow belt of grazing, hitherto fairly constant as to width and area, suddenly shot out into the wilderness and spread with amazing rapidity until it covered a region larger than all that part of the United States devoted to crop raising. This region became the so-called "cow country," where ranching was carried on for several years upon a scale vastly greater than ever before until the homesteaders, advancing slowly but steadily westward, had at last invaded nearly every portion of it and taken over all of the lands suitable for cultivation.

A number of factors influenced this sudden rise of the "cow country." The close of the Civil War released from the armies many young men who came west in search of adventure and fortune. Over the western plains roamed countless herds of buffalo, a potential source of food, clothing, and shelter for the fierce Indian tribes that occupied that region. Buffalo hunting became at once a popular and profitable pursuit. Within two decades the great herds had been exterminated, and the In-

dians, finding their food supply cut off, moved more or less willingly to reservations set aside for them where they lived to a
great extent dependent upon the bounty of the federal government. The plains were thus left open to occupation by herds of
the cattlemen and the latter were not slow to take advantage of
the opportunity presented to them.

Even so, ranching could not have spread so rapidly had there
not existed a great reservoir from which animals might be drawn
to stock these western plains. That reservoir was the great state
of Texas. Even from earliest times everything in Texas seemed to
promote livestock raising. Range, climate, and the land system
were all distinctly favorable to grazing. The early Spanish settlers brought with them cattle of the lean, long-horned type
that the Moors had raised on the plains of Andalusia for a thousand years. These increased rapidly and American settlers coming into Texas brought with them cattle of the North European
breeds. These, crossed with the original Spanish type, produced
animals that were larger and heavier than the Spanish cattle,
and yet with the endurance and ability to take care of themselves, so necessary on the open range.

Spain, and later the Republic of Mexico, gave out large grants
of land to individuals and later the Republic of Texas continued
this liberal land policy. Also when Texas was admitted as a state,
it retained possession of its own unoccupied lands, and these
the state sold in large tracts and with liberal terms of payment.
Thus at the outbreak of the Civil War Texas was, largely speaking, a region of great landed proprietors, nearly all of whom
owned herds of cattle.

The war came and the Texans, "ever eager for a fight or a
frolic" and sometimes willing to regard the fight *as* a frolic, hurried away to join the armies of the Confederacy. For four years
they fought bravely for the Lost Cause, proving their mettle
upon many a bloody field. During all this time Texas was less
touched than any other state of the Confederacy by the ravages
of war. While Virginia was devastated by the armies of both
sides; while Sherman's army ate a hole fifty miles wide across
Georgia; and while the fields of Mississippi and Alabama lay

fallow or grew up in bushes and briers for want of laborers to till them, the cattle on the broad plains of Texas grew fat and sleek and increased rapidly under the favorable conditions of range and climate. The result was that when the war closed and the Texans returned to their homes, they found their ranges fairly overflowing with fine, fat cattle for which there was no market, though cattle and beef were selling at high prices in the North. Stock cattle could be bought on the Texas prairies in 1866 at from one to three dollars a head, and fat beeves sold at from five to six or seven dollars. Even in 1867 three-year-old steers were quoted as having an average value of $86.00 in Massachusetts, $68.57 in New York, $70.58 in New Jersey, $40.19 in Illinois, $38.40 in Kansas, $46.32 in Nebraska, and $9.46 in Texas.

Out of this condition grew the so-called "northern drive." The Texas soldiers from the Confederate armies mostly reached home in the summer of 1865, too late to attempt to drive their cattle to market that year. In the spring of 1866, however, large herds were collected preparatory to starting north as soon as spring was sufficiently advanced to make the venture practicable. Most of these herds belonged to Texas ranchmen who were themselves driving them to market, though in some cases Northern men came to Texas and purchased herds to drive up the trail.

The start was usually made late in March or early in April. The usual route followed by these earliest drovers was north from central Texas, passing just west of Fort Worth, and on past Denton and Sherman to Red River. Beyond that stream the line of travel was north across the Indian Territory past Boggy Depot, thence northeast past Fort Gibson to the Kansas line near Baxter Springs.

Just how many cattle were started north from Texas in the spring and summer of 1866 is uncertain, but estimates made a few years later place the number at 260,000 head. The drive proved on the whole disastrous in the extreme. Immune as the Texans were to privation and hardship and accustomed as they were to handling cattle, few had at this time much experience

in driving herds for long distances on the trail. Accounts left
by some of these early drovers are little better than one long
wail of trouble and misery. Rain, mud, swollen rivers, stampedes,
hunger, and dissatisfied men are but a few of the difficulties
of which they complained before Red River was reached. Beyond that stream there was added to all these miseries endless
annoyance from Indians, who demanded payment for grass consumed by the cattle, stampeded herds at night in order to collect
money for helping gather them again, and in other ways proved
themselves a constant source of worry and vexation. The war
had but recently closed and conditions along the border and in
the Indian Territory were lawless and unsettled. White thieves
and outlaws, together with pilfering Indians, stole horses, mules,
and cattle and made it necessary to be watchful at all times.

When the drovers reached the Kansas or Missouri line, they
found themselves confronted by fresh difficulties. The settlers
along the border of these states had suffered losses from Texas
fever when some small herds had been driven up from the south
just before the war, and were determined not to risk a repetition
of such loss. Armed bands of farmers met the drovers at the
border and warned them that they would not be permitted to
proceed, at least until cold weather had come to lessen the
danger.

The question was complicated by the mysterious and subtle
nature of the disease, Texas fever, which the Northerners professed to fear. We know now that it is a malady to which Southern cattle are immune but which they carry to Northern cattle
by means of the fever ticks which drop from their bodies and
attach themselves to other animals. The Texans asserted that
their cattle were perfectly healthy and that it was absurd to
think that they could bring disease to others. The Kansans declared that, absurd or not, when Texas cattle came near their own
animals the latter sickened and died, though they were forced to
admit they did not understand why.

Yet numerous theories were evolved. It was declared that a
shrub of Texas wounded the feet of the animals and made sores
from which pus exuded to poison the grass. Others asserted that

the breath of Texas cattle upon the grass brought disease to other animals, a kind of bovine halitosis which no scruples of delicacy prevented the Kansans mentioning in no uncertain terms. Some felt that cattle ticks might be responsible, but most people ridiculed such a theory.

The Northerners did not, however, concern themselves much with theories. It was enough that their cattle had died in the past and might die in the future. They were fixed in their determination to take no chances.

There were conflicts in some cases—sharp conflicts in which the Texans, far from home and the support of their friends and kindred, were foredoomed to failure. Drovers were assaulted and beaten, some were killed and in a few cases small herds of animals were shot down and killed to the last animal. Some turned back into the Indian Territory and moved westward until far beyond all agricultural settlements, then turned north and continued until opposite their destination in Iowa or St. Joseph. Some of these succeeded in some measure, but the long drive and heavy losses seldom left them with enough animals to make the venture profitable. Of the 260,000 head of cattle driven north in the summer of 1866 very few reached a profitable market.

The Texas ranchmen were almost in despair, but the following year was to see a solution of their problem. At this time the Kansas Pacific Railway was building west up the valley of the Kaw and had reached the town of Salina. In the spring of 1867 Joseph G. McCoy, a prominent and wealthy cattle feeder of Illinois, came to Kansas City and, journeying westward on this railway to Abilene in Dickinson County, decided to establish there a great cattle depot and shipping point.

Abilene was far west of all agricultural settlements. Here McCoy built a hotel and large shipping pens. He made with the railway a contract by which he was to have a share of the freight receipts from Texas cattle shipped to Kansas City and then sent a rider south to seek out herds on the trail and tell the owners to bring them to Abilene. From Abilene they might be shipped to Kansas City, and thence to Chicago or any other market that seemed desirable.

The advantages of this plan of reaching market were soon apparent. The route followed was far to the west of the old trail to Baxter Springs, and so avoided the wooded and mountainous areas of eastern Oklahoma as well as most of the Indians, and above all the hostile agricultural population of eastern Kansas. Late in the season as the project was started, 35,000 head of cattle were shipped from Abilene in 1867, while the following year, or 1868, 75,000 head were brought up the trail. By 1869 the number had risen to 350,000 and in 1871 the best estimates indicate that no less than 600,000 head were driven from Texas to the cow towns of Kansas.

Abilene was only temporarily the great Texas shipping point. As the settlers began to come in to take homesteads near it, the cattle trade shifted farther west. New railroads were building and new cow towns sprang up. Among these were Newton, Ellsworth, Wichita, Caldwell, and especially Dodge City. Ogallala, Nebraska, on the Union Pacific also became an important shipping point.

Most important of all the cow towns was Dodge City, which for ten years was the greatest cattle market in the world. To it flocked the gamblers, saloon keepers, and lawless riffraff of the underworld to meet and prey upon the Texas cowboys who arrived with their summer's wages in their pockets and a thirst accumulated during the months of toil on the hot and dusty trail.

Dodge City's first jail was a well fifteen feet deep, into which drunks were lowered and left until sober and ready to leave town. Two graveyards were early established, "Boot Hill" on one side of town where were buried those men who died with their boots on, and another cemetery on the opposite side for those who died peacefully in bed. The latter cemetery remained small, but "Boot Hill" soon came to have a large and constantly growing population.

The first trail drivers who took herds from Texas to the cow towns of Kansas, or the northern Indian agencies to fill beef contracts, frequently knew little of the region to be traversed and had little to guide them. Yet no trail boss ever turned back. He merely set his wagon each night with the tongue pointing to the

North Star and the next morning pushed on with a grim determination to make his ten or fifteen miles that day. In a real sense he "hitched his wagon to a star" and did not shrink from difficulties and dangers.

In time, however, certain well-defined trails were established. Prominent among these was the Western Trail crossing Red River at Doan's Store and extending north past Fort Supply to Dodge City. East of this was the famous Chisholm Trail, following roughly the line of the present Rock Island Railway across Oklahoma. Still farther east was the West Shawnee Trail and beyond that the East Shawnee Trail that crossed into Kansas near Baxter Springs.

During the two decades following the Civil War a vast stream of Texas cattle poured northward over these trails. The drive to the Kansas cow towns, moreover, frequently became but the first half of a drive from Texas to ranges on the Northern plains. The possibilities of that region for ranching became apparent to many men very soon after the close of the war. Some men with small herds established themselves along the line of the newly constructed Union Pacific Railway. Others living near the overland trail established small herds through the purchase of lame and footsore cattle from emigrants. The development of mining camps in the Rocky Mountains brought in men with cattle to furnish beef to the miners, while the government made contracts with cattlemen to supply beef to the Indians on northern reservations, and large herds were driven up the trail for that purpose. As the buffalo disappeared from the plains, however, leaving large areas of attractive pasture lands without animals to consume the grass, many men began to establish ranches in various parts of Wyoming, Colorado, Dakota, and Montana, and these frequently purchased herds in the Kansas cow towns to stock their new ranges. The cattle industry was spreading with marvelous rapidity. It was found that the animals grew fatter and heavier on the Northern plains than they did in Texas. As a result the mature animals from that state were shipped to market for slaughter, but tens of thousands of younger cattle were sold to Northern buyers to stock ranges on the North plains. Eventually the drives came to consist largely of young steers for this purpose. A division of labor was growing up. Texas, because of its low altitude and warm climate, came to be regarded as a great breeding ground, while the high plains of the North became a great feeding and maturing ground. Cattle feeders from the corn belt began to purchase Western steers for their feed pens. Profits grew and the range-cattle business grew proportionately.

By the late seventies an interest in the range cattle of the United States had extended itself to Europe. In 1875 Timothy C. Eastman of New York began the shipment of dressed beef to England. Eastman had purchased outright the patent for the new "Bate Process" of refrigeration, by which beef was hung in refrigerator rooms and kept at a temperature of about 38 degrees Fahrenheit by means of cold air circulated by fans.

The first shipment by Eastman was in October, 1875. In that month he sent 36,000 pounds of beef to England, to be followed by the same quantity in November, and by 134,000 pounds in December. By April, 1876, his shipments had risen to over a million pounds a month; by September to over two million, and in December to more than three million. Other men in New York, as well as some in Philadelphia, took up the business. In 1877 the shipments of dressed beef to Europe, mostly to England, was nearly fifty million pounds. In 1880 this had risen to eighty-four million and in 1881 to a hundred and six million pounds. This trade was accompanied by the annual shipment of many thousand head of live cattle.

As the trade grew, markets for American beef were established in many British cities; and as the supply grew in volume, the English and Scotch cattle raisers became alarmed when they saw their business threatened by this competition of American meat.

In 1877 the *Scotsman*, a Scotch newspaper devoted largely to the agricultural interests of North Britain, sent to America James McDonald, a prominent writer on its staff, with instructions to investigate the livestock business of the United States and make reports in the form of a series of articles for publication. These articles described the great ranches of the West and to glowing terms of the great profits of the industry which, it was stated, averaged in most cases as much as 25 per cent annually.

The interest of the British Government was aroused, and in 1879 it dispatched two commissioners to the United States to study and report upon the range-cattle industry. The men chosen for this mission were Clare Read and Albert Pell, both members of Parliament. They spent several months in the West and reported that the profits of the range-cattle industry ordinarily averaged about 33 per cent a year.

Canny Scotch and British businessmen had already seen the possibilities of ranching in America as a field for investment. In 1870 the Scottish American Investment Company had been founded by W. J. Menzies. It financed a number of cattle companies in the Great Plains area, including the Wyoming Cattle Ranch Company and Western Ranches Limited. Another great Scottish syndicate formed quite early was the Scottish American Mortgage Company, which established the Prairie Cattle Company, one of the largest enterprises in the West.

The articles of McDonald and the report of Read and Pell served to increase greatly the interest of Scotch and English investors in cattle raising in America; and during the next three or four years many companies were formed and a vast stream of Scotch and British capital was poured into the West to promote the range-cattle industry. Besides the cattle companies previously mentioned Scottish capital founded numerous other ranch enterprises. Prominent among these were the Matador, the Hansford Land and Cattle Company, the Texas Land and Cattle Company, the Swan Land and Cattle Company, and numerous others.

By 1882 it was asserted that not less than thirty million dollars of English and Scotch capital had been invested in ranching on the Western plains. Not a few of the investors came over to give their personal attention to the business, and with them came others from the continent of Europe. Prominent among the latter were the Marquis de Mores, a French nobleman, and Baron von Richthofen, ancestor of the famous German ace. De Mores had

married a New York girl and established with his father-in-law's
money a ranch near the border of Montana and Dakota where
he built and named for his wife the town of Medora. Among the
English and the Scotch were the Adairs, Murdo McKenzie, John
Clay, and a host of others.

Along with the foreigners there came to the western plains an
ever increasing swarm of enterprising young men from the eastern part of the United States. Young college men, among whom
Theodore Roosevelt may be mentioned as a conspicuous example, hastened west to engage in the cattle business.

An enthusiasm for ranching amounting almost to a craze
swept over the country. United States senators, representatives,
and judges were financially interested in range cattle, as were
bankers, lawyers and manufacturers. A machinery was built up
for financing the business. Great cattle-exchange banks and loan
companies were established. The great stream of Texas cattle
flowed steadily northward in spite of quarantine regulations and
fluctuations in prices, and spread itself over the northern plains
until the most remote ranges had been occupied. By the middle
eighties the cattle business had reached its zenith and the vast
cow country stretched from the Rio Grande to the Canadian
border, and from the western edge of agricultural settlements to
the Rocky Mountains and far beyond.

So came into existence the "cow country," a pastoral empire
greater than any of its kind the world had ever seen, on whose
broad plains grazed millions of cattle cared for by men whose
lives and deeds will be heralded in song and story so long as the
American nation shall endure.

Throughout the whole vast region conditions of life and work
were somewhat similar, yet the industry rose so rapidly and suffered such a speedy decline that it never became entirely stand-
ardized. As a result generalizations are always difficult and are
never more than approximately correct. Ranching was an extremely technical business that was little understood except by
those actually engaged in it, and myths and misunderstandings
with respect to it have been all too common.

Democratic as were the men of the cow country, that region

nevertheless presented the picture of a curious kind of "American feudalism," in many ways not unlike that of medieval Europe. The great ranchman built his ranch house or headquarters which might be compared to the baronial castle; his cattle roamed over an area larger than that of many a principality of Europe; his bold riders were as numerous as were the men at arms of many a petty German princeling. The brand of XIT, the spur, frying pan, or J.A. were more widely known perhaps than were the bleeding heart of the Douglas, the clenched hand and dagger of the Kilpatricks, or the white lion of the Howards. The raids of Indians, or white cattle thieves, strife with fence cutters, or episodes like the "Lincoln county war" furnished quite as much excitement as did the forays of the mosstroopers along the Scottish border. The livestock associations bore some resemblance to the federations entered into by groups of Old World nobles, and while the tilt or tournament did not exist, the rodeo or roping contest furnished a very fair substitute.

Yet with all of these similarities to feudal Europe, there were striking differences. There was little of show, formality, or ceremony, and complete democracy was the universal rule. Cattle baron, cowpuncher, cook, and horse wrangler rode, ate, worked, and played together upon terms of absolute equality. Circumstances had made one the boss and the other the "hand" today, but tomorrow or next month or next year the situation might be reversed.

Little has been written about the great leaders of the cow country and yet their influence upon American history has been enormous. They were men of wisdom and they had the energy and strength of purpose to be willing to endure all manner of privations and dangers in order to make their dreams come true.

As for the cowboy, that most picturesque figure among all the children of the Great West, he has received better, or at least more voluminous, treatment at the hands of writers. Yet it must be admitted that much which has been written about the cowboy is untrue. He is sometimes pictured as a sort of modern Sir Galahad, a knight without stain and a champion without reproach, who rode about slaying villains and rescuing damsels in distress. By others he is described as a rough, wild, and lawless creature, crude and uncouth in speech and manner. Both views are equally distorted and incorrect. The cowboy was much like Kipling's "Tommy" who said:

> We ain't no thin red 'eroes
> And we ain't no blackguards, too,
> But single men in barracks
> Most uncommonly like you.

"Just folks," remarked an old cowboy. "Just common everday bow-legged humans! That's cowpunchers."

The description fits. The cowboy was after all not unlike any other young man who lived in the open an active and at times a somewhat hard and adventurous life. For while his work sometimes brought long periods of comparative ease and leisure, it also brought periods of terrific exertion, of hardship and privation, of exposure to cold and rain and the "bright face of danger." Such being the case he learned to take life as it came. Complaints could not change conditions, so why complain? Unconsciously he became a philosopher. He ate thankfully the flaky sour-dough biscuit, and juicy beefsteak in time of plenty, and tightened his belt with a grin in time of famine.

Happy-go-lucky and full of the joy of living, he sang and whistled at his work and play whether it was a bright morning in spring when he cantered over the green flower-spangled prairies to make a friendly visit, or a cold, rainy November night when he must crawl from between his wet blankets at the glad hour of 2:00 A.M. and circle slowly around a restless herd until daylight.

Much has been written about cowboy songs, and they were indeed of infinite variety. There was the plaintive, mournful song so commonly regarded as typical like "Bury me not on the lone prairie," and there was the light lilting one as:

> Twas in the fall of '71
> I thought I'd see how cowpunchin' was done,
> The boss said cowpunchin' was only fun
> There wasn't a bit of work to be done

All you had to do was just to ride
And go a-drifting with the tide
The son-of-a-gun, Oh, how he lied
In seventy one!

Then there were the songs in which love formed the theme as: "Remember the Red River Valley and the cowboy that's loved you so true," and frequently a deeply religious note crept in as in this:

Last night as I lay on the prairie
Looking up at the stars in the sky
I wondered if ever a cowboy
Could go to that sweet bye and bye.
I wondered if ever a cowboy
Could go to that sweet bye and bye.

Someday there will be a grand roundup
Where cowboys like cattle will stand
To be cut out by the riders of Judgment
Who are posted and know every brand.

The road that leads down to perdition
Is posted and blazed all the way
But the pathway that leads up to Heaven
Is narrow and dim so they say.

Whose fault is it then that so many
Go out on that wide range and fail
Who might have honor and plenty
Had they known of that dim, narrow trail.

Such songs are folklore, and are typically American. They reveal the very heart and soul of the cowboy. He was lighthearted and frivolous at times, and he was often lonely. His reverence for pure womanhood is too well known to require comment. He was religious, too, after a fashion and according to his own way. He lived in the open air in God's big out-of-doors. He had seen men die with their boots on in most unpleasant fashion, and the thought of death and the world beyond grows strongly familiar when one lives close to it for so many years. This deeply religious nature is expressed in a little poem written by a real cowpuncher, which has in it the majesty and beauty of real poetry:

> O Lord, I never lived where churches grow
> I like Creation better as it stood
> That day you finished it so long ago
> Then looked upon your work and called it good.
> I know that others find You in the light
> That's sifted down through tinted window panes,
> And yet I seem to feel you near tonight
> In the dim, quiet starlight of the Plains.

The words of but few cowboy rhymes rise to such heights of poetic grandeur as this. Many of them deal with the life and work of the rough riders. Some men formulated tunes as well as words; they improvised, they sang parodies on the then popular songs of the day.

Carrying still further the comparison to feudal Europe it may be noted that some men with good voices and a great repertoire of songs became almost famous throughout large sections of the cow country. They were welcomed gladly at every camp and round-up wagon because of their ability as entertainers. They were minnesingers of the range, troubadours, wandering minstrels, and their songs were of wide variety. Many were of the type just described; some were ballads dealing with certain individuals who had lived beyond the law, but who had possessed personal qualities much admired by some of these wild riders of the prairies. Such men as Jesse James, Sam Bass, and other outlaws were the subject of ballads that were widely sung throughout the cow country. The words of two or three such songs are given in part in another chapter in this volume.

Outlaws as they were, the heroes of these songs had many admirers. Legends not unlike those that cluster about the names of Robin Hood, Rob Roy, and Captain Kidd were associated with them.

Picturesque as was the life of the cow country of the middle eighties, it was doomed to a speedy passing. Its rise had been spectacular but its decline was hardly less spectacular and certainly was much more tragic. The year of 1885 is the high-water mark of the business. During the summer of that year President Cleveland issued a proclamation ordering all cattle to be removed within forty days from the lands of the Cheyenne-Arapaho Indians in what is now Oklahoma. These 210,000 head from this great reservation were thrown upon already overstocked ranges near by, and the following winter saw heavy losses.

Prices were still high in the spring, however, and the drive north out of Texas was heavy. Tens of thousands of head were moved up the trail and spread out in the most reckless fashion imaginable over the already heavily stocked ranges of Wyoming, Montana, and Dakota.

Winter came early and laid his icy hand upon the Northern prairies. A terrific blizzard bringing sleet and snow came roaring out of the north and the thermometer went down as though it would never stop. The cattle drifted before the bitter winds into ravines and coulees where they died by thousands. Heavy snows fell and intense cold continued throughout the winter. Hunger-maddened cattle gathered along the little streams, and gnawed the bark from the willows as high as they could reach before they at last gave up the struggle, and lay down to die.

Spring came to find every cattleman on the Northern plains flat broke. Swan, Sturgis, Kohrs, Granville Stuart, Dickey Brothers, Worshams, the Continental Cattle Company, and a host of others either failed or were in the shakiest possible condition. Theodore Roosevelt quit the cattle business, leaving his range thickly strewn with bones.

No such winter had ever before been known in the history of the cow country. Charlie Russell, the cowboy artist, was in charge of a herd of five thousand head belonging to a group of Eastern capitalists. Toward spring his employers wrote him a letter asking how the cattle were doing. Russell's painting which he sent as a reply has become famous. It is a picture of a gaunt and lonely old cow in the midst of great snow drifts, standing with drooping head like a bovine peri at the gate of

Paradise, and in the corner Russell had written the title, "The Last of Five Thousand."

Most of the Northern ranchmen never recovered from the effects of that frightful winter. Losses of between 50 and 60 per cent were common. As high as 80 and 90 were hardly exceptional. Money lenders who had been financing the industry were panic-stricken. In a desperate attempt to pay interest and to liquidate a part of their loans ranchmen poured a stream of lean and unmerchantable cattle into the markets. Prices went down until cattle would hardly be accepted as a gift, especially since the summer of 1887 was very dry and crops throughout the corn belt almost a failure. There was no demand for feeders and the range cattle were too thin for slaughter. A great industry was prostrate and recovery was slow and uncertain.

As a matter of fact the range-cattle business never again rose to the heights it had attained in the middle eighties. Its glory had departed forever. The cow country was changing. Trunk lines of railroads heading out from the great markets had penetrated Texas, making it possible to ship cattle to market by rail. The great drives began to lessen in volume. A realization that the Northern ranges had been overstocked, the competition of the railroads, the stringent quarantine laws of Kansas, and the general depression of the industry all served to check the northern drive.

Pioneer settlers in prairie schooners were, moreover, drifting westward in large numbers and taking up homesteads in the range-cattle area. Their little dugouts and sod houses appeared mushroomlike almost overnight on the more fertile lands in various parts of the cow country. The Indian lands of western Oklahoma were opened to settlement and a great area changed from grazing to crop growing.

Brief periods of prosperity came again to the ranching industry at times, but the magnitude of the earlier operations steadily declined. Some of the big ranches began to subdivide their holdings and sell out lands in tracts to suit the purchaser. Fenced pastures, winter feeding, and small-scale production became the rule.

The range was shrinking, cattle disappeared from many regions, and farmers armed with hoe and spade sprang up on all sides as though an unseen hand had planted dragon's teeth on every hill and in every valley. Steadily the ranchmen were forced out of the agricultural lands and pushed back into the barren deserts, the hills and mountains, or onto forest reserves and Indian reservations. Here the business still exists, though large-scale operations are about gone, and the life at its best or worst, depending upon the viewpoint, is only a faded and washed-out copy of the life of the earlier days.

The men who once rode the boundless ranges of the Great Plains or who followed the long herds up the dusty trail are with few exceptions no more. Gone with the things of long ago they have, to quote their own language, "passed up the dim, narrow trail to that new range which never fails, and where quarantine regulations do not exist." Gone it is true, but I trust never to be forgotten. For if it is true that

> You may break, you may shatter
> The vase if you will
> But the scent of the rose
> Will cling to it still

so it is also true that you may enclose the green prairies and plow up the sweet wild flowers, you may build towns and cities on sites once occupied by the cowboy's dugout and branding pen, but always something of the fragrance of the romance of those early days will cling to the region which the bold range riders once called their own, to remind us of those picturesque days now gone forever.

The period of the range-cattle industry constitutes in a sense the heroic age of the great West. Those of us who know something of it at first hand look back upon its passing with a tinge of regret. Yet we realize that society is never static, never still. The cowboy has given place to the settler, the city builder, the manufacturer, the merchant, the scholar. The tale of their rise in the West is another story, but there too lies romance.

II

Our fare was mostly bacon and beans
With plenty of beef from the range,
And we et our own which some I've known
Figgered was mighty strange.
Our biscuits, always of sour dough,
Were flaky and brown and light
And we had a stew called son-of-a-gun
When we wanted to be polite.

It was long ago that I left the range
To travel the world so wide
But I can't forget the way I et
In th' days when I used to ride.
I've learned in many a grand hotel
And restaurant swank or club
That the old trail cooks weren't much for looks
But they shore turned out th' grub!

The Chuck Wagon

II
Cowboy Cookery

COWBOY FOOD and the methods of preparing it differed from those of any other group of people in the world. Some knowledge of how the ranch cooks were able to produce tasty and satisfying meals from comparatively few raw materials should prove not only interesting but of considerable value to many persons.

A COW OUTFIT no less than an army moves like a snake—on its stomach. As a matter of fact, any man responsible for the accomplishment of a task requiring the services of many people for a long period of time quickly learns how important is good food for the preservation of morale and the smooth functioning of the human machine whose parts are the men who must get the job done.

This is as true of cowhands as it has always been of the army and navy, a crew of lumberjacks, a railway construction gang, or any other body of men engaged in hard manual labor. Those who must work long hours at tasks involving much physical effort have little interest in knickknacks, nor is it necessary to tempt their appetites by dishes served in attractive forms. What they want is an ample supply of good, nourishing food that is clean, well cooked, and of a type calculated to "stick to the ribs" through long periods of arduous labor.

This every ranch foreman, trail boss or round-up captain, as well as every cook who was worth his salt, sought to provide. True, some outfits were notorious for the poor fare they served their men just as others were famous for excellent food; but when the fare was hopelessly bad, responsibility for it usually lay with some owner or general manager who operated from a distant office in a town or city rather than with an experienced range man who rode and ate with the men themselves.

The cowboy's work consisted largely of driving cattle on the trail, sharing in the round-up, or riding the range. In the case of the first two, he ate at the wagon such food as was prepared by the cook, and in the last-named, he lived in camp and ate his own. Every cowboy was a cook of sorts and the great majority developed considerable skill, though obviously some were far better than others.

A good cook in the cow country, as everywhere else, was regarded as a real treasure. Usually he commanded wages of at least five to ten dollars a month higher than the riders even when the latter were top hands. On the trail or with the round-up he drove the four horses or mules that pulled the chuck wagon, prepared the meals, washed the dishes, loaded up the wagon each morning, and was something of an autocrat second only to the boss in importance.

Every chuck wagon was equipped with bows and a canvas cover to protect the supplies and bed rolls of the men from rain. Fitted into the wagon bed at the rear and held firmly in place by wagon rods extending through it was the chuck box. This was usually some four feet high with its front wall perpendicular, while the rear one, sloping outward from top to bottom, was hinged at the base so it could be let down to form a cook table supported by a sturdy leg. This leg was attached to the outer edge by a small hinge so it folded flat against the outside when the box was closed.

Shelves and perpendicular partitions divided the interior of the chuck box into compartments. The lower ones were large and held the sour-dough jar or keg as well as the larger pans and tin plates, cups, knives, forks, and spoons. The middle ones, of smaller size, were for sugar, syrup, lard, rice, beans, or dried fruit, while the smaller ones at the top held salt, pepper, baking powder, or other less bulky commodities. Most things were usually put in tin cans with close-fitting lids, and these were placed in compartments of a suitable size so that they could not turn over as the wagon jolted over the rough and bumpy prairie.

It is doubtful if any better camp kitchen has ever been devised than the well-built chuck box attached to the rear of every trail or round-up wagon. By unscrewing the wagon rods, it could be lifted out and nailed to the wall in one corner of the range rider's dugout camp and so become the usual kitchen cabinet of the cow country. Naturally, on the trail or during the round-up only lighter articles and a supply of the more bulky groceries sufficient for a day or two were carried in the chuck box. The major part of the flour, beans, bacon, beef, dried fruit, sugar, and coffee was in the wagon bed, while a rack was built beneath it to carry the big Dutch ovens, pots, spade, axe, camp hooks, and other large and heavy utensils.

On the trail the cook ordinarily had the job of providing three square meals a day for about a dozen men, most of them with surprisingly healthy appetites. Reaching the spot designated by the boss, usually by the bank of a stream, he unharnessed and hobbled the team, brought up wood and a pail of water and after excavating a short, shallow trench, built a fire in it. On this he put the lids of the big Dutch ovens and then let down the back of the chuck box to form his cook table and set to work at the task of preparing dinner, or supper as the case might be, for the hungry men some miles to the rear slowly moving the herd along the trail.

Ordinarily the first job was making bread. There is a tradition that the owners of the first herds driven north out of Texas frequently started with little in the way of food except corn meal and salt and so ate corn bread for most of the journey. If this is true, it must have been only during the first year or two after the close of the Civil War, for the staff of life throughout the cow country during most of its existence was sour-dough biscuits. At their best, sour-dough biscuits are delicious but it must be admitted that at their worst, the less said about them the better.

In any case, however, they were the staple article of diet throughout the entire length and breadth of the American frontier for a generation or more.

Their basis is the sour dough which is made by filling a stone jar or small keg nearly half full of lukewarm water, adding a handful of sugar and then stirring in flour with a flat wooden paddle to make a batter as thick as it can be stirred. The jar is then set in a warm place and within 48 hours, or less, it has become sour and has increased to twice its original bulk. The cook merely filled a large tin pan two-thirds full of flour, and pushed it back from the center to leave a depression in the middle into which was poured half the contents of the sour-dough jar. A teaspoonful of soda was then dissolved in a little lukewarm water, put into the sour dough, and a little salt and lard or bacon grease added.

The flour was then worked in from the sides, care being taken that the dissolved soda was well distributed throughout the mass. The table was thickly dredged with flour and the dough lifted on to it and kneaded thoroughly for several minutes. A large spoonful of lard or some bacon fat had been placed in the Dutch oven and melted and pieces of the dough about the size of an egg or slightly smaller were pinched off, rolled into balls, and placed in the Dutch oven and turned over in order to give to the entire surface of each a coating of grease so that they would not stick together. When the oven was full it was placed near the fire, or in the summer time set out in the sun for half an hour or more so that the biscuits might rise while the rest of the meal was being prepared.

The huge coffee pot with a wide base usually well blackened was brought out and nearly filled with water. A generous supply of coffee was ground on the mill attached to the side of the chuck box and dumped into the pot, which was then placed on coals shoveled from the fire. The coffee used was often one of the standard brands put up in one-pound packages and an enormous quantity was required, for the cook firmly believed that there is no such thing as strong coffee but only "weak people," and the men for whom he must provide were surely not of that type!

The next step was the preparation of the meat. Usually a fat heifer was slaughtered every few days and the quarters of beef after being hung up overnight to cool were packed in the wagon. Half a quarter was brought out and the meat cut in fairly thick slices with a sharp butcher knife. A couple of big skillets were placed on a bed of coals and in each was put a generous handful of suet cut into small pieces.

While this was frying out, the steaks were cut into liberal-sized pieces and pounded with a hammer if there was any suspicion that the meat might be tough. Each piece was then sprinkled with salt and dredged with flour, and the suet "cracklings" were lifted out or pushed aside and the steaks dropped into the sizzling hot fat, which should ordinarily be half an inch or more deep. A tin lid was often put on each skillet to keep out the dust and keep in the steam and flavor.

The oven of biscuits was then put on a few coals and covered with the hot lid lifted from the fire with a camp hook. Coals were placed on top and the cook could then devote himself to turning the steak and at the same time keep an eye on the coffee, and lift the lid from the oven once or twice with the camp hook to be sure that the biscuits were browning properly. The secret of baking bread in a Dutch oven is to see that there are not too many coals below and plenty above so that biscuits may be produced with each one having a deep brown upper and lower crust enclosing its delicious, soft, spongy interior.

Correct timing was necessary in order to have everything ready when the herd appeared and was spread out along the stream to water and graze while all the men except a couple left to "day herd" came in to eat. If they were a little slow, the cook took the bread and meat off the coals but placed them near the fire to keep warm.

At the last minute all of the steaks were put into one skillet and into the fat of the other was stirred a couple of tablespoonfuls of flour. Salt and water were then added and the mixture briskly stirred until it had boiled sufficiently to produce a thick gravy commonly known as "sop."

A jug or can of syrup was then set out together with a stone jar or tin pail full of dried apples, peaches, or apricots, which had usually been stewed the night before. When the men appeared, the more persnickety ones washed in a tin basin. Then each loaded up his plate and sat down cross-legged on the grass to enjoy a meal that food experts might not regard as properly balanced but that was nevertheless very satisfying.

None of the three meals of the day—breakfast, dinner, and supper—departed very much from this standard pattern. Bacon cut in thick slices and fried to a golden brown might replace the beef, and beans boiled with bacon or salt pork were often served —and rice at times—but the name "moonshine" by which the latter was commonly called is evidence that it was not regarded very highly as food for a real he-man.

As has been indicated, the cook was an important man who was always treated with a considerable degree of respect, and the old cowboy saying "Only a fool argues with a woman, a mule, or the cook" is significant. Often the boss felt it necessary to stop the herd for a few days to allow the cattle to rest and graze. Upon such occasions the cook had ample time and opportunity to exercise his talents. Moreover, the riders had a good deal of leisure, since only a couple of men were usually required for day herding.

This leisure they sometimes employed in fishing, often bringing in a string of perch or catfish and dressing them to be fried and so breaking the monotony of the daily fare. Also they would help the cook by dragging up dry wood with a rope or doing other minor chores about camp, while in some instances they spent hours in gathering pecans, walnuts, or, in the summer, wild plums and grapes. Also it was upon such occasions that a beef was slaughtered, sometimes a fat stray, for there is some element of truth in the saying "No cowman ever liked the taste of his own beef."

Relieved for a few days of the task of harnessing and unharnessing the team, of loading the men's bed rolls, and of driving for several miles each day, the cook often took advantage of the opportunity to prepare some especially delectable type of dish which he thought the men would like. One of these was beef and dumplings. Pieces of fat beef were placed in a pot and simmered slowly over the fire until perfectly tender. When the biscuits were put in the oven a good-sized lump of dough was put aside to rise for some three-quarters of an hour. Bits of this, the size of the end of the finger, were snipped off and dropped into the pot with the beef and cooked for a few minutes. A little flour was then dissolved in half a cup of water and added to the contents of the pot in order to thicken the gravy. The small lumps of dough puffed up to three or four times their original size and a plate filled with this tender beef and light dumplings swimming in rich gravy was about all that was required for a meal which was truly "soothing, sustaining, and satisfying."

When a calf or other young animal was killed, the cook sometimes made the favorite dish of the cowboy which in his more polite moments he called "son-of-a-gun stew" or merely "son-of-a-gun." No recipe for it can be given for the reason that every cook had his own and in consequence there were as many ways of making it as there were cooks. Ordinarily the tongue, sweetbreads, heart, brains, and perhaps the liver of the freshly killed animal were chopped into small pieces and put into a big kettle. If more meat was needed, a choice cut also chopped fine was added. In cowboy parlance, you "put in everything except the hide, horns, and holler."

The meat was covered with water and any vegetables available were added. Some cooks put in chopped potatoes and onions, a can or two of tomatoes, a couple of cans of corn, or whatever could be had. In fact, it might be said of "son-of-a-gun," as the colored man replied to the query of how the soup was made, "We don't usually make it at all; it just sort of accumulates."

The "accumulation" in the kettle of "son-of-a-gun" was covered with water and boiled slowly for a long time. In fact it was commonly said that "the longer you cook it the better it is," and also "if you can tell what's in it you know it ain't made right."

On the whole the man who supplied the gastronomic needs of a bunch of cowhands had no easy task and few doubted that he earned every dollar of his wages. In pleasant weather his job was not too difficult; but when it rained and the soaking wet wood refused to burn in anything like adequate fashion, his patience and temper were both sorely tried. Even in clear warm weather he must rise long before day to prepare breakfast and rouse the sleepy men with loud yells of "Roll out, you waddies! It's getting daylight. Come git it 'fore I throw it in the creek."

Fortunately, he was not expected to provide pies, cookies and doughnuts as do many of the cooks in the camps of the lumberjacks of the Northern woods. Plain food and plenty of it was demanded by the cowboys but, as has been said, they did not expect any frills or fancy fixin's and, in most cases, would have been astounded if anything of the sort had been set before them.

The diet of the cow country on the whole rested upon seven pillars—flour, beef, bacon, beans, coffee, syrup, and dried fruit. With these essentials—plus salt, sugar, and soda—any man, whether a regular cook or a cowhand in some remote line camp which he occupied all alone or with a single companion, could prepare tasty and nourishing meals with a surprisingly wide range of variations. True, a few cases of canned tomatoes or corn helped a good deal, as did a keg of pickles or a few onions and potatoes from time to time, but not many men expected these as a regular part of their fare.

With the basic materials so few in number it was highly important that every dish be prepared with care and made as nearly perfect as possible. The biscuits must be brown and light, the beef well cooked and tender, the beans properly seasoned and thoroughly done. Unlike the person seated at a well-loaded dinner table where if one article of food is not pleasing something else can be selected, the cowhand had no choice. If any article of food was badly cooked, the entire meal was ruined.

As a rule the cook for a dozen or more men seldom had either the time or inclination to experiment, but the lone cowboy in his line camp often tried out new things, sometimes with surprising and even disastrous results! Yet, there was always an ideal to be sought for in the preparation of these basic foods, and the making of good biscuits was one art that was to be cultivated at all times.

Every cowhand literally loved sour-dough bread. Baking-powder biscuits he would eat upon occasion without too much complaint, but they were commonly not considered healthful as a steady diet. The buttermilk biscuits affected by the nesters, and that he occasionally got at headquarters if the foreman had a wife who demanded a supply of milk and butter, he admitted were good though still somewhat below the sour-dough variety. Corn bread he disliked as a rule and baker's bread, often called "wasp nest bread," he abhorred. Moreover, the finest of home-made "light bread" did not appeal to him.

Buck Rainey, who had been visiting for a day or two with a friend whose wife was well known locally for the quality of her homemade bread, could see nothing about it to admire. When other visitors expressed enthusiasm for the big snowy loaves that came from the oven, Buck only remarked plaintively: "Yes, I guess it must be fine but somehow it don't seem to do me the least bit of good."

In fact the making of such bread was a mystery to most cow-hands. A ranchman's wife has related that when Johnnie Thomp-son dropped in Saturday afternoon to spend the week-end with the family she served him homemade bread for supper. The next morning he was up early and came out to the kitchen just as she was starting breakfast. "Miz Brown," he said hopefully, "I'll help you get breakfast and let's not cook no light bread for breakfast this mornin'—what do you say?"

In addition to the methods of cooking beef already mentioned there were many others. Sometimes a sort of pot roast was pre-pared by salting a large piece of beef, dredging it lightly with flour and putting it in a Dutch oven with a cup or so of water to bake slowly for half a day. When it was nearly done some peeled potatoes and onions were added, upon those rare occasions when they were available, and more coals put on top of the lid to bake them to a golden brown. Such a dish, with biscuits and syrup or dried fruit, made a full meal.

There were several schools of thought with respect to cooking steak, but on two points there was universal agreement. It must be well done and must be fried—broiled steak being virtually unknown in the cow country. Also it should never be fried in lard except as a last resort but in beef fat secured from a little chopped suet. From this point on, differences of opinion crept in. Some asserted that it should first be dredged with flour. Others declared that this was not only unnecessary but undesirable. Still others went even further and insisted that each piece of meat should be dipped in batter before frying. Some wanted it cut thin and others thick, some wanted it served with pan gravy made from the hot fat and a dash of water, while others insisted on "sop." All agreed, however, that it should be fried in suet and must be well done.

Steak and sour-dough biscuits were the twin essentials of cowboy diet. Even a man who accompanied a trainload of cattle to Kansas City or Chicago would walk into a restaurant, look the bill of fare over from top to bottom and, passing up the fish, oysters, lobster, and other strange delicacies, at last would say: "Guess I'll have a nice steak." Once in a great while one might be found with sufficient imagination to order ham and eggs but this was most unusual.

It is true that most men who rode the range agreed that bacon had its points and a skillet full of thick slices fried brown was not to be despised. Plenty of bacon was essential in the cow country for it was not only fried but also boiled with beans, and boiled beans and bacon would stay with a man throughout a hard day of work. In fact, Badger Clark voiced a fundamental truth when he wrote:

> You always came in when the fresh meat had
> ceased
> And the road of the pathway of empire was
> greased
> By the bacon we fried on the way.

After a few days of bacon as the only meat, however, the cowhand began to pine for beef and cast about for a suitable animal to slaughter. In case he must eat bacon a considerable length of time he began to devise ways and means to change the flavor and so make it more palatable. Thick slices of bacon or salt pork were often parboiled for a few minutes and then rolled in flour and fried. It was still bacon or pork but at least the taste was different!

Deeply respected as was the cook, the boys would occasionally indulge in a bit of good-natured joking at his expense, but this always stopped short if he showed the least indication not to take it in good part. "Don't you go to squattin' and snortin' at Sim's biscuits," remarked a cowhand when one of his companions had declared that these were "mighty firm biscuits." "Every one of them biscuits is about two pounds lighter'n it looks."

Milk and butter were of course virtually unknown in the range area except once in a while at headquarters and were, as a matter of fact, articles of food from which the average old-time cowhand shied as does a range horse from corn. Upon rare occasions a few cans of condensed milk might be seen but this was seldom. Sometimes a newcomer would complain bitterly, and one tenderfoot from the hills of Arkansas after a month on the range insisted that he was going back home where he could get some milk and butter instead of staying any longer "in a country that had nothing in it but cows!"

Since he was needed to do certain chores about camp, the boys at last rounded up an elderly brindle longhorn with a young calf and put her in the corral as a milk cow. After the first milking she was promptly dubbed "Old Sahara." For a week the men risked life and limb each night and morning in the perilous task of attempting to secure a little milk. Then they decided that two or three cupfuls a day were not worth the effort, to say nothing of the danger, and in disgust turned Old Sahara out on the range again.

In planning and preparing a meal few cooks felt that it was necessary to provide any dessert except the inevitable dried fruit stewed with plenty of sugar. Even this was sometimes lacking and the dinner or supper was merely "topped off" with syrup. This might be sorghum, ribbon cane, sugar drip, corn syrup, or any one of half a dozen other varieties. The fruit was usually dried peaches, apples, apricots, or occasionally prunes or raisins.

Sometimes a bread pudding was made by soaking cold biscuits

in warm water and adding sugar and raisins. After the mass had been beaten to a pulp, it was poured into a well-greased Dutch oven and baked to a golden brown. With some sugar syrup poured over each serving it was not bad, though of course not so light as is the bread pudding made with eggs. It was often called "slumgullion" though this is a somewhat elusive term applied to beef stew in some parts of the cow country.

As has been indicated, a lone cowboy in some remote line camp had more time and opportunity for experimentation in the culinary art than did the professional cook who must prepare three meals a day for a crew of hungry men. Sometimes such a cowhand had a companion, the two men riding out from camp in opposite directions each morning, but in many cases he was all alone. Every cowboy was judged in great measure by the way in which he kept his camp. Contrary to common opinion he was in most cases an excellent housekeeper. The dirt floor was sprinkled and carefully swept every day with a broom made by tying a large bunch of long grass to the end of a stick. The pans and tin plates were scoured and polished until they shone, and the bed was carefully made up each morning. Only a bum, it was asserted, was willing to live in the midst of dirt and disorder. Moreover he was usually clean and orderly in his cooking as he was in everything else.

About once a month a wagon came out from headquarters bringing him the staple articles of food previously referred to, except beef which he ordinarily supplied himself by slaughtering a young animal in time of need and hanging up the quarters in a tree if one were near camp. He often had a shotgun at camp and would at times kill a few quail, prairie chickens, wild turkeys, plovers, or ducks to vary his fare. Quail were skinned, drawn, and split into halves. They were then salted, rolled in flour, and fried in fairly deep fat with a lid turned over the skillet. For a change they might be stewed and dumplings made from small pieces of biscuit dough dropped in when the birds were tender. Prairie chickens were unjointed, rolled in flour and fried, or boiled with dumplings, or in some cases baked in a Dutch oven with a stuffing made of bread crumbs. Drop dumplings were made with baking powder and flour stirred into water to make a stiff batter which was dropped into the pot a teaspoonful at a time.

Sometimes wild blackberries or dewberries were found along the streams and an enterprising cowhand might decide to try his hand at making a pie. Lard, flour, and water were mixed to make "pie dough" and a deep tin plate was floured and lined with this. The berries that had been stewed and sweetened were then poured in, a top crust added, and the pie baked in a Dutch oven. If it proved successful, others might be attempted with a filling of dried apples, peaches, or apricots.

Some men even declared that a cake made by kneading sugar and raisins into a lump of dough, made up as for sour-dough biscuits, was quite good. Others asserted that sugar could be added to the biscuit dough and after this had risen a little, strips could be cut off, made into twists, and fried in deep, hot fat to make quite tolerable doughnuts.

Once started on such experiments the ambitious cowpuncher found few limits to his ingenuity in devising toothsome delicacies. Fried pies, or turnovers, were easily made and were especially delicious. By frying up a couple of dozen at a time, some containing one kind of dried fruit and some another, an excellent dessert for several meals was insured.

Potatoes were seldom a regular item in the cowboy's bill of fare because they were bulky and would freeze in winter or rot in summer. When they were available a favorite way of cooking them was by frying. They were peeled, cut in thin slices, and dumped into a skillet containing half an inch of hot bacon fat. Salt was added and a lid placed on the skillet to retain the steam. From time to time the slices were turned over with a broadbladed knife. When they were tender and part of them browned, they were scooped out on tin plates, and a generous serving of fried potatoes plus three or four slices of bacon, some biscuits, and coffee made an excellent meal.

Apples were sliced with the peelings left on and fried in exactly the same way except that they were sprinkled with sugar instead of salt. Canned corn was also fried in bacon fat, sometimes with a little water added, while canned tomatoes were stewed and some crackers or crusts of bread broken up and cooked with them.

Hot cakes or "flapjacks" were a standard article of food in every cow camp. They could be made with sour-dough by adding soda, a little salt, and enough water to make a batter of the proper consistency. It was better to let the batter stand for half an hour in a warm place so that bubbles would form, making the cakes lighter. Flapjacks were also made by mixing a liberal supply of baking powder with flour and stirring this gently into a pan of cold water to make a batter. Care was taken not to beat the batter since this made the cakes tougher. If the cook had some condensed milk and could use one part of this to three parts of water, so much the better.

Hot cakes should be baked on a griddle or in a skillet very lightly greased with a bacon rind rather than fried in a considerable quantity of grease. They were served with a spoonful of bacon fryings on each one in lieu of butter, and a generous supply of syrup. If the flavor of the latter had begun to pall, sugar syrup was often made merely by boiling two or three cups of sugar with a cupful of water.

Maple syrup was of course virtually unknown, but an ingenious cowhand would sometimes stew dried fruit with a considerable quantity of water and then pour off the surplus juice, add to it two or three cups of sugar, and boil for several minutes. In this way syrup could be made with apricot, peach, or apple flavor which was an agreeable change from that made merely with sugar and water. Also preserves were made by soaking dried peaches or apricots overnight, adding an equal bulk of sugar and a cupful of water, and boiling until the fruit was tender and a thick syrup had been formed. The result appealed greatly to the taste of many.

If the supply of sugar was low, a man would sometimes prepare what was called "fried molasses." Three or four slices of bacon were fried in a skillet and after they had been lifted out, a pint of sorghum was poured into the hot bacon fat and boiled briskly for five or six minutes. The change in taste is surprising and no matter how tired a man had grown of the same old sorghum three times a day he usually found the "fried molasses" extremely good with hot biscuits or flapjacks.

Returning to the subject of coffee, which was regarded as an essential accompaniment of every meal, it is only necessary to say that the pot two-thirds full of cold water was placed on the coals and the coffee ground and dumped in. When it had boiled for three or four minutes, a dash of cold water was added to settle the grounds. So made, it was clear and of excellent flavor if the quality of coffee used was good. The only requirement was that it be strong, for as Bill Jones once remarked, "It seems that a lot of people never realize how little water it takes to make good coffee!"

It is impossible to give any complete list of cowboy dishes since the food varied with the season, the region, and the source of supply. Many ingenious cowhands devised new ones. Beef ribs were barbecued over a bed of coals by placing them on an improvised grill made of peeled green poles. Canned corn and tomatoes were stewed together. Potatoes were sliced and fried with onions. Sometimes in the spring a rider in a remote camp would feel a hunger for fresh vegetable food and gather some form of wild greens, as poke salad or lamb's quarter, to be boiled with a slab of bacon or salt pork.

Wild onions, a favorite food of some Indian tribes, might be pulled and fried in bacon grease. Biscuit dough was rolled thin, cut into strips, and dropped into smoking hot fat to make fried bread. In rare cases a wild turkey's nest might be found and the extraordinary treat of eggs enjoyed. There are even instances of a cowpuncher's finding, along some timber-bordered stream, a bee tree which was cut and a supply of honey added to the resources of the camp. Such cases are, of course, exceptional. Ordinarily the seven standard food staples named were the chief dependence of the cow country and with these available few men complained of any lack in either the quality or variety of their daily fare.

Most dietitians would probably hold up their hands in holy horror over both cowboy food and cookery. They would doubtless assert that so much starch and protein and the constant consumption of fried foods must inevitably cause grave digestive disturbances and result in bad health and a weakened physical condition. But "there is nothing so tragic as a beautiful theory assassinated by a fact!"

No hardier, healthier or more robust men ever lived than were the riders of the cow country. Digestive troubles were virtually unknown among them. On the fare described they rode from dawn until dark and often far into the night, day after day, in heat and cold, rain or snow, or worked at the hard labor of branding calves all day and never seemed to tire. Upon occasions they would ride all day and dance most of the night and then get back to camp a little sleepy perhaps but ready and willing to tackle the day's work.

III

They say we had no culture
Which I guess is really so,
But I can't forget the roses
That my mother used to grow.
And her patchwork quilts and mottoes
With their colors gay and rich
Revealed her love of beauty
In every single stitch.

The books we knew were very few
But we were always sure
That the Bible which our father read
Was the best of literature.
And we sang the songs of long ago
And made us up some more
Which the scholars have collected
And called them "true folklore."

Home in the Hills

III
American Frontier Culture

THE COWBOY had little time for cultural things, but the people who migrated west to establish new homes on the American Frontier were far from gross materialists interested only in improving their economic welfare. It is true that most of these pioneer settlers hoped to build in this new land a better future for themselves and their children. Yet among them were certain elements who sought to promote those cultural and spiritual values without which any society is poor indeed. As a result their lives were far from drab or sordid and gracious living was often found even in the most humble homes.

ONE DOES NOT HAVE TO BE a historian to realize that behind the great ocean liner proudly plowing the seas lies the crude dugout canoe in which primitive man poled, or paddled, his way along the more sluggish streams, or across the still waters of lakes and land-locked bays, with an occasional daring soul venturing far out from land upon the broad bosom of the ocean itself. We know that back of the streamlined train rushing over the rails at ninety miles an hour is the creaking ox cart, or that behind the majestic skyscraper reaching high toward Heaven is the rough bark lodge or hut of palm leaves constructed by some enterprising aboriginal man, and for which he left his earlier cave dwelling despite the jeers of his more conservative neighbors.

What is true of material values, however, is equally true in the realm of those things which we call cultural. Behind the greatest of symphonies is the booming kettledrum used by the chief to arouse the martial spirit of his warriors, or the notes of the reed or bone flute with which the young savage wooed his dusky mate. The forerunners of the priceless masterpieces of painting or sculpture were the crude drawings on skins or birch bark depicting exploits of war and the chase, or rough figures modeled in clay or chipped from stone. The beginnings of grand opera or the Russian ballet were the ceremonial songs and dances of primitive peoples, and of the great works of literature the picture writing by which primitive men recorded the story of important events in their lives.

Culture is, moreover, a relative term. The tribesman who was most adept at beating the drum, playing the flute, or painting designs on buckskin or pottery was an artist in the eyes of his fellows. The most graceful dancer, the ablest orator, the cleverest story teller or picture writer, or the most melodious singer was a cultivated man among his own kind regardless of how crude the results of his efforts might appear to the people of what we are pleased to call a more civilized social order.

It is not to primitive peoples of an alien race and a different color, however, that America owes most of its present-day culture. Much of it is rooted in Old World soil, though perhaps more of it than we think is the product of our own plains and forests. Even that part of it originally brought from Europe has been so colored and transformed by a new environment as to affect greatly its tempo and pattern. It has changed or been modified to such an extent as to be scarcely recognizable by its originators.

From the beginning of our country's history to the present, many people of Europe have asserted that America is a nation of money grubbers whose people have little interest in scholarship, and above all, no understanding or appreciation of art, music, and literature. Emerson's immortal essay, *The American Scholar*, was in a sense our intellectual declaration of independence, but even today, over a hundred years after it was written, not a few people of the United States are still all too willing to accept the dictum of Europe as law and gospel and to insist that only by long and patient study abroad can one hope to become a real artist.

In the older settled regions of the East, moreover, even those who are willing to admit that America may have something of an intellectual and cultural nature to contribute to the world are likely to think that the people of the frontier regions of the West were gross materialists, interested only in things of the flesh or in supplying their own physical needs. This is far from true and has never been true of any frontier area, whether it was that of Piedmont Virginia in 1690, of Kentucky and Tennessee in 1790, or of Oklahoma and Texas in 1890. Since pioneer life in America has always been essentially the same, however, it seems well in discussing the cultural life and interests of the frontier to choose the most recent one, which is that of the West approximately sixty to seventy years ago.

Obviously it would be impossible to give in a brief chapter any complete discussion of the cultural life of frontier people in all of its aspects. In consequence attention will be directed only to three phases of the pioneer settler's culture—art, music, and literature.

The roots of the cultural interest of pioneer peoples must be sought in the self-selection of those who migrated west to occupy virgin lands on the American frontier. As a rule they belonged to a certain type. When Longfellow, speaking of the Pilgrims, said:

> God had sifted three kingdoms
> To find the wheat for this planting
> Then had sifted the wheat
> The living seed of a nation,

he was but voicing a general truth which might be applied to the settlers of every new land quite as well as to those who sailed in the Mayflower to establish the little colony of Plymouth. The bold, hardy, and restless migrated while the timid, the weak and contented remained at home. Nor was the pioneer settler always primarily interested in improving his worldly condition by removing to a new country. Often the lure of strange lands attracted him. He was eager to see what lay beyond the far horizon. In many cases he was an idealist, often an incurable romanticist, imbued with a spirit of daring and filled with an eager desire for change and adventure. He was a dreamer who looked far off into the future and saw there wonderful things. He was quite willing to endure hardships and suffering and frequently real danger if only in some remote future his dreams might become realities. Such a man was not "stolid and stunned, a brother to the ox." He was eager, ambitious, and vital. Often he sought escape from sordid surroundings in the land of his birth and hoped in a new home to find a fuller and more abundant life.

There was, moreover, much in a new and unpeopled land to stimulate the imagination of the new settler. The vast forests, the wide stretches of green prairie reaching out to meet the purple horizon, the blue mountains and swelling hills all served to stir his love of beauty. Everything was on a grand scale. The distances were great, the rivers and mountains much bigger than those he had known farther east. The clear air made distant objects appear very near. The stars at night seemed almost within reach of his hand. The violent winds, the heavy downpours of rain which turned dry stream beds into raging torrents, all were indicative that nature operated on a scale as huge as was the pattern of the country itself.

The frontier settler's interest in the field of art in the narrower sense of the word may be treated very briefly. In very rare instances did he paint pictures or model in clay or stone, and very few such artistic objects were to be found in his home. In many other ways, however, did he evidence his love and appreciation of the beautiful. One of these was in the choice of a location for his new home. Often it was placed in the midst of a grove of trees on the crest of a hill so that he had a magnificent view of the surrounding landscape. In other cases it was nestled in an attractive glen or narrow valley in such fashion as to permit an outlook upon the encircling hills or mountains with their ever-changing colors brought by sunshine or shadow and the march of the seasons. Those of us who are familiar with the frontier have frequently observed a primitive home placed in so perfect a setting that it seemed a natural part of the scene, or as though it belonged exactly there and nowhere else, and without it something would be lacking. It must have taken a real sense of the artistic to make such a choice of the site for a home.

The actual residence of the pioneer had about it little of architectural beauty. In most cases it was only a log cabin, sometimes with a lean-to at the back, or in some instances was a double log house with a "dog trot" between the two rooms and a stone, or stick and clay, chimney at either end. In the prairie regions it might be a sod house, a dugout, or a crude structure built of rough lumber. Yet he and his family were very proud of the new house and worked diligently to improve its appearance and that of its surroundings. Often the settler's wife had brought flower seeds with her to the West, a few tulip bulbs or rose bushes from her former home.

Promptly her husband was drafted to spade up beds beneath the windows, in the yard, and on either side of the path leading to the front door, and here she planted the seeds, set out the roots, bulbs, and cuttings and tended the young plants with true motherly care. Before the end of the first season, the doors and windows were framed in a luxuriant growth of vines including morning-glories, balsam apples, mock oranges, and Jack beans, while the flower beds flamed with a riot of colors. Here were zinnias, bachelor buttons, four o'clocks, phlox, and the sweet spicy pinks and other so-called "old-fashioned" flowers, though exactly why there should be fashions in flowers must always remain to some of us an unsolved mystery. Within a year what had been a rough, primitive habitation had become a real thing of beauty fitting as naturally into the landscape as though placed there by the hand of God Himself.

Inside the home there had also been wrought interesting changes. No works of art adorned the walls, but the rag rugs on the floor and patchwork quilts on the beds were often of a quality and appearance to attract the attention of any lover of beautiful things. Not a few frontier housewives were known far

and wide for their beautiful quilts of which there were almost
as many patterns as are to be found in early American pressed
glass. Among these patterns were the "log cabin," "evening star,"
"sunrise on the walls of Troy," "double wedding ring," "way to
the Black Hills," and numerous flower patterns. In addition
many a frontier housewife did crochet work, knitting, and
needlepoint and made hooked rugs, hand-woven coverlets, and
artificial flowers. Her husband also did his bit at times and constructed ladder-back chairs with hickory seats, wove baskets,
and fashioned in wood household utensils such as bowls, bread
trays, piggins, and other articles all with such graceful lines as to
indicate considerable artistry on the part of the maker. Women
also did embroidery, or made mottoes and samplers to hang on
the walls, while the huge bed in the "front room" often had at its
head two great pillow shams on one of which had been worked
in Turkey red the legend, "I Slept and Dreamed That Life Was
Beauty," while on the other the couplet was completed with the
words, "I Woke and Found That Life Is Duty."

Perhaps few of these objects mentioned would qualify as art
according to our present-day standards. Yet they were seldom
made to satisfy any particular physical need but only to gratify
the love which these pioneer peoples had for what they considered beautiful things. Moreover, the eagerness with which
modern collectors seek out these products of the skill of our
pioneer forebears is some evidence that they are regarded even
today as having an artistic value.

Turning to the field of music, a study of pioneer life reveals
that the frontiersman must have truly felt that "He whose soul is
not moved by the concord of sweet sounds is fit for treasons,
stratagems, and spoils." Just as he all too often lacked the means
of gratifying his love for beauty, however, so did he in many
cases lack the means of gratifying his love of music. Certainly
musical instruments were decidedly scarce on the frontier of
even a half century ago. The children, of course, strummed
Jew's harps and played on harmonicas or French harps, often to
the accompaniment of doleful howlings by the family dog, but
that their efforts produced anything remotely resembling music

is open to grave question. Yet a young man was occasionally found who lacked little of real artistry in playing a French harp, though they were quite exceptional. As a rule a harp was regarded as a childish toy merely to be played for the edification of the owner and his young friends and often to the considerable irritation of their elders.

Few as were the musical instruments on the frontier, virtually every community had at least one violin, the owner of which was the local fiddler who played for the square dances and also in his own home for the entertainment of guests. His repertoire included many of the old "breakdowns" such as "The Downfall of Paris," sometimes known as the "Mississippi Sawyer"; others called "The Waggoner," "The Irish Washer Woman," "Arkansas Traveler," "Pop Goes the Weasel," "Sugar in the Gourd," "Turkey in the Straw," and "Hell Among the Yearlin's." To these should be added an occasional waltz such as "Evelina," or some other production as "The Drunkard's Hiccup." Occasionally a girl or man could be found who played the accordion, guitar or banjo in indifferent fashion, but it was rare to find more than one or two of all these instruments in a single neighborhood. Pianos were almost entirely unknown since the cost was prohibitive to people as poor as were these pioneer settlers, but a cottage organ might be found in at least one home in nearly every community.

With instruments so few, the well nigh universal craving for music must on the whole be satisfied by singing. This meant that virtually everyone sang or tried to do so. Children learned to sing almost as soon as they learned to talk. Women sang as they went about their housework and men as they toiled in the fields, cowboys as they stood guard over a sleeping trail herd at night or to "keep themselves company" during long and lonely rides. Wrinkled old grandmothers sang in quavering voices the old songs of their girlhood days and taught them to their grandchildren. People sang as naturally as a bird sings, and a visitor approaching a house would sometimes pause to listen to the words of some old ballad such as "The Gypsy's Warning" which the housewife sang as she washed dishes or scrubbed the floor.

Trust him not, O gentle lady
Though his voice be low and sweet,
Heed not him, that dark-eyed stranger
Softly pleading at thy feet.

I would only guard thy future,
Shield thee from the tempter's snare
Heed me now, O gentle lady,
I have warned thee, now beware.

Songs were by many people divided into only two groups—
hymns, or sacred music, and "Opery songs." The first named
were usually about the only ones which were commonly seen
with words and music complete. They were to be found in the
song books bought for use at church or Sunday School, though
hymn books were also common. These contained only the words,
for the singer was expected to remember the tunes. They included many songs which have come down to us today un-
changed by the lapse of a century or more. Familiar examples
are "How Firm a Foundation," "On Jordan's Stormy Banks I
Stand," "Washed in the Blood," "Amazing Grace," and "Jesus
Loves Me." The number of such hymns, however, was enormous, and many people knew the tunes and at least some of the
words of scores of them.

The so called "opera songs" to many people were any songs
not of a religious nature. Strictly speaking, however, the term
probably meant only recent songs by professional song writers
of the East. In this group might be included "Silver Threads
among the Gold," "The Court House in the Sky," "In the Baggage Coach Ahead," "Ta-ra-ra-boom-de-ay," "A Cottage by the
Sea," "White Wings," "Down on the Farm," "After the Ball," "A
Hot Time in the Old Town," "Two Little Girls in Blue," and a
host of others. Most of the three or four last named did not appear until the late nineties, and just at the end of the century, the
Spanish American War produced a new crop as "My Sweetheart
Went Down with the Maine," "After the Battle," and "Just as the
Sun Went Down." All of the songs named followed one another

in successive waves of popularity just as best-selling novels do today.

A stanza of one of the older ones, "The Court House in the Sky," is as follows:

> The angels on the picket line
> Along the milky way,
> Are seeing what you're doing boys
> And hearing what you say.
>
> And when you get unto that gate
> You'll think it's mighty slow
> When they ask you 'bout that chicken scrape
> That happened long ago.
>
> To that Court House in the sky
> I will spread my wings and fly
> To stand examination
> At the Court House in the sky.

In addition to the two classes of songs mentioned, however, there was a third group of great importance. This included the old ballads and folk songs of which "The Gypsy's Warning," already mentioned, is a type. Many of these were of Old World origin but had been brought to America very early by people who had settled in the mountainous districts of the East. Here they had been sung for generations by a people living in a more or less static society, and from here they were brought farther west by home seekers in covered wagons. Others were clearly rooted in American soil, but all were alike in that they had almost never been reduced to writing but had been passed on from generation to generation by word of mouth alone. In consequence, many variations appear, all directly traceable to a common source.

Of the old English songs "Barbara Allen" is a conspicuous example, beginning as follows:

> In Scarlet Town where I was born
> There was a fair maid dwellin'

As all young men were well aware,
Her name was Barbara Allen.

All in the merry month of May
When green buds they were swellin'
Young Jimmy Grove on his death bed lay
For love of Barbara Allen.

There was another dealing with Young Randall the Proud, who
was "justly hanged to the door for shedding the blood of the fair
Fanny Moore." There were many others, including one about

The rich old farmer
Who lived in the country close by
Who had an only daughter
On whom I cast my eye.

Some of those probably of American origin are "Nellie Gray,"
"Kitty Wells," "Beautiful Mabel Clare," "The Flowers I Saw in
the Wild Wood," "Gentle Annie," and numerous others. Most of
them were of a highly romantic nature, and in not a few instances fairly slopped sentiment.

Any girl whose family owned an organ was certain to be very
popular if she could play and sing for visitors. Young men would
ride long distances to pay her a call, and after a brief period of
preliminary conversation, would always ask her to play and sing.
The songs chosen were in most cases of a deeply sentimental kind
varied occasionally by one or two of a more flippant and frivolous
nature. In most cases, however, they were of a type calculated to
wring the heart of a wooden Indian, and in consequence they
brought the romantic cowhand or granger lad to the very verge
of tears. The words of one favorite called "Too Late" began as
follows:

And so you have come back to me-e-e
Since time alone has set you fre-e-e
And offer me again the heart
Whose early hopes were bound in me-e-e
And so you have come back again
And say the old love lingers yet.

You've tried through all these weary years,
You've tried though vainly to forget.

Come close and let me see you now-ow
Your chestnut locks are tinged with snow
But yes, it is the dear old face
I loved so fondly years ago-o-o.
The same as one summer's eve
Bent over me and kissed my brow
Oh, happy hour of trusting love
Ah, well, it is all over now.

Such doleful words sung to an even more doleful tune while the wailing organ sobbed its accompaniment were calculated to arouse in the heart of the bug-eyed listener the deepest emotion, which threatened to make him break down completely and bawl like a lost calf!

In addition to the old songs brought from the East, the pioneer settlers of the prairie West soon picked up those of another type indigenous to the new land to which they had come. These were the cowboy songs too well known by most people today to require any extended description. Usually they were mournful and plaintive in nature as "Bury Me Not on the Lone Prairie," "The Dying Cowboy," and "Dying Ranger," and "The Dying Californian." As a rule they consisted of many stanzas, indicating that the central character must have died a long and lingering death! In addition there were ballads of the "picaresque type" extolling the virtues of some dashing individual such as Jesse James or Sam Bass who had lived beyond the law and died bravely with his boots on. A stanza of one called "The Forbidden Fruit" is as follows:

Frank James in jail drinks it out of a pail
Governor Crittenden orders to suit,
There's Lee and Bob Ford drink it out of a gourd
The juice of the forbidden fruit.

Another relates that

Jesse left a wife
To mourn all her life

> Three children they were brave,
> But a dirty little coward
> Shot Mr. Howard
> And laid Jesse James in his grave.

Still a third states that

> Sam Bass was born in Indiana
> It was his native home,
> And at the age of seventeen,
> Young Sam began to roam.
> He first came out to Texas,
> A teamster for to be
> A kinder-hearted fellow
> You seldom ever see.

It then goes on to detail Sam's exploits and adventures until the time when

> Sam met his fate at Round Rock
> July the twenty-first
> They pierced his body with rifle balls
> And emptied out his purse.
>
> Poor Sam now sleeps in Texas
> Beneath six feet of clay
> And Jackson's in the bushes
> A-trying to get away.

These prairie settlers wrote very few songs descriptive of their own lives, though one or two became widely known. Perhaps the most popular was "The Little Old Sod Shanty on the Claim," of which the first stanza and chorus are as follows:

> I am looking rather seedy now
> While holding down my claim
> And my victuals are not always served the best
> And the prairie dog keeps barking so
> That I can scarcely sleep
> In my little old sod shanty in the West.

Oh! the hinges are of leather
And the windows have no glass
While the board roof lets the howling blizzard in
And I hear the hungry coyote
As he sneaks up through the grass
'Round my little old sod shanty on the claim.

While singing was so often an individual matter on the frontier, there was much group singing as well. Young people gathered Sunday afternoons at any home which boasted an organ to spend some hours in singing. So-called "singings" were also held at the country schoolhouse at more or less regular intervals and an "all-day singing with dinner on the ground" was a popular social event. Singing conventions were also held, attended by the people of an entire county, at which considerable good-natured rivalry among "teams" coming from various communities was evident.

From the time of Ichabod Crane and perhaps long before, a few men were to be found on the frontier who lived for music even though they were not able to live *by* it. Such an individual was usually a homesteader like his neighbors, but to him farming was only a more or less sordid means of acquiring a living, while his primary business was singing and directing the singing of others. With his trusty tuning fork in his pocket, he ranged far and wide, never missing an all-day singing or a singing convention, and in fact he was likely to appear at any place in perhaps an entire county where people had met to sing. He conducted the song service at revival meetings, sang at weddings and funerals, and was well known throughout a wide area.

In the field of literature, the pioneer often showed quite as much interest as he did in that of music or of art. As a producer, he was naturally a complete "washout" unless we accept the idea that his pungent, colorful speech, tall tales told orally, and occasional ballads are literary contributions, but he was frequently an omnivorous reader and sought reading matter wherever it might be found. As to what he read, generalizations are dangerous but as a rule he had little choice. An old pioneer in speaking of food on the frontier once remarked that "we ate what we could get and not much of that." The same might be said of what the early settler read. The people were so poor that newspapers and magazines were decidedly rare, and if a family in the language of the time "took a paper" at all, it was likely to be a semi-monthly journal such as *Farm and Fireside* or *Comfort* with its pages devoted largely to farming, gardening, household hints, recipes, and perhaps two or three stories.

Yet its coming was eagerly awaited, and every issue was read and reread until its contents were almost "known by heart." Often the father or mother would read the stories aloud to the entire family assembled about the fire on a winter's evening, and the characters and incidents were discussed for days afterward. Even the advertisements were diligently studied, and many a child learned new words and developed skill in reading from the glowing accounts of "Radway's Ready Relief" or "Sloan's Liniment, good for man or beast" and warranted "to heal cuts, wounds, burns, scalds, bruises, and abrasions." The children, accustomed to the coarse and often scanty fare of their pioneer home, also derived a sort of vicarious pleasure from reading recipes for the making of delectable dishes which they had never tasted and in all probability never would. Once the contents of the journal had been carefully mastered, it would be lent to a neighbor and sometimes passed about throughout an entire community.

Books were as rare as newspapers and magazines, though virtually every home had a family Bible and perhaps a copy of *Pilgrim's Progress*. These, together with the children's school books, sometimes constituted the entire library, though many households had a few others ranging from dime novels, the *Adventures of Buffalo Bill* or *Peck's Bad Boy*, to Shakespeare, Dante's *Divine Comedy*, and Milton's *Paradise Lost*. Yet people with the barest rudiments of an education tackled any and all of them with enthusiasm and deep interest, and seemed to derive from them considerable pleasure, and in their own minds at least, much profit. An ill-featured cowhand who once saw on my own table a copy of *Festus* by the English poet Bailey asked to

borrow it and returned it a month later with the remark that
"there's an awful lot of mighty good readin' in that there book."
Those familiar with the volume will doubtless wonder just how
much of it he was able to understand.

Some of the works of Dickens or Scott's *Waverley Novels* were
often found in a frontier home, as well as volumes of George
Eliot, Bulwer-Lytton, or Thackeray. All of these were enthusiastically read and discussed, but it must be confessed that there
were other books which were more numerous and which were
often read with even greater interest. These included the Beadle
Dime Novels usually dealing with the Wild West, the Old Sleuth
series of detective stories, and the saccharine effusions issued by
the F. M. Lupton Publishing Company. The last named included
such novels as *Thrown on the World, A Mad Passion, Lord
Lisle's Daughter, Heron's Wife, Reaping the Whirlwind,* and a
host of others. Frequently the scene was laid in England, and
the chief characters were lords and ladies. Authors were Bertha
M. Clay (Charlotte M. Braeme), Mary Cecil Hay, and a host of
others. All of them tossed in adjectives with a reckless abandon,
and every story always started with a bang, moved at hair-raising speed, and skidded to a sudden and dramatic stop. Other
writers whose books were widely read on the frontier were the
Duchess, Mary J. Holmes, H. Rider Haggard, E. P. Roe, and a
dozen others. Their books include *Airy Fairy Lillian, Tempest
and Sunshine, She, King Solomon's Mines, Nature's Serial Story,*
and a great many more. Some authors would give their novels
a double-barreled title as: *Dora Dean;* or, *The East India Uncle;
Breakneck Farm;* or, *The Merriman Twins;* and *Boys Will Be
Boys;* or, *A Harvest of Wild Oats.* Apparently the idea was to bag
the interest of the prospective reader, and if you missed with
the first barrel, you were nearly certain to get him with the
second.

Any such device to attract readers was entirely unnecessary
so far as the people of the frontier were concerned. A book was
a book, and leisure was abundant and books scarce. When one
was available, it was to be seized upon with avid curiosity and
eagerly read with scant regard to the title. Many of those read by

the pioneer settlers were trashy enough, being merely blood and thunder or sickly love stories filled with impossible, or at least highly improbable, characters, but in most cases they were quite harmless. They did, however, take these pioneers temporarily out of their drab surroundings into a world of romance and adventure, and no doubt permanently influenced their mental outlook and attitudes toward life. As a matter of fact, most frontier settlers would have been horrified by some of our modern novels—even the best sellers—and would have refused to have them in their homes lest they contaminate the children, or even adults. With this view there are still a few of us old-fashioned enough to have some sympathy.

Books, like periodicals, were of course freely lent to neighbors, and the temporary acquisition of a new one, or rather one not yet read, was an event of major importance. They too were read aloud of evenings, and doubtless many a man plowing in the field or housewife toiling over the washtub found the hours shortened and the work lightened by thinking over what had already happened to the fantastic hero and heroine of the book they were reading, and speculating on what would take place in the succeeding chapters to be read aloud that evening when the day's work was done.

Women had some advantage since a little reading might be done while waiting for the dinner to cook or the clothes to boil, and it is possible that many a husband was served scorched beans or burned gingerbread because of the tragic adventures of Wolfgang Wallraven or Lady Jane de Courtland. One old-timer relates that stopping at the home of Sam Smith, he found Mrs. Smith sitting on the back porch churning with one hand and holding in the other a copy of *Lady Audley's Secret*, which she was reading with wide-eyed interest, the tempo of the churndasher diminishing or increasing with the ebb and flow of action in the story!

Perhaps it is not so much what they read as it is their interest in reading, their attitude toward it, and the way in which it affected their own lives which should be considered in any discussion of literature on the frontier. That these pioneers thought a great deal more about what they read and were more influenced by it than are people today seems certain. Of course there were a few deeply religious souls who felt that reading novels was a waste of time and even slightly immoral even though their definition of the term "novel" was likely to be slightly naive. These were, however, quite exceptional. As a rule people read everything available and wished for more. Also the characters in the books were very real to them and were sometimes compared with their own friends and acquaintances in the community. Mrs. Gray once remarked that Lady Clare de Vere in *The Earl's Daughters* reminded her a great deal of Lottie Miller, a neighborhood belle, and further asserted that Sir Ralph Hadden, Master of Hadden Hall, was the "spittin' image" of Jim Haddock, who was never master of anything more pretentious than his one-room sod house a mile farther down the creek. Other such comparisons were common. Surely a people with that much imagination must have been deeply and permanently influenced by the literature which they read, regardless of the character of that literature as judged by modern standards.

It seems that enough has been given to show that the people of the American frontier were far from being rank materialists interested only in their own physical welfare. Perhaps it may be urged that the interests described can hardly be classed as cultural since their efforts, productions, and interests fall considerably short of being in the fields of what we, today, would call art, music, and literature. Yet they were humble beginnings or roots from which have grown greater things and wider interests. It is certain that many of our greatest artists in all three of these fields grew up under frontier conditions, and in all probability they found their inspiration for a later distinguished career in exactly those rudimentary cultural activities which have been described. Cyrus Edwin Dallin, the sculptor who created *The Appeal to the Great Spirit,* was born at Springville, Utah, and grew up in a frontier environment. George Grey Barnard was the son of a village preacher who came west when the lad was quite small. John Noble was born in 1874 at Wichita, Kansas, while Hamlin Garland was born and reared in Wisconsin, and as a young man took up a homestead in Dakota. William Dean Howells was born in Ohio when that region was still frontier and worked with his father, who published a village newspaper. Numerous other men well known in the realms of art and literature spent their childhood on the frontier, while in the field of music, we all know men and women who grew up in pioneer homes and whose interest in a musical career was doubtless awakened by some itinerant teacher or the crude efforts of local musicians.

Not only do we find many great artists who have emerged from such an unpromising environment, but throughout our entire country are thousands of highly educated men and women deeply appreciative of the best in literature and the fine arts who lived as children in sod houses, dugouts, or log cabins, attended all-day singings, drew pictures on their slates when the teacher thought they were doing problems in arithmetic, and read Nick Carter as avidly as their own small sons and daughters listen on the radio to the story of the exploits of the Lone Ranger or follow adventures of their favorite hero on television or in the daily newspaper strips.

IV

I left my old log cabin
In the hills of Tennessee
For I couldn't see much future there
For the kids and Mary and me.
So we loaded our stuff in the wagon
And told the friends good-bye
And journeyed westward day by day
To a region of grass and sky.

We're happy here on our prairie claim
Though our little home is of sod
And neighbors are few and the land so new
As to seem just created by God.
We miss our friends of other days
And yet we would rather be
In our sod house rude on the level plains
Than back in Tennessee.

Sod-House Folks

IV

From Log Cabin to Sod House

PIONEER LIFE IN AMERICA was not always the same. The settlers of
new lands in the West all faced common hardships and often common
dangers. Moreover, from the time of Bacon's Rebellion to the era of
Bryan Democracy they felt that their needs were ignored in the
legislation enacted by the people of the East. These factors gave to
all frontier residents a degree of regional consciousness, but geographic and physiographic conditions made life in the eastern wood-
lands very different from that on the prairies of Nebraska or Kansas.
This chapter seeks to give the problems of the pioneers in these two
areas.

THE CULTURAL AND ECONOMIC PATTERN which, broadly speaking, is the life of the people of any region grows from certain
distinct roots. Some of these, as climate and geographic conditions, lie close beneath the surface while others are deeply
rooted in the subsoil of history. From these grows a pattern of
life which reaches full flowering and eventually produces fruits.
It would seem that if these fruits produced by various regional
cultures could be gathered and placed in a great wine press and
the juice extracted, the resulting brew would have certain distinct qualities. For in it one might find the wholesome but
slightly acid touch of Puritan New England, the mellow sweetness of the Old South, the substantial body of the Middle West,
the wild raw tang of the Great Plains and Rocky Mountain Pla-
teau, the peculiar spiciness of the Spanish Southwest, and the
exotic flavor of the Pacific Coast all mingled in the peculiar

blend that we call Americanism which, lacking any one of these elements, would not be the same.

In addition to the regions named and some others, there existed for many generations in America another area in which conditions of life were in most cases essentially the same and whose people usually had a distinct regional consciousness. That area was the American frontier. The characteristics of the frontier did not vary much for at least two centuries and the people who occupied it, whether in the northern, middle, or southern zones of settlement, felt themselves bound together by common experiences, hardships, and dangers and by the necessity for solving the same problems. Remote from markets and from industrial and commercial centers, they usually felt themselves either neglected or exploited by the people of the more thickly settled regions farther east, and this too was a bond of union.

The purpose of this chapter is to discuss very briefly the life of the people of two American frontiers—that of the log-cabin dwellers of the timbered regions east of the Mississippi, and largely speaking, of the first tier of states west of that stream; and the frontier of the early settlers of the prairie plains beginning as a rule some distance west of the great Father of Waters.

As agricultural settlement moved slowly westward from the Atlantic seaboard and passed the fall line of the rivers, there was always along its western rim a pioneer society composed of people who lived under frontier conditions, and who looked to the West as an area of free land and economic opportunity, rather than to Europe as the source of culture, as did the people of the coastal plain. On beyond the fall line to the foot of the mountains these settlements were gradually extended, then they jumped the first range of the Appalachian Highland into the great valley, poured westward through the Cumberland Gap or down the Ohio to occupy the Mississippi Valley, and eventually crossed the great river to settle Missouri, Arkansas, Louisiana, eastern Texas, and Iowa. Before 1840 Missouri and Arkansas had been admitted as states and half a dozen years later both Texas and Iowa had become members of the Federal Union.

By the time of the outbreak of the Civil War the edge of the great prairie plains had been reached and here this advancing agricultural population hesitated, reluctant to attempt to cope with a region so unlike any which it had known in the past. While certain portions of Ohio, Indiana, Illinois, Iowa, Kentucky, and some other states had fairly extensive areas of prairie, the life of the American pioneers had largely been that of forest dwellers and was shaped and conditioned by the wooded lands on which they lived, or which lay in more or less close proximity to their homes. Pioneer life in America up to this time had been a woodland life. The occupation of the vast stretches of level prairie plains lying to the west was still in the future.

Without too much logic we are always likely to judge the characteristics of any individual by the type of home which he occupies. By no means all of the people of the wooded regions of the frontier lived in log cabins and certainly less than half of those of the plains of Nebraska, Kansas, western Oklahoma or Texas resided in sod houses but log cabins seldom appeared on the prairie plains and the sod house was unknown east of the great prairies. In consequence, it is not without some reason that these two areas may be called the log-cabin and the sod-house frontiers.

Up until the middle 1840's many of the pioneers who migrated westward came down the Ohio by boat, thence to the mouth of either the Missouri or Arkansas and up those streams to a suitable spot from which they spread out into the interior. This ability to penetrate the West by means of rivers was largely responsible for the admission of Missouri and Arkansas to the Union in 1821 and 1836 respectively while that of Iowa was delayed until 1846. By no means all of these westward emigrants, however, came by water. Many came overland in covered wagons, some on horseback, some on foot with their possessions strapped to the backs of pack horses, and some on foot. Period!

The story has been told of a family consisting of husband, wife, and two very small children who set out from eastern

Missouri to reach free land in the western part of that state. Having no domestic animals, they had to carry all their household goods and utensils on their backs. Both husband and wife were so heavily burdened that the former could in addition carry only one child and the latter none at all. This did not discourage them. The husband would pick up one child, carry it half a mile, and deposit it together with his axe, gun, and other impedimenta beside the trail. He would then walk back and carry the second youngster half a mile beyond the first, after which he would return for his property and the remaining junior member of the little group. In the meantime, the wife plodded steadily onward pausing occasionally to rest, while the father did his own resting during the return trip for his offspring waiting more or less patiently beside the trail. In such intermittent fashion did the little family proceed toward the end of their own particular rainbow. Surely the lure of the West must have been well-nigh irresistible to induce even the most courageous of pioneers to undertake a migration under such difficulties.

While this story was told in all seriousness and was abundantly vouched for, it must have been a very exceptional case. Most of the pioneers who removed overland to the wooded frontier region journeyed either by covered wagon or with their worldly goods on pack animals. Choosing a tract of land, they settled down, built a shelter from the weather, and set to work at the task of felling the forest trees in order to provide logs for the new home.

The first shelter occupied by the family was likely to be a "half-faced camp" such as the Lincolns are said to have occupied for a time. This was a rude shed open on one side except for quilts or blankets that might be hung there to keep out the rain and wind. This was only a temporary habitation, however, to be occupied while the log-cabin home was constructed.

Apparently the house built of logs notched at either end and slightly flattened on the sides, with any possible cracks plastered with clay, was first erected in America by the Swedes of Delaware and was modeled on similar structures of the Scandinavian Peninsula. The log-cabin homes of the American pioneers were of several types. Perhaps the commonest was simply a square, or rectangular, structure of one room with a puncheon floor and a roof of rough, split shingles. Because timber was so abundant, however, many pioneers sought to provide a more commodious home by building the walls high enough to provide an attic bedroom, reached by a ladder, and by reducing the pitch of the rear roof and extending it back far enough to cover a "lean to" or second room, which might be used either as a kitchen or bedroom. A chimney, either of stone or sticks and clay, was built at one end of the main room—which usually served as a kitchen, too, unless the smaller rear room also boasted a fireplace. Cookstoves did not appear very much in the rural districts of Illinois or Missouri until the 1840's. Even then they were at first viewed somewhat askance by some conservative souls who had heard of boilers bursting on the river steamers and feared that the strange iron contraption might blow up and kill half the family.

The more enterprising settlers of a community frequently built a double log house with a fireplace and chimney at each end and a wide hallway, sometimes called a dog trot, between the two rooms. In this hall were hung the tools, saddle, and harness. Here the dogs slept in winter and here the housewife sat on hot summer days to do her churning, sewing, or preparing vegetables for cooking, since this wide hall open at either end was the coolest part of the house. If in addition to the two rooms and open hallway the exterior walls were built high enough to provide attic bedrooms, and if a shady front porch were added, the family felt that the home was little short of luxurious.

The spot for the location of the home had been chosen with due regard both to the practical and the artistic. Sometimes it was in a sheltered glen where it would be protected from the cold winter winds. More often it stood on a low tree-crowned hill from which might be had a view of the surrounding country. If possible it was built near a spring which not only furnished a supply of water for domestic use but over which a springhouse might be built where milk, butter, and other perishable foods could be kept cool in summer.

Once the home had been erected, however, often with the help of kindly neighbors, the pioneer's task was only well begun. Unless he happened to be located at the edge of some small prairie the forest lay all about, so after building cribs, lots, and shelter for the domestic animals came the labor of clearing and fencing fields for planting. From dawn to dusk the settler toiled at the task of felling trees, splitting rails, and building the worm fences with stakes and riders to tie the panels together. All day long, in many cases, his axe sang a song of triumph over the forest, interrupted at times by the crash of a falling tree. Moreover, what the woodland pioneer could do with an axe would make the city dweller or one born and bred on the wide prairies gaze at him in goggle-eyed wonder. The curiously curved axe handle, which is purely an American invention and is even yet virtually unknown to Europe, was evolved quite early. In order the more quickly to provide a sizeable area for planting, some of the larger trees were often merely "deadened" by girdling and left standing. Once the field had been cleared, it must be fenced, since the livestock usually ran at large.

The logs not to be used in building or for fencing were rolled together into great heaps at the neighborhood "log rollings" and burned, and the stumps and girdled trees were also burned as far as possible when they had become dry. The settler could not foresee a time when the American people would deplore the passing of the forests and need so desperately the vast store of timber thus so wantonly destroyed. Even if he had, it is doubtful if the possible wants of the future would have prevailed over the necessities of the present. Whether it was timber, game and fish, soil or mineral resources, the average frontier American has seldom thought much of conservation for the sake of future generations. "Have you no regard for posterity?" an old pioneer was once asked. "Regard for posterity?" was the answer. "No, I should say not. Why should I? What did posterity ever do for me?"

To the log-cabin settler the forest was a horrible impediment to progress and civilization—an enemy to be fought every day. Moreover, the forest fought back with a persistence and vigor that must at times have proved most discouraging. After a field had been cleared and the logs and slash burned, roots still remained deep in the soil and from these, each spring, sprouts shot up with an enthusiasm that must have been most discouraging to one who had worked so hard to prepare a field for tillage. These must be cut down annually, and if possible, the roots from which they had grown, destroyed. The labor required to hold and utilize what had already been wrested from the forest made additional clearing proceed very slowly. In consequence, the area of cultivated land usually remained small for several years.

In most cases, however, there was little need that it should be large. Remote from markets, the settler sought only to provide for himself and family those fundamental needs of food, clothing, and shelter. Even this was not always easy and the ambitious man who sought each year to widen the clearing and so provide more land to produce more food for his family found his life one of unremitting toil. Corn was the staple breadstuff of most of the woodland pioneers and hominy, corn pone, griddle cakes and corn dodgers—sometimes known as "hush puppies"—were staple articles of diet.

At first, meat was largely obtained from hunting, and the long rifle and skill in its use furnished the best guarantee of an adequate meat supply for the family. It was not long until game began to grow scarce but by this time the first pigs brought in had increased to such numbers as to provide an ample supply of pork, ham, and bacon. Two or three lean cows provided a somewhat inadequate supply of milk and butter while the only fruit during the early years consisted of wild blackberries, huckleberries, plums, grapes, persimmons, and pawpaws gathered in the woods. A few peach, apple, and pear trees were usually planted, however, and when these came into bearing the situation with respect to fruit was greatly improved. The garden supplied an abundance of fresh vegetables, and turnips, potatoes, sweet potatoes, and cabbage were stored in a cellar or buried in the ground for winter use.

Clothing was often homespun for there were at least a few

sheep in almost every community, though they required considerable care due to the ravages of wolves and other predatory animals. Shoes were made at home from home-tanned leather and a warm coat was often made from the skins of animals while the buckskin shirt and coonskin cap were also common. Furniture for the cabin was likewise made at home. This consisted of bedsteads on which were placed feather beds, straw ticks, or shuck mattresses; hickory-bottomed chairs; tables of rough boards; or a bench on which the children sat at meals and which was usually placed behind the dining table next to the wall. Often two or three rag rugs were on the floor and one or two pictures on the walls. Light was furnished by tallow candles and in the later period by kerosene lamps.

With the passing years life grew a trifle easier. The log-cabin home was weathered by the elements. Gay morning-glories climbed over the windows or the front porch, and beds of old-fashioned flowers such as pinks, phlox, bachelor's buttons, and zinnias beside the front door or along the path leading to it added splashes of color to the scene. In time the humble home, which had at first appeared new and out of place, nestled into its setting and merged with the landscape as though always a part of it.

The horizon of the woodland pioneer and his family was necessarily limited. Seldom did he know many people beyond walking distance from his own cabin though "walking distance" is a relative term and was greater than most people would regard it now. Yet, in spite of long hours of hard labor, time was found for social contact with neighbors. Often on Sunday morning the entire family would rise early, and with the numerous youngsters washed and scrubbed to within an inch of their lives, all were loaded into the wagon for a drive of two or three miles to spend the day with friends. Here they always received a warm welcome. When the horses were stabled and fed, the men sat in the shade of a tree and talked while the women went into the kitchen and prepared dinner and the children ran wild about the farm or played such games as marbles, town ball, or prisoner's base. Eventually dinner was announced and the older people went in and sat down at the long table, while the children were required to wait since there was no room at the table nor were there enough dishes for everyone to eat at the same time.

After grace had been said, the guests and hosts alike fell to with an enthusiasm that the abundance before them fully warranted. When they had finished, the dishes were washed, the second table was set, and the children attacked the food with appetites considerably sharpened by the delay. Those Sunday dinners in a frontier home, especially after the first two or three years of pioneering had passed, would make the modern housewife turn green with envy. Chicken and dumplings, fried ham with red gravy, turnip greens and other fresh vegetables from the garden, blackberry cobbler, cool buttermilk, coffee, corn bread, and golden butter were only a few of the items likely to grace the table in the early summer season. In winter, baked sweet potatoes, dried corn, and beans boiled with pork, turnips, or cabbage were substituted for the fresh vegetables, and nearly always there was chicken, or in some cases baked spareribs, country sausage, fried pork, or bacon and cream gravy.

Such all-day visits were frequently almost the only form of social relaxation for many a busy housewife though there were occasional quilting or sewing parties, and sometimes an itinerant preacher held services in one of the homes or under a rude brush arbor.

The men, however, had more social contacts than did their wives. Eventually a gristmill would be erected beside some convenient stream which furnished the necessary water power, and men and boys bringing a "turn of corn" to mill would sit in the shade and gossip or swap stories while waiting for the grain to be ground, often commenting sarcastically but in good-humored fashion on the length of time required for that work. "Most persistent mill I ever saw," asserted Hank Johnson. "Just as soon as it gets one grain ground, it tackles the next one right off." "Yep," replied his companion, "my boy Sam sez, sez he, 'Why, paw, I could eat that meal as fast as this mill grinds it.' 'Maybe you could, son,' sez I, 'but how long could you keep it up?' 'Well, paw,' sez he, 'I figger I could keep it up till I starved to death!'"

Soon some enterprising settler usually built a general merchandise store near the mill or at some crossroads and dispensed as much sugar, coffee, calico, and other commodities as the pioneer settlers could purchase, frequently bartering his merchandise for coonskins, buckskin, cowhides, tallow, and beeswax, or butter and eggs if not too remote from a larger market. The crossroads store also became something of a social center where people met their neighbors and exchanged neighborhood news while transacting business. A schoolhouse was soon built and this too became a center for social activities. Church services might be held there once or twice a month, a literary and debating society was organized, box suppers were held, and meetings for singing arranged on Sunday afternoons. The younger people also held parties, socials, play parties, and in some cases square dances at the more commodious homes. So the little community soon began to enjoy some social life.

As the years went by, the character of the log-cabin frontier began to change. The settler's family increased and he found it necessary to widen his fields by clearing additional acres in order to produce more food for so many hungry mouths. Families were, as a rule, large: half a dozen children being only an average number, and ten or a dozen not unusual. With little hired labor available and money to pay for it very scarce, even if it had been procurable, children were a distinct asset to people faced with the heavy task of clearing and improving a woodland farm. In consequence, the settler "raised his own help" just as he raised his own meat, fruit, and vegetables. Once the writer and an elderly farmer from the wooded hills of northern Arkansas were walking along the streets of a small city with a huge Navy base located nearby, weaving their way in and out of an almost continuous procession of baby buggies pushed by young Navy wives. Presently the old farmer shifted his chew of tobacco to the other side of his mouth, spat generously over the curb, and remarked: "Well, it looks like that in eighteen or twenty years we're sure either agoin' to have to start another war or clear more land."

Here spoke a voice from the past—stating in succinct fashion the problem of the log-cabin pioneer of three quarters of a century ago. With his family increasing so rapidly, he must clear more land, but the limits to which his fields might be extended were marked by the boundaries of his farm and before many years these had been reached. Except in certain parts of eastern Texas—a state always generous with land which was its most plentiful commodity—very few of the forest pioneers had originally acquired a large acreage. The famous advice given by Mrs. Means to her husband who sought land, "Git a plenty while you're a-gittin'," was seldom followed by the pioneer farmer. Few actual farmers had money enough to purchase a large tract and, moreover, there seemed little reason for it since years would be required to clear and put in cultivation even 40 acres. There seemed no point in holding title to extensive pasture lands which could hardly be enclosed at a time when the only fences must be made of rails or poles. Even if the settler owned as much as 80 to 160 acres a large part of it was likely to consist of hills or rocky land unfit for tillage.

As more and more settlers entered a new region, government land passed into the hands of individuals until no public land remained. Many of these individuals were the small subsistence farmers though naturally some large tracts were early acquired by speculators, in many cases nonresidents, who sold off their holdings at a generous profit in tracts of a size to suit the purchaser, and gradually increased their prices to "as much as the traffic would bear." Eventually some of these larger landholders came out to settle on their holdings bringing capital enough to build themselves large farmhouses and to develop their extensive acres. Other men, farther east where land was high, sold out their farms and came to this secondary frontier to purchase larger tracts of relatively cheap land and establish themselves as prosperous farmers. Some of these rented a part of their holdings and the tenant farmer began to appear in a region where he had hitherto been unknown. Thus in time a differentiated society began to grow up in what had been the former log-cabin frontier. There were the original settlers on their small woodland farms, and on the one hand these larger and more prosperous landowners who were growing so called "money crops" of cotton and tobacco in the South or of wheat, corn, and hogs in the North, and on the other tenant farmers renting land from these larger landowners.

Under such circumstances what was the log-cabin dweller with half a dozen boys fast growing up to do? Clearly his little farm would not support the entire family. Once these lads had reached manhood they must, if they continued farm life, either migrate or become tenant farmers, giving a large share of the fruits of their toil to the landlord. Prices of farm land were by this time too high for them to purchase farms in the community.

Of course from 1840 to 1865 events of nationwide importance came to confuse the picture. The migration to Oregon, the California Gold Rush, the Pike's Peak boom, and the Civil War took many thousands of young men from the log-cabin frontier, some of them permanently but in most cases only for a temporary absence. Those that returned came back only to find opportunities for them less promising than when they had left.

There were factors other than providing for the future of a growing family that caused many a log-cabin dweller to leave his hard-won clearing and seek his fortune on the western prairies. The fertility of the soil declined due to erosion and lack of crop rotation. The little farm, which now produced less than formerly, must provide a living for a larger number. Also on every frontier there have always been certain restless individuals who pioneer for the sheer love of pioneering. This applies not only to the hunters, mountain men, and other characters of the Great West but to settlers as well. It is in a sense the manifestation of the creative urge. Such men love the thrill that comes from building a home and carving a farm from the wilderness and helping to develop a new community. Once that has been done they are eager to push on and repeat the process.

All these factors and many more must be considered in determining the reasons for the rapid settlement of the prairie plains in the decades immediately following the close of the Civil War. Just to the west of the last log-cabin frontier lay the enormous stretch of level prairies. At their eastern edge settlement had hesitated for approximately a generation but, not long after Appomattox, the migration began and soon swelled to a flood covering all that part of the plains region suitable for crop growing and extending at times into other parts which we now realize were not suitable, due to lack of rainfall. In the two decades from 1870 to 1890, according to census figures the population of the Dakotas grew, in round numbers, from 14,000 to 719,000; that of Nebraska from 122,000 to 1,058,000; Kansas from 364,000 to 1,427,000; and Texas from 818,000 to 2,235,000. Even in the next decade, from 1890 to 1900, there was a great increase in the population of some western states and territories, that of Oklahoma Territory rising from 61,000 to over 400,000. While a considerable part of this population, particularly in the North, was European-born, much of it in the Central and Southern area came from the log-cabin frontier of the next tier of states to the east.

The log-cabin dweller who sought a new home on the prairies, like every other man who migrates to a new land, always did so despite the urgings and oft-expressed misgivings of his friends and neighbors. "Wild geese migrate, owls stay at home," declared the friends of Nathan Wyeth of Massachusetts when he expressed his intention of removing to Oregon. When Hiram Wick, a tenant farmer of the Texas Cross Timbers, who had a large family of girls and owned no property except a wagon and team, a few tools and household goods, and a number of "hound dogs" and a shotgun, announced his intention of going to Oklahoma, his old father-in-law was vociferous in his objections. Sitting at a neighbor's dinner table one day the old gentleman expressed himself in no uncertain terms. "Let me tell you, Mr. Smith," he exclaimed, pounding the table to give emphasis to his words, "whenever Hiram Wick goes out West with that big family of girls of his'n and no cattle—it'll break him—it'll break him—just as shore as I'm a-settin' here a-eatin' your grub." Yet Hiram had nothing to "break" except a pack of hounds and a shotgun.

Once he had acquired what was called the "Western fever," however, a man seldom gave much heed to the objections of his neighbors. The Homestead Act of 1862 gave 160 acres free of charge except for land-office fees to every citizen twenty-one years old or the head of a family, or to those who had declared their intention of becoming citizens. Migration for the tenant farmer involved few preliminaries. Ordinarily he had only a wagon, team, and a few tools and household goods. Once his crops had been gathered, all movable property could be loaded into the wagon and a start made for the West. The same was true of a newly married couple who went west to establish their first home. Ordinarily the parents of the groom and bride each made some contributions toward providing the necessary outfit for the journey and the establishment of a new household.

Not much was required. Many a young couple set out for the Prairie West with high hopes for the future though their sole worldly possessions consisted of a pony team and an old wagon in which was stored a plow, hoe, spade, axe, and gun, together with a feather bed, half a dozen quilts, a couple of chairs, and a box containing a skillet, kettle, coffee pot, a very few dishes, and a meager supply of food for the journey. Often the young husband did not have twenty-five dollars in real money tucked in the pocket of his faded jeans, and in some cases it was much less.

For the small landowner migration involved more complications since in most cases a buyer must be found for the farm. Seldom did the purchase price amount to more than a few hundred dollars, and not more than one third of this was ordinarily paid in cash while the remainder was likely to be due in installments paid annually for three or four years. When the farm had been sold, with some misgivings and regrets, there remained the work of finishing the harvest of the crops, selling the livestock and such other property as could not be taken in the wagon, and a hundred other little chores and errands. The wife carefully packed her most treasured belongings and the junior members of the household went about swelling with importance while their young friends and playmates gazed at them with respectful admiration. They were going West—out into a land of romance and adventure—a region of wide plains traversed by mighty mysterious rivers and they already felt themselves "wild westerners."

To any questions from the unfortunate youngsters that must remain in the drab and monotonous surroundings, they responded with imagination and enthusiasm. Yes, it would be a long and dangerous journey but their dad was a brave man and would see them all safely through to its end. Once there, life was certain to be filled with adventure! Surely there were Indians out there and cowboys and wolves, bears, and panthers! They themselves were going to learn to be great riders and hunters and perhaps scouts or ranchmen. Maybe some day they would come back mounted on dashing horses with silver-mounted saddles and dressed in buckskin with boots, and spurs, and all the regalia of real cowboys! It is little wonder that their youthful comrades were impressed by such flights of eloquence.

At last came the day of departure. Nearly everything had been packed into the wagon the day before. Old Rover could go west too, trotting along beside the wagon or beneath it, but sorrowfully the children carried the family cat to the house of a nearby neighbor, who had promised her a good home, because there was no way of taking her with them and besides, "it is bad luck to move cats." Probably several friends came over early to see the emigrants off. The last box and bundle was packed in the wagon box and the children climbed to their seats on rolls of bedding beneath the canvas cover which had been looped up on either side so that they might view the landscape. Then the husband and wife climbed to the spring seat and, followed by the final good-byes and good wishes of the assembled neighbors and with old Rover barking excitedly and capering about the wagon, out toward the mysterious West drove this family of pioneers.

Perhaps in most cases the husband kept his eyes steadfastly fixed on the road ahead and the children chattered excitedly, but we can believe that it was a very unusual wife who did not look back and wipe her eyes with her handkerchief as the old home which she had loved and helped so much to create faded into the distance. One who has himself journeyed west in a cov-

ered wagon and who has lived beside a road along which many
migrating families have passed with the husband and wife sitting on the spring seat, and three or four children peeping out
from beneath the brown, travel-stained cover, has never had any
doubt as to which was the tragic figure in each such little family
group. It was never the man, going out into a new region of free
land and what he felt were great opportunities. It was not any
of the children, for to all of them such a journey was one continuous picnic. Always the tragic figure was the woman sitting
by her husband's side going away from home and church and old
friends and all those little things which mean so much more to a
woman than they can ever mean to a man—yet cheerfully and
willingly going with those she loved to a far-off country. How
many times had she packed away beneath the wagon cover,
among the tools and household goods, two or three pictures,
some lace curtains, a white tablecloth and napkins, a few choice
pieces of glass, china, or silver, a few packages of flower seeds
and some roots of the old rose bush by the window—packed
away with tender, loving hands in moist earth to be transplanted
into the alien soil of a new home which as yet existed only in
her dreams.

Probably the husband, knowing the desperate need for space,
had urged that such useless things should be left behind. Perhaps he had asserted that they would be out of place in the crude
frontier society of which they must for many years be a part,
but the wife usually had her way and she was right. It was only
the possession of a few such little treasures that sustained many
a homesteader's wife through the cruel first years of life on a
prairie claim, because these things represented to her at once a
memory of her own old home, where she had a great pride in
these possessions, and the hope of a time in the future when she
would have a home into which these things would properly fit.

The journey westward might be long but as a rule it was a
happy one. When the edge of the great prairies was reached the
character of the farms and houses began to change. Log cabins
gave place to structures of stone or lumber. Then the distance
between houses lengthened as they entered the more thinly

peopled region. When they saw the first sod houses and dugouts they realized that they were truly in a new land and the sight of the first prairie dogs convinced the children that the real West had been reached at last. Finally, they came only to scattered settlements with long stretches of unoccupied land between, and here a tract of 160 acres was chosen and their long trek was at last ended.

Many factors were considered in choosing the land upon which to settle. Most important of all was fertile soil, but distance to railroad, the possible source of a supply of water, and of firewood and timber for framing a habitation, all had to be considered. Also, it was desirable not to be too far from neighbors and to locate in an area where others were likely to settle in the near future so that it would be possible to have a school, church, and perhaps a store. More, perhaps, than the woodland pioneer, did the prairie settler hope for the rapid peopling of the region about him. This may have been due in part to the bigness and loneliness of the land. Or perhaps it was partially a hope for increased land values that were certain to come with more population, or merely the eager desire to see his own courage and faith justified and the region grow quickly to a thickly peopled and prosperous region.

The preliminaries of visiting the land office and making entry of the tract chosen if it were a homestead, or of arranging with the railway land department for the purchase and first payment if it were railroad land, did not usually take long. Then came the building of a home and the task of creating a farm on a tract of virgin prairie.

As has been indicated, by no means all or even a majority of the prairie pioneers built and lived in sod houses. Only in localities where the soil is of firm texture, with its particles firmly bound together by the roots of a thick coat of grass, can a sod house be built. In areas of sandy soils covered by bunch grass, some other type of construction is necessary. Like the forest dweller, the prairie settler utilized for his house the material which he had available. In some cases it was stone, in others, sod, in still others rough lumber. In many instances, the home was a dugout, or half dugout, partially underground but usually with the sides built up sufficiently to admit of two small windows.

Ordinarily, the cover was removed from the wagon and used as a tent while the first home was constructed. If it were a sod house, long ribbons of sod usually eight to ten inches wide were cut into blocks about eighteen inches long and walls were made of these with spaces left for a door in front and windows on either side. These spaces were framed with rough boards to hold the windows and door. A fireplace was usually put at one end of the structure with the chimney also built of sod. The earthen floor was beaten hard and smooth, and the roof, supported by the heavy ridgepole which extended the entire length of the building, was made of blocks of sod resting on willows or rushes placed on poles extending like rafters from the ridgepole to the side walls. Properly made, a sod house would last for several years, though some repairs might from time to time be necessary.

The dugout was often constructed by excavating a rectangular space in the side of a low hill and building up the front portion with sod, stones, or short logs. Its interior differed little from that of the sod house. In some instances stone was available to build the walls of the new home and in others the settlers had enough money to purchase lumber for a crude box dwelling of one or two rooms made of twelve-inch boards with the cracks between them covered by narrow strips of lumber. Such a house had a shingle roof and a floor but the great majority of people did not have sufficient funds for such a luxurious dwelling. The first home of the majority in many areas was either a sod house or dugout.

Once the home was finished and the scanty possessions moved inside and bestowed to the best advantage, the settler set to work at the task of improving the farm and at the same time providing a living for his family. Sod was broken and harrowed, a little crop and a few fruit trees planted, shelter provided for the livestock, and arrangements made for water and fuel.

From the very first the settler was acutely conscious of the wide differences between his present environment and his former one. The most impressive thing about the prairie was the prairie itself. A young man born and bred among the wooded hills of Arkansas once went out to western Oklahoma to visit his brother and reached his destination late at night. The next morning his brother conducted him outside and said: "Well, Bill, what do you think of the country?" Bill gazed for a full minute at the wide expanse of green prairie stretching out on every side to meet the purple horizon before he replied: "I don't rightly know, Sam, but it looks to me like the Lord or somebody else has done the best job of clearin' here I've ever seen!"

How to live in a region almost completely devoid of timber was a major problem. For the first time the settler realized the value of the forests and often yearned for just a few of the trees which he had so wantonly destroyed. Wood for fuel was scarce and must often be eked out by the use of cow chips or twisted hay. The few timbers required for framing the sod-house home must be hauled for many miles. The matter of enclosures was a problem. Locust or Osage orange seeds were planted about the fields and pasture lands but it would require some years for the young sprouts to grow sufficiently to form a hedge and in the meantime the horses and even the milk cows must be picketed out on the prairie or in some cases herded by one of the children throughout the day and driven up each night to a small corral made of poles often hauled from some distant ravine, or tract of land too rough for farming.

Securing water for domestic use and for the livestock was also likely to be difficult. Regretfully, the settler thought of the cold, flowing springs of his former homeland or of the shallow well near the log-cabin door from which an ample supply of cool water was drawn by means of a bucket and sweep or with rope and pulley. Springs on the prairie plains were few and far between and while in some localities good water might be had by digging a well to the depth of thirty feet or less, there were many other regions where it was necessary to drill for hundreds of feet before a supply of water was reached.

The prairie pioneer also quickly discovered that he must adjust to new climatic conditions. Nature worked on a grand scale.

Long periods of drought were followed by torrential rains. The summers seemed intensely hot and the winters were often very cold. Then, too, there was the wind which seemed to blow eternally and often proved most nerve-racking, especially to the women.

In addition, he found that he must revise his former conceptions as to distance. The nearest railroad town was likely to be forty or fifty miles away and from it must be transported most supplies. Even the little frontier store might be six to ten miles distant and the nearest neighbor at least a mile or more away. No longer was the settler's horizon bounded by the distance that he could easily walk. Trips to the railroad, to the store or little hamlet, or even to the homes of any but the nearest of neighbors, must be made on horseback or by wagon. This ordinarily meant the acquiring of another horse or two, a better saddle, and far wider contacts than had been known in the past.

Even today the resident of the prairie plains has a conception of what constitutes distance that is puzzling to the rural or small-town people of the East. Often he may drive forty to eighty miles to attend a show, for a few hours' shopping, or to have dinner with a friend. A traveler across western Texas suddenly remembered that he had a cousin living somewhere in that portion of the state and stopped at a ranchman's house on the remote chance of securing some information as to this relative. "Could you tell me where Jim Blevins lives?" he inquired of the old cattlemen sitting on the front porch. "Sure can, stranger," was the reply, "he lives exactly ninety-five miles straight down this road and on the right-hand side, in a two-story white house with a big cottonwood tree in the front yard. You can't miss it!"

Undoubtedly the prairie settlers were also affected by attitudes and viewpoints of those who made up the pastoral society which in many cases they came to displace. Unlike the woodland pioneer who found the region occupied only by an occasional Indian, the plains dweller came into contact with the ranchman and was doubtless influenced by the range rider's indifference to money and distance, as well as his buoyant cheerfulness, youthful spirit, and light-hearted attitude. This is another story, however, which has already been told and would require an exclusive monograph for any full discussion. At any rate the prairie pioneer felt at least that his viewpoint had been broadened by the bigness of the wide land in which he had settled. He felt that he was doing things worthwhile and was distinctly sorry for his old neighbors farther east. He believed that they were cramped by a narrow life and earnestly urged that they come out and join him in the development of a new country.

The sod-house dweller also soon found his food habits radically changed. His prairie land could easily be prepared for wheat and this rather than corn became his staple breadstuff. Bacon and pork were common but grass-fed beef appeared on his table far more often than formerly. Wild game was still an important addition to his food supply but instead of squirrels, pheasants, or venison, it was likely to be prairie chickens, plovers, curlews, or in some cases antelope. The garden supplied vegetables but the newly planted orchard would not come into bearing for years, and the mouths of the settler and his family often watered as they thought of the luscious blackberries and strawberries or the succulent pawpaws and persimmons that grew so plentifully in the woods of the old homeland, or of the apples, peaches, and pears produced by their trees planted in a sheltered spot near the log cabin which they had left behind.

Lack of fruit was one of the real hardships of the sod-house frontier but the ingenious pioneers sought substitutes so far as possible. Watermelons and cantaloupes often grew in astonishing fashion. Tomatoes, rhubarb, and several types of small melons known as pomegranates, or "poor man's apples," were common. Pies were made from pie melons and preserves from citron melons or watermelon rinds, and pumpkin butter or even a marmalade made from cantaloupes appeared on many tables. Trips were made to the sand hills bordering the nearest river to gather wild plums or grapes from which were made jelly and preserves, so far as the scanty supply of sugar permitted. On the whole, the sod-house pioneers seldom lacked food, though it might be coarse and lacking in variety. Yet with milk and

butter, eggs, and fried chicken now and then—mostly then—
they were reasonably well fed.

Perhaps the most significant change in the life of the man who
migrated from the log-cabin frontier to that of the sod house
was his enormous increase of leisure. In his old home he had a
job three hundred and sixty-five days in the year and three
hundred and sixty-six in leap year! Land had to be cleared,
sprouts cut, stumps grubbed out, rails split, and new buildings
erected from the abundance of material at hand. All such tasks
were in addition to the ordinary labor of plowing, planting,
cultivating, and harvesting plus the daily chores of living. Out
on the wide prairie the first few months were busy ones while he
was building a home, erecting a shelter for domestic animals,
and plowing the prairie sod. When this had been done, however,
long hours of labor every day were no longer necessary or
profitable. If he was located forty to fifty miles from a railroad
town there was little need to grow crops for sale. Even when
wheat was a fair price at the market centers, it brought very
little at the frontier railroad town due to the long haul by rail
and the high freight rates. Any surplus grown yielded slight
returns and besides, for the first few years, drought, hot winds,
grasshoppers, greenbugs, and the scanty yield of newly turned
sod kept the surplus down to a minimum. Under such circumstances it is not surprising that the settler merely practiced
subsistence farming, seeking only to provide a living of sorts
for his family while he "held down his claim" and waited hopefully for the coming of a railroad bringing nearer markets, more
settlers, increased land values, and all the good things of civilization. Long, leisurely trips to the railroad or for wood might be
necessary, but of hard labor, to which he had once been accustomed, there was very little.

Unfortunately this did not apply to the mistress of the sod
house. For her there were still the daily tasks of cooking, sweeping, washing clothes or dishes, mending, caring for the children,
and all that work of women which it has been said "is never
done." Life on the prairie frontier was hard for women and one

can sympathize with the woman newly arrived in western Texas who wrote to her sister back in Tennessee: "Texas seems like a good country for men and dogs but a mighty hard place for oxen and women."

While the prairie wife did not have as much leisure as her husband, it seems probable that life in this new land was not without its advantages even for her. Back in the old home, particularly in the South, the average woman, recognizing the heavy toil of her husband, sought to relieve him of some of the labor often recognized as properly "a man's work" and took over most of the care of the garden, chickens, and cows. She felt with some reason that a man who had split rails all day should not be expected to milk three or four cows at night or feed and care for chickens, and so cheerfully did this herself, only claiming as her reward the "butter-and-egg money" if there should happen to be any. With equal cheerfulness, she planted and cultivated the garden, only asking that her husband plow the land and make it ready for planting. Unless such habits had become too deeply ingrained, there was likely to be some readjustment on the sod-house frontier of this division of labor. Here the man of the house was likely to use some of his abundant spare time to do the milking and gardening, and at least to help with the poultry.

Also the clean pure air of the prairies promoted good health. Seldom was there any malaria, commonly known as "chills and fever," such as was all too common in portions of the woodland region, and strong healthy children, free to run wild on the open prairie, required comparatively little care. In addition the prairie settler's wife was largely relieved of such labor as making soap or hominy, grinding sausage, rendering lard, picking berries in the woods, or weaving rag rugs—tasks which had at times seemed all too common in the old home. So, on the whole, she too, perhaps, did less hard work than formerly, though not to the same degree as her husband.

The effects of this more abundant leisure upon the cultural and social pattern of the sod-house frontier were soon apparent. Hard labor from dawn to dusk ceased to be regarded as a virtue, and people no longer felt it necessary to apologize for taking time to go fishing or hunting or for spending long hours at the country store or tiny prairie town.

Social activities were promoted. There was much visiting of neighbors and friends and many picnics, parties, dances, fish fries, barbecues, and meetings for the purpose of singing. Such social activities did not hinder work too much for apart from "holding down the claim" and watchfully waiting for the country to grow up, there was comparatively little useful work to be hindered.

That some years of virtually enforced leisure often affected the habits and outlook of the people was inevitable. Years later when, due to the coming of the railroads and markets, some farmers had become prosperous enough to employ additional help, it was a common saying: "If you want a good farm hand, get you a young fellow from the woods of Arkansas or Missouri. He'll make you a fine hand for the first year or two but as soon as he's learned the ways of this prairie country, he'll get just like these boys that have grown up here." Undoubtedly, there was some element of truth in this.

While the prairie claim did not always afford the settler steady profitable employment, there were such tasks as planting trees or building an addition to his sod-house home by which he could utilize some of his spare time. Then, too, since no labor could be found in his own community, he might in time of stress or distress leave the family at home for a month or so while he took the wagon and team and drove east to a more thickly settled region to pick cotton or work in the harvest fields, thereby earning enough money to provide shoes, clothing, and groceries for his little flock during the coming winter.

Enough has been said to make it apparent that the sod-house frontier was very different from that of the wooded region from which many of its people came. Topography, soil, climate, vegetation, remoteness from market, and the bigness of the land all combined to form a new economic and social pattern of life which America had formerly never known. It was a good life, on the whole, and not without its attractive features, for these settlers were a great people. The humble home was, as a rule, always kept neat and clean. Flowers were planted in beds beside the sod-house door and the windows were framed with morning-glories or other vines. Family ties were close while hospitality and neighborly kindness were universal. On Sunday morning the children were washed and dressed in their pitifully poor best clothes and the day was one of rest and recreation. Lives were motivated by a simple but deep and sincere spiritual faith which to most people was literally "a rock in a weary land, a shelter in the time of storm."

All of this applies to the typical settler of the better class. There were trashy people and even near degenerates on both the log-cabin and the sod-house frontiers and of these a few authors have written books in the name of realism that have attracted wide attention. Such writers have mistaken facts for truth. The conditions and the people they have described may have existed but they were very exceptional and their descriptions are untrue in the larger sense of the word.

The period of the sod-house frontier was of short duration. Railroads were rapidly penetrating the western prairies, their builders encouraged by the level nature of the land and the comparatively cheap cost of construction. Towns sprang up mushroomlike along their lines, to which flocked men eager to erect elevators and mills, or to establish stores, banks, and other business enterprises. More settlers poured in and the ranchmen either turned to stock farming or drifted farther west to lands too arid or rough for successful crop growing. With markets close at hand, the settler sowed a larger acreage of wheat, and a bounteous crop enabled him to erect a two- or three-room house of lumber to replace the crude structure that had been his first prairie home. Successful farmers of the Middle West came out on excursions promoted by the railroads and were so much impressed that they promptly sold their high-priced lands and returned with money to buy these cheaper ones and to erect commodious homes and barns.

The original settler sought to follow their example. With the proceeds of two or three more good crops and all too often with the aid of a mortgage, he too built a big white house and red barn and purchased more farm machinery which the mechanical and industrial pioneers so soon made available. Barbed wire came into universal use, deep-well drilling machines and windmills provided an adequate water supply. The old "sod buster" was replaced by a gangplow, drills, binders, headers, and eventually combines came into general use. The internal-combustion engine brought in cheap automobiles and tractors. Rural mail delivery and telephones became common. Some of the busy small towns grew to the stature of little cities, the road over which the covered wagon jolted westward was widened to a broad highway, and the old-time pioneer life passed into the realm of things that used to be.

Just as a well-built log cabin will endure almost indefinitely, while the life span of any sod house is but a few years, so did the log-cabin frontier, together with all that it represents, persist for many generations while that of the sod house quickly disappeared. Even today one may find in certain remote districts of the Appalachian Highlands or in the hill regions of Oklahoma, Arkansas, or Missouri, families living in log houses and little communities in which conditions are strangely reminiscent of the woodland frontier of nearly a century ago. On the western prairies, however, one is likely to search in vain for a sod house or dugout or for a social and economic order resembling that of this same region in the latter part of the nineteenth century.

Though the frontiers of the log cabin and the sod house are largely gone and the pattern of life which each produced is only a memory, their influence still lingers and is of real significance to this new America of ours. For it takes no great stretch of imagination to make us believe that some of the qualities shown by our men all over the world in the two bloody conflicts of world-wide war may be in part due to that heritage of courage, resourcefulness, stamina, hardihood, and spirit developed on these frontiers of other days. It may be urged that a majority of the men in our armed forces were born and bred in towns and cities. Yet it is certain that the forebears of a large part of our urban population were rural people lured to the city by what seemed greater opportunities and not a few of these came from one of these two frontiers.

Whether or not one accepts the idea that frontier characteristics persist as a cultural heritage long after the conditions which produced them are gone forever, few will deny that these pioneers had certain qualities or characteristics that America will need in the crucial years that lie ahead. Very much shall we need the courage, patience, persistence, energy, and industry of the log-cabin dwellers, the buoyant optimism, breadth of vision, and belief in the future of the prairie settlers, and the tolerance, kindness of heart, and deep spiritual faith of both.

V

I never thought to see the day
I'd burn cow chips and twisted hay
To keep us warm and cook the grub
Or load the washin', soap and tub
Into the wagon once a week
And drive six miles to a little creek.
We'd rather haul the clothes becuz
They don't slosh out like water does.

I must admit that I've sometimes yearned
For some of the logs I piled and burned
Or the flowing spring so clear and cold
Back on the hillside farm I sold.
But when I think of its rocky soil
The sprouts and stumps and the constant toil
Of cutting or grubbing them out by hand
I'd rather be here in a prairie land.

Prairie Land

V

Wood and Water

Twin Problems of the Prairie Plains

THE PIONEER SETTLER of wooded areas found himself confronted by the arduous task of clearing fields, grubbing out stumps and cutting sprouts. When he later migrated to the Western prairies he quickly discovered that he had flown from old familiar ills to others of which he had formerly known nothing. Chief of these was the almost complete absence of timber for fuel, buildings, and fences, and of water for household use and livestock. Something of his efforts to solve his twin problems with respect to wood and water until the invention of barbed wire, well-drilling machinery, and the coming of railroads brought a measure of relief is told in this chapter.

THERE IS A VENERABLE STORY of many variations to the effect that an old gentleman from the wooded hills of Tennessee once paid a visit to his two nephews who were ranching on the plains of western Texas. The two young men met him at the nearest railroad point with a spring wagon and camping outfit and the trio set out in the early afternoon for the ranch some seventy miles distant. A little before sundown they stopped to make camp near a windmill that stood not far from the banks of a dry, sandy arroyo which meandered across the level prairie. One of the young men took a pickaxe from the wagon and began digging in the dry earth near by from which grew a few mesquite sprouts.

Soon he had unearthed an armful of large mesquite roots,

brought them to the wagon, and kindled a fire. In the meantime his brother had unharnessed the horses, watered them at the big circular metal stock tank beside the windmill and staked them out to graze on the thick buffalo grass. He then seized an iron pail and hung it over the end of the iron pipe leading from the windmill to the stock tank. There was not a breath of air stirring, but the young man climbed the steel ladder leading to the top of the windmill tower and turned the great wheel with his hands until a stream of fresh, clear water poured from the pipe and filled the pail. Returning to the campfire, he filled the coffee pot and began to prepare supper.

The old uncle who had been sitting on the wagon tongue watching these proceedings with a jaundiced eye but considerable interest suddenly inquired: "Is there ever any water in that creek?" "Oh, yes," was the answer, "when it rains and for a few days or weeks afterward." "What's the name of it anyhow?" continued the old man. "José Creek," answered the nephew, "J-O-S-E, pronounced *hosay*." The old man snorted indignantly: "I don't know why you boys want to stay out here. I wouldn't live in any country where you have to climb for water and dig for wood and spell hell with a *J!*"

While it was only in the Southwest that the Anglo-American pioneers had to struggle with the vagaries of Spanish spelling and pronunciation, it must be confessed that the early settlers of all the prairie states from the Dakotas south to western Oklahoma and Texas found that their twin problems were always the securing of an adequate supply of wood and water. Many settlers on the Southwestern Plains for a time depended largely upon mesquite roots grubbed from the hard earth to cook their food while, unless a handle had been attached to the pump rod of a windmill, it was always necessary to climb the tower and turn the wheel by hand to pump fresh water when the wind was not blowing, though it must be admitted that this was not often.

Explorers of this region as well as the "mountain men," Indian traders, Mormons en route to Utah, gold seekers headed for California, and the emigrants to Oregon have all commented upon the difficulties encountered due to the arid nature of the area and the almost complete absence of timber. W. A. Ferris, journeying west for the American Fur Company in 1830, complained of the shortage of fuel as had many before him. James Akin who went with a party from Iowa to Oregon in 1853 kept a diary in which a short entry of three or four lines was made each day. Of the thirty entries made in June when they were crossing Nebraska, twenty-four refer to fuel or water or both, indicating that these two necessities held a most important place in the minds of the emigrants.

To these early explorers and travelers, however, the vast prairie plains formed only a barrier to be crossed as quickly as possible to reach some predetermined destination beyond. The thought of establishing permanent homes there had never entered their heads. In fact, it was not until much later that any considerable number of people began to believe that these wide prairies would ever support a great population of agricultural settlers. For the American people who had pushed relentlessly westward ever since the early years of the seventeenth century hesitated for approximately a generation at the edge of the dry, treeless plains, reluctant to attempt to cope with a land so unlike any which they had known in the past. It is true that there were fairly extensive prairies in portions of Ohio, Illinois, and many other states east of the Mississippi. These, however, were comparatively small. Timber for fuel and building purposes was usually available within a few miles. Moreover, the rainfall was sufficient to mature crops virtually every year and numerous streams, springs, and ponds, together with wells, which in most cases were comparatively shallow, insured a bountiful supply of water.

This western land was very different. The level prairies stretched away for scores of miles unbroken by a single tree. Streams were few and far between and many of them were only broad strips of sand for a large part of the year even though heavy rains occasionally turned them into raging, muddy torrents. Springs were even fewer than streams and in large areas nonexistent, while whether or not pure water could be had by digging or drilling wells was a question that in many cases seemed likely to demand a negative answer.

It was not mainly a reluctance to face hardships or the fear of hostile Indians which caused would-be settlers to pause at the edge of these western prairies until after the close of the War Between the States. The American pioneers had never shrunk from the hardships of frontier life in the past and the early settlers of the eastern portion of the Mississippi Valley had been confronted by forest Indians quite as warlike and dangerous as were the plains tribes west of that stream. Primarily it was the lack of timber for fuel, buildings, and fences, and of water for domestic use and livestock which halted the pioneer settlers at the edge of the prairie plains for so long a period.

Eventually, however, the increasing scarcity of agricultural land which could be purchased at what was considered a reasonable price and the eager desire for homes caused some of the more hardy souls to venture out into a land where most of what they had learned of pioneering in the past was of no value and where new methods must be devised to solve new problems.

Certainly from 1866 to 1900 there was an enormous outpouring of settlers to the Prairie West. Obviously, this movement was greatly accelerated by the Homestead Act of 1862 but there were other factors that were almost as important. These were the westward advance of railroads promoted by huge grants of land from the Federal government, which the railway companies offered for sale at comparatively low prices. Still others were the taming of the Plains Indians and their concentration upon reservations, the influx of immigrants from Europe, and increased travel back and forth across the region due to the settlement of the Pacific Coast and the development of mining operations in the Rocky Mountains.

Along the eastern edge of the prairies there were in some places a few groves or islands of timber and a considerable fringe of trees along the streams; but as the settlers advanced westward into a land which ever grew higher, dryer, and more nearly level, the dual problem of securing wood and water became increasingly acute. Most of the lands east of the Mississippi and of the first tier of states west of it were wooded, and the people who first occupied them were faced with the immediate task of clearing fields for cultivation. To these settlers the forest had seemed largely an unmixed evil. It appeared to them only an inpediment to progress. With enormous energy they set to work to fell or girdle the trees in order to provide a clearing for the growing of crops. The first logs cut were utilized for building a home, barn, and outbuildings or split into rails for fencing the fields. The surplus ones were burned after being rolled into great heaps with the assistance of kindly neighbors who gladly came to participate in these "logrollings," at which a jug of corn whiskey often stimulated the efforts of the participants.

In time the clearing became a symbol of economic and, to some extent, cultural progress. To widen the clearing in order to provide more tillable land for growing crops to feed his family and to sell, in order to get money for clothing and other necessities, became the settler's chief task. After the trees had been felled, the stumps must be pulled or grubbed out, or in some cases burned or blasted out with gunpowder.

The forest trees which bordered the clearing not only shaded and drew sustenance from a wide strip of soil but also sent out long roots which when broken by the plow sent up shoots which if not promptly destroyed seriously threatened again to "let in the jungle."

One who migrated from the wooded regions to the wide prairies at first viewed his new homestead with pride and admiration. Here he need no longer wrestle with the tasks of clearing land, grubbing out stumps, and cutting sprouts. Furrows entirely across his land could be plowed without encountering a root or stone. He soon discovered, however, that he had fled from ills which he had formerly borne only to encounter others that he had hitherto "known not of." For the first time the American pioneer began to realize the value of those forests which in the past he had striven so hard to destroy. His entire pattern of life was changed and much of that change was due

to the great scarcity of the two commodities which in the past
he had accepted as a matter of course because they were so
abundant—timber and water.

His first task was to provide housing for himself and family.
In the old homeland the pioneer settler had found it necessary
only to hew and notch logs and lay them up to form the walls
of a comfortable log house, which was covered with rough
shingles split with an axe and smoothed down a bit with the
axe or a plane. In a prairie region he must utilize for constructing
a home such material as was available and this was in most
cases sod or earth. Moreover, to decrease the height of the walls
it was sometimes advisable to build it partly underground. Even
a sod house or dugout required some timber for its construction,
however, since it was necessary to provide a ridge pole, corner
posts, and stringers along either side to support the roof made of
narrow poles covered with hay on which were placed sods or a
thick layer of closely packed earth.

The settler accordingly erected a small tent from his wagon
cover as a temporary shelter and then set out in search of the
required timbers to frame the new home. This often required a
journey of ten to thirty miles to reach a stream bordered with a
thin line of cottonwood, elm, and hackberry trees or some ravine
or canyon in the bottom of which there usually grew at least a
little timber. Such ravines were usually in a hilly region where
there was little land suitable for cultivation. In consequence
these lands were not occupied by homesteaders until all of the
level, fertile prairies had been settled and so remained for some
years a part of the public domain. Eventually Congress enacted
a law permitting settlers to take timber from unoccupied government lands "for domestic use." This, however, was largely a
meaningless gesture since the pioneer settler had never hesitated
to take timber anywhere he could find it except from the land
of another settler. This might be the public domain, state or
territorial school lands, railroad land, some ranchman's range,
or an Indian reservation. Cutting and removing timber from
Indian lands was contrary to law and deputy United States
marshals sometimes derived a considerable revenue from arrest-

ing "wood haulers" on the great reservations of Oklahoma, South Dakota, and some other western states, since they received not only a fee for making the arrest but mileage for the distance traveled in taking the luckless timber cutter to the nearest United States court. The lands of the Cherokee Outlet, in northern Oklahoma, before they were opened to settlement in 1893 had been largely denuded of timber for many miles south of the border of Kansas by the pioneer settlers of that state as were those of the Kiowa-Comanche reservation by settlers of Greer County, until 1896 a part of Texas. The Indians, seeing that the activities of the wood cutters could not be stopped, sometimes patrolled the border of their reservations and collected twenty-five cents a load for wood taken from their lands. In the middle 1890's the author paid fifty cents for a load of wood to an old Comanche Indian who had displayed an official-looking paper which he apparently thought was his authorization from the Department of the Interior to demand such payment. The document, however, was only a circular letter signed by the Secretary of the Interior warning white persons not to purchase wood from Indians since the latter were not permitted to sell timber from their lands!

Regardless of their source, enough timbers were eventually secured to frame the proposed dwelling and the homesteader set to work to construct it. If the soil happened to be firm in texture and thickly interlaced with the roots of a thick coat of grass, a sod house wholly above ground might be built. In areas of sandy soil, however, it was necessary to construct a dugout or half-dugout, though its walls were usually built sufficiently high above the level of the ground to allow the insertion of from two to four half windows. For window frames, a little lumber was required, though in a pinch they might be made from three or four wooden boxes or packing crates. No boards were required for a floor since it was in most cases only the hard, beaten earth, while the roof was also of earth or sod. From this, plants often sprouted, and the newcomer from the East was sometimes astonished to see a house on the roof of which were growing weeds or sunflowers.

After the house had been completed and the family moved in and the furniture arranged, there still remained the task of providing shelter for the livestock. This usually took the form of a hay-covered shed, but this also required some timber, and in addition, enough poles had to be secured to build a small enclosure about it, variously called a lot, pen, or corral. All of this construction necessitated several more trips to the all too distant source of timber.

In the meantime the problem of fuel for cooking the food and heating the home was an acute one. The majority of people who migrated to the prairie plains did so in the early autumn in order to erect buildings before the coming of cold weather and to break the sod and prepare the ground for planting in the spring. Consequently fuel for heating was not required at first but by the time a home and outbuildings had been constructed the "eager and nipping air" warned the settler that winter was fast approaching and provision must be made to keep the family warm once its icy winds began to sweep the prairies.

Also, from the first, fuel was required for cooking and in most cases was not easy to obtain. In preparing the timbers for framing the new home some scraps of wood were inevitably left and these were carefully saved to be burned in the cookstove. These were too few to last long, however, and it became necessary to utilize the only fuel which the prairies afforded. This was "prairie coal" as buffalo chips or cow chips were commonly called. These had been largely used for campfires on the westward journey once the edge of the treeless plains had been reached and were equally dependable for burning in the cookstove or fire place of the sod house or dugout. They made a hot, though somewhat smoky, fire that was about adequate for cooking the meals and keeping a room fairly warm in mild winter weather. Cow chips formed the principal fuel of many settlers during the first two or three years of life on a prairie claim. During the early years of the settlement of Nebraska, Kansas, and western Oklahoma a common sight was a homesteader slowly driving a team hitched to a farm wagon across the prairies while his wife and children walked beside it, picked up cow chips, and tossed them into the wagon box until it was filled to overflowing despite the fact that it was equipped with "sideboards." Once back home the family unloaded the wagon, stacking the "prairie coal" in a neat rick beneath a hay-covered shed where it would remain dry, for wet cow chips persistently refused to burn. Moreover, even when they were perfectly dry it was almost imperative to have some wood to mix with them so additional trips to the school section, unoccupied lands of the public domain, or Indian reservations where some timber might be found, were necessary.

As more settlers came in the supply of "prairie coal" eventually became pretty well exhausted, and if trees could be found only at a great distance the problem of fuel became increasingly acute. Corn cobs, corn stalks, and sunflower stalks were all utilized as fuel for cooking the food, and in some cases wisps of twisted hay provided enough fire to boil coffee and fry bacon and hot cakes. One stanza of the old song "The Little Old Sod Shanty on My Claim" refers to this as follows: `

> And when I left my eastern home
> So happy and so gay
> To try to win my wealth and fame
> I little thought that I'd come down
> To burning twisted hay
> In the little old sod shanty on my claim.

In some parts of Nebraska, Kansas, western Oklahoma, and other prairie states a stove was sometimes fitted out as a "hayburner." The equipment consisted of several metal cylinders half the length of the fire box and open at one end. Inside each was a coiled wire spring attached to the closed end while the walls of the cylinder were pierced with a number of large holes. The spring was pushed down by packing the cylinders tightly with hay and two were placed in the fire box of the stove with open ends together and the hay lighted at one of these holes. As it was consumed, the spring pressed a fresh supply into the fire and when it had all been burned, the cylinders were replaced with fresh ones. Another type of hayburner had a large drum filled with hay above the fire box of the stove and this was fed into the fire by a coiled spring. In either type a hot fire could be produced, but almost constant attention was required to keep it burning.

When more bountiful crops were produced, some people in the remote prairie regions of the North burned corn at times when the cold was intense and corn prices low, while those of the southern plains occasionally used cottonseed for fuel. The feeling was common, however, that it was immoral to burn commodities so much needed for food by hungry persons and animals throughout the world. In consequence, it is doubtful whether any considerable quantity of corn and cottonseed was used for fuel except in cases of grave emergency.

Scarcity of wood for construction and fuel were only two aspects of the problem faced by the prairie settler because of lack of timber. A third and very serious question was the age-old one of enclosures. Once he had chosen and settled a tract of land, he was faced with the problem of restraining his own domestic animals, and as soon as fields had been plowed and crops planted, some means had to be devised of protecting them from his livestock and that of his neighbors, as well as from cattle of the ranchman who still lingered in the region even after the coming of many homesteaders.

In the wooded area the pioneer had no such problem. Once a field had been cleared the branches were trimmed from the tree trunks with an axe and used to construct a "brush fence" about the clearing which served reasonably well until such time as enough rails could be split to replace it with the more stable and permanent "worm fence" properly "staked and ridered." Lacking any suitable material for fencing, the prairie homesteader had to adapt himself to his environment in this as in so many other things. If he had only a team of horses and a milk cow, the animals could be picketed out with long ropes and the stake pins moved every day to insure fresh pasturage. The rope soon became as much of a necessity to the prairie pioneer as the axe had been to his ancestors of the forest regions. In the summer a mother would sometimes tie one end of a rope about the waist of the two- or three-year-old toddler and stake the youngster out on the prairie where he could play unharmed while she did her washing and other household tasks. If the settler had a number of cattle, it was necessary to herd them during the day and at night put them in a pen or corral which usually required some poles for its construction.

The prospect of herding the cows and staking out the work animals indefinitely was an appalling one, however, and many homesteaders planted hedges of *bois d'arc,* commonly called "Osage orange," about their fields. Since it would be at least two or three years before these had grown sufficiently to protect crops, the settlers of most communities promptly voted a "herd law" requiring all persons owning livestock to restrain their animals and to pay for any damage resulting from their failure to do so. Ranchmen grazing their herds on the public domain complained bitterly but usually without effect.

In addition to planting hedges about their fields, most settlers also set out young trees, or cottonwood slips, near their homes. Congress, tardily recognizing the need of the prairie farmers for more trees, enacted the Timber Culture Act, granting an additional hundred and sixty acres of land to any homesteader who would plant forty acres of trees and care for them ten years. Nebraska, owing to the efforts of J. Sterling Morton, made provisions for Arbor Day, specifying a certain day each year on which its citizens were urged to plant trees.

Moreover, necessity is the mother of invention, and the great need of the prairie settlers for more adequate means of fencing their lands eventually brought about the invention and manufacture of barbed wire. J. F. Glidden of DeKalb, Illinois, had perfected before 1875 a barbed wire which became the pattern for most types, and by 1885 the new type of fencing was widely used throughout the West. For some years there was much prejudice against this type of fence, however, and even after it had become generally accepted, many poor homesteaders lacked the money to purchase wire. In addition, posts to which it must be nailed had to be secured, and this added to the settler's problem of finding more timber. Eventually, however, barbed wire fences replaced the hedges but often not until the trees of the latter had grown large enough to make posts. Even today one can see many hedge fences, or the remains of them, in Kansas, Nebraska, and some other western states.

Apart from the practical need of timber for improving the homestead and for fuel, the complete absence of trees must have had a profound psychological, or spiritual, effect upon the prairie settler. He missed the fine old oaks and elms of his ancestral home quite as much as he missed his old friends and perhaps more than he missed his own and his wife's relatives! When the summer sun beat down relentlessly on the brown prairie, the pioneer women especially must have longed for the shade of the great trees that grew about the old homestead. The monotony of the landscape where one "could look farther and see less" than in any other region they had ever known must at times have proved most depressing.

On no other basis can be explained the feverish energy with which so many of these people planted trees and the solicitous care with which they cared for them. On the first Arbor Day over a million trees were planted in Nebraska. One who reads the impassioned plea for tree planting made by J. Sterling Morton in his article in the Omaha *Herald* for April 17, 1872, must feel that this subject was almost a religion to the great founder of Arbor Day. This can be better understood by viewing a picture of his birthplace—an attractive little home surrounded by trees, or when one remembers that his youth was spent among the wooded hills of Michigan. It was only the second generation of prairie pioneers, born and bred on the level plains who loved them intensely and felt themselves shut in and stifled when they visited the wooded areas from which their parents had migrated. Many of the first generation endured the prairies but zealously sought to break the monotony of the landscape by planting trees.

Grave as was the prairie settler's problem of securing fuel and timber for constructing buildings and enclosures, that of providing sufficient water for domestic use and livestock was equally acute. While not much fuel was required in the summer months, water had to be available every day of the year. For the first few weeks of life on the homestead this almost certainly had to be hauled in barrels sometimes as much as eight to ten miles, and this period of time might be extended to several months or even years.

In some favored localities an adequate supply of pure water might be had by sinking a well to the depth of twenty to forty feet but on the high plains of western Texas and portions of western Oklahoma, Kansas, Nebraska, and some other states, it was necessary to drill a well to a depth of from three hundred to six hundred feet or even more to reach water. The cost of such a well was, of course, prohibitive for the average pioneer settler and he was forced to haul water from the nearest source of supply. The author as late as 1907 found an old gentleman in the Panhandle of Texas hauling water nine miles for household use and livestock. When asked why he did not drill a well, he replied that it was "just as near to water one way as the other" and he preferred to get his "along horizontal rather than perpendicular lines!"

Under such circumstances water was a precious commodity and must be used as sparingly as possible. Domestic animals could, of course, be made to travel to the source of supply under their own power, and many a housewife found it far easier to load wash tubs, kettles, and soiled clothing into the wagon and take them to water and do her washing there rather than to bring water for that purpose to her home. If the latter were done, however, the soap suds might be used to scrub the floor if it were of wood, which was not often the case, and children were bathed in the tub of water in which clothes had been rinsed.

Even if water were found by drilling or digging a well, it was in some areas likely to be impregnated with mineral, usually gypsum, and so unfit for human consumption. "Gyp water" was a sore trial to many a family, while livestock often died from the effects of drinking "alkali water."

Obviously, the first settlers of a region had no idea at what depth water might be found and were puzzled as to the exact spot where the well should be dug. Sometimes a neighbor supposed to be peculiarly gifted at "finding water" would be summoned to give advice. Such an individual would walk about grasping in his hands the two ends of a forked switch until it curved down and pointed at a spot where water presumably could be found. In some areas of western Oklahoma, where it was necessary to sink a well to a depth of nearly a hundred feet, settlers, since they had no money to employ a driller, dug wells with a pick and shovel, a task which must have been laborious and even dangerous. In many small towns the problem of securing an adequate supply of water was an acute one. Water sold at twenty-five cents a tub in Woodward, Oklahoma, for a time and at an equally high price in Lawton during the first three or four months of the town's existence. Towns that derived their water supply from shallow wells were frequently swept by typhoid fever which in some cases assumed epidemic proportions. In the early 1900's the author assisted in analyzing samples of water from nearly a hundred wells of a small town in western Oklahoma and found eighty per cent of them contaminated by typhoid. Even in the rural districts of the shallow-water areas typhoid was often very common in earlier days.

Difficult as were the twin problems of securing an adequate supply of wood and water on the prairie plains, the passing years eventually saw their solution. Railroads were rapidly penetrating the entire prairie plains area. These brought in coal, lumber, and farm machinery. With a market for grain established at the little towns along these railway lines, the settlers increased their wheat production and with the money obtained from its sale purchased coal. They also were able to buy lumber, and the sod house or dugout was replaced by a modest frame or box structure of two to four rooms. With a shingle roof over his head the prairie farmer in the "bad water" areas often placed gutters under its eaves, acquired cement and constructed a cistern, thus insuring an ample supply of pure water for household use. Also if a suitable spot could be found on the farm, an earthen dam was thrown up to impound the rain water and so form a pond. Improved well-drilling equipment soon began to

be brought to the plains and many of the more prosperous settlers had wells drilled and erected windmills. These pumped
water for domestic use and for the steel or wooden stock tank in
the pasture or corral. The trees of the groves and hedge fences
within a few years had grown large enough for fence posts, thus
not only giving the homsteader a supply of home-grown fuel but
making it possible for him to cut down the hedges and replace
them with wire fences as barbed wire came into general use.

Eventually came the opening up of oil pools in the Mid-Con-
tinent Area and the eager search for oil further promoted improvements in well-drilling machinery. Also many gas wells
were opened and for many people oil and gas became available
for fuel as numerous pipe lines were constructed. Oil stoves
were installed in many homes to be used in cooking, especially
in summer.

As the settlers grew more prosperous through the greater production of grain and livestock, many of them constructed a
new home, sometimes securing additional money for that purpose by mortgaging their land to which they had by this time
received a patent in fee, thus making it possible to use it as collat-
eral for a loan. A large two-story farmhouse was accordingly
built and water piped to it from an elevated steel tank set up
near the windmill. An oil-burning furnace was sometimes installed in the basement since oil was a cleaner and more satisfactory fuel than coal. In regions where natural gas was available, it was used both for heating and cooking. Rural electrifi-
cation became common in some areas and electric lights and
equipment were installed in those homes near a "high line." An
electric motor or gasoline engine in some cases was acquired to
pump water to the house for domestic use and the windmill used
only to provide a supply of "stock water." The era of sod houses
and dugouts, of "prairie coal," and wood hauled for twenty to
thirty miles, or of hayburner stoves, and water brought in barrels
from some distant spring had largely passed away.

There is little shortage of fuel and water in the prairie states
today. At least a few trees have been planted on virtually every
farm and even the "shelterbelt" activities of the United States

government some years ago which brought considerable criticism from many people have in some areas been remarkably successful. In those communities where the people depend for a water supply upon shallow wells and ponds long periods of drought may bring inconveniences, but not nearly to the extent of earlier years. An occasional farmer, on marginal or submarginal lands may still load his water barrels into a wagon and fill them at the well of one of his more fortunate neighbors or in years of crop failure be hard put to find enough money to buy his winter's supply of coal, for "the poor we have with us always" even in the Prairie West. Largely speaking, however, the twin problems of wood and water which proved so difficult for the settlers of the prairie plains half a century or more ago are now only a memory.

VI

Getting the kids up for breakfast
Was not such a chore in my day
For the odor of frying sausage cakes
Brought us right out of the hay.
We knew there would be hot biscuits
With butter and jelly or jam
And syrup and stacks of brown flapjacks
Or a platter of eggs and ham.

So if the youngsters lie in bed
Perhaps there is some excuse
In not getting out of a nice warm bed
For toast and orange juice.
But give 'em the kind of breakfast
My grandmother served to all
And watch 'em roll out each morning
The moment they hear you call.

Grandma's Kitchen

VI

Food of the Frontier

ALTHOUGH FOOD has had a great influence upon American history—even the discovery of America came about as a result of the quest for the spices of the Orient—this chapter is concerned with the opposite phenomenon, how the dietary habits of the pioneers were changed and remolded by the living conditions of the frontier.

FOOD, THOUGH THE MOST FUNDAMENTAL of all human needs, varies widely among the different peoples of the world and is subject to numerous curious taboos and prejudices. "What's one man's meat is another man's poison" seems to have a large element of truth. The Comanche and Kiowa Indians never ate the wild turkeys which swarmed along the streams of their homeland in such abundance. Yet they were very fond of dog stew, roasted terrapins, or the broiled entrails of buffalo and cattle.

Diet and dietary habits are, moreover, national or regional in their nature, and various peoples seem to be characterized by a certain article or articles of food. Since the American frontier was essentially a region, the food and food habits of its people were always much the same, whether it was the frontier of Piedmont Virginia in 1690, of Kentucky in 1790, or of Kansas and Oklahoma in 1890, subject only to such variations as might be due to climate, local resources, and the former homes of the pioneer settlers. Naturally, all of these had their various effects, and yet a study of the diet and cookery of all these pioneer peoples will reveal that they had striking similarities.

The first frontier in American history was along the Atlantic seaboard, for our earliest pioneers were those hardy souls who had sailed some three thousand miles westward to establish settlements at Jamestown or Plymouth. The little ships in which they came to America were too small to carry more than sufficient provisions for the trip, with only enough additional to subsist the crew on the homeward voyage. Any small surplus that might be left behind for the colonists was quickly consumed and the pioneers soon had to provide for themselves.

It was instantly apparent to these people that their eating habits must undergo a radical change. The red roast beef, Yorkshire pudding, and kidney pie of "Merrie England" belonged to the past. In the future, their fare must be derived from such small crops as they might grow and the native products of the sea, stream, and forest.

For a people accustomed to pioneering these should have been ample. The forests abounded in game, the rivers and streams were teeming with fish, and oysters, crabs, and mussels were to be had everywhere along the coast. Blackberries, gooseberries, wild plums, grapes, persimmons, and several varieties of nuts were to be found in many places, but these early colonists were, in modern parlance, "tenderfeet," who knew little of how to sustain themselves under wilderness conditions. Virtually all of the earlier colonists imported food from Europe for twenty years after their arrival in America, and it was not until a second generation had grown up that the English colonists had become sufficiently familiar with pioneer life to take full advantage of the food resources which the country afforded.

The settlers at Jamestown landed in May, at which time spring is far advanced in the latitude of Virginia. Despite the lateness of the season, however, they quickly spaded a plot of ground and sowed wheat—the grain with which they were most familiar. It grew amazingly and their hopes were high until they discovered that these rank stalks produced no grain. The Pilgrims at Plymouth were more fortunate in the growing of food. They had settled on the site of a former Indian village which had been ravaged a year or two before by pestilence—probably smallpox.

Many of the former inhabitants had died and the remainder had
fled in terror and established a new settlement some distance
away. The Pilgrims inherited the little cornfields which lay about
this former village and so had a considerable area of land already
cleared and ready for cultivation. They had landed, moreover,
in December, and thus had ample time to prepare the ground
for planting before winter was over. Also, Squanto and other
friendly Indians visited the little settlement in the early spring
and taught the colonists the best methods of planting and cultivating Indian corn which eventually became the chief breadstuff
of New England. In consequence of the early use of corn, the
friendly character of most of the Indians, and perhaps their close
proximity to the sea, the people of New England, despite their
more rigorous climate, did not suffer from famine to anything
like the same degree as did the early settlers of Virginia. The
latter usually established themselves on the banks of one of the
broad, tidal rivers, at considerable distance from the ocean. As a
result they were not able to secure so much of their living from
the sea as did the Northern colonists. In addition, the Indians of
Virginia were often hostile and did not teach the whites their
own primitive methods of agriculture, or the utilization of the
resources of the forest. In consequence, it was only after a long
"starving time" and some years of hardship and misery that these
Southern colonists, at last learning how to utilize the abundance
of the country's natural resources and grow the proper crops,
began to be well fed and to develop some semblance of prosperity.

The change in food habits doubtless came hard for these people. Yet they eventually learned, though perhaps not as quickly
as did the early inhabitants of New England. Later colonists
landing on our shores must have been surprised by the strange
dishes which the firstcomers set before them. Instead of roast
beef or mutton chops they were offered venison, fried squirrel,
or other wild game. Hominy or hoecake took the place of the
wheat bread to which they were accustomed, and in lieu of tea
they were given a strange brew made from sassafras. Plum pudding was nonexistent, but as a substitute they were given Indian

pudding made of corn meal and molasses cooked together, with possibly the addition of a few of the rare imported raisins or currants. Probably not many of them liked this fare at first, but in time they, too, became accustomed to it even though their mouths no doubt often watered at the memory of some of their favorite dishes of bygone days.

So long as the colonists remained in fairly close proximity to the sea, a large part of their living was not only derived from the ocean itself but there was always the possibility of securing at least some small quantity of imported foods. Fish of various kinds —oysters, clams, crabs, and lobsters—were common on the tables of those dwelling near salt water. There were, in addition, importations of sugar, tea, cheese, butter, spices, wines and liquors, and at times salt or pickled beef or pork as well as marmalade, jam, and jellies. Such articles were too expensive for the poorer people but the well-to-do planters apparently consumed huge quantities of imported wines and liquors and some of the more bulky food products.

As the years went by, however, and population steadily advanced westward beyond the fall line of the rivers into the Piedmont or the interior of New England, the western settlers found themselves remote from any food supply either from overseas or from the sea itself. This forced them to depend almost entirely upon the resources of the forest and the crops which they could grow for themselves. Before the dawn of the eighteenth century there was a distinct West in the American colonies—a definite frontier so regarded by the people of the seaboard. Here prevailed American food and food habits little touched by European influences. By the time of the American Revolution settlers had crossed the mountains and begun to occupy Kentucky and Tennessee. After the close of that struggle the westward advance was much more rapid. The purchase of Louisiana added a vast new region and the peopling of the present states of Arkansas and Missouri soon began and rapidly grew in volume. By this time the Old Northwest was fairly well settled by a frontier population, and settlements were made in Iowa, Michigan, and eastern

Texas. In all of these regions the hardy frontiersmen lived in much the same fashion and their food was distinctly similar, subject only to such variations as the resources of each particular region made necessary and modified somewhat by the traditional customs, likes, and dislikes, in the matter of diet, due to environment in their earlier homeland in the East.

In advance of actual settlers always went those vanguards of the frontier—the trappers, traders, and hunters. Most of these were men without wives and families and their food was of a peculiarly "masculine nature." Living among the Indians or in close proximity to them, some of them married Indian wives and, to a greater or less extent, "went native" in diet as in everything else. Such men, however, were few in number and may be disregarded in this particular study which deals primarily with those people who journeyed west to establish homes and develop a raw and untamed land.

Most of the regions mentioned were wooded, or at least partially so, though there were areas of prairie land especially in the Northwest and to some extent in the regions farther south. Throughout the frontier area the basic vegetable food was Indian corn. It was easy to grow and harvest, and it yielded a large quantity of grain which could be utilized in a wide variety of ways. Also, it matured quickly; the ears of the dwarf varieties were sometimes ready for boiling within sixty days of the time of planting. By making several plantings a week or ten days apart green corn could be had on the table over a very considerable period of time. Once it had passed the "roasting ear" stage but was still not hard enough to grind, it could be grated by hand to make what the pioneers called "gritted bread" which was particularly delicious.

Green corn was cooked in a variety of ways. The most common was by boiling the ears in a pot after the husks and silks had been removed, though some preferred to boil or roast it in the husk. Also, it was cut from the cob with a sharp knife and seasoned with milk or butter or fried in a little pork or bacon fat. An especially delectable dish was obtained by slitting each row of kernels in the center with a sharp knife, scraping out the pulp, and frying it in butter. This involved some time and effort but the result was well worth it.

After the corn had matured and been harvested, it furnished the staple bread supply of most families for the year. Hominy was made by boiling the shelled corn in a weak lye (made from wood ashes) until the husks had been loosened and could be rubbed off by hand. The corn was then taken from the lye, washed several times in cold water, and put in a stone jar and stored in a cool place. It was fried in bacon fat for breakfast, boiled with the addition of milk and butter for dinner, and was frequently warmed up for supper. It furnished an excellent substitute for bread as well as for the various types of breakfast food in use today, and when properly made and cooked was one of the most palatable and nourishing of foods in the frontier diet.

For pounding corn into meal the Indians utilized a mortar made by hollowing out a section of a tree trunk and a pestle made from hickory or some other hard wood. The white settlers sometimes did the same but it was not long until gristmills for grinding corn were common throughout the frontier. Power was usually furnished by a water wheel and many old-time pioneers still solemnly assert that meal ground by a water mill makes far superior bread to that ground by steam. There was also the endless argument over the relative merits of white and yellow corn meal. Taking "a turn of corn" to mill was one of the regular duties of nearly every pioneer lad, the expression doubtless originating from the fact that everyone had to wait his turn to get his corn ground. The miller, in most cases, derived his pay from a toll taken for every bushel ground and so usually had meal to sell and would exchange it for corn when the customer was impatient or too busy to wait. This was seldom the case, however, for going to mill furnished an opportunity for social contacts with the neighbors, and the men and boys waiting their turn had ample time to exchange gossip and swap stories. Those who tended to grow impatient could relieve their minds by sarcastic remarks as to the slowness of the grinding operations.

South of the future Mason and Dixon line and in many areas

north of it, corn bread was literally the staff of life of most frontier settlers. The simplest form was made by salting the meal and scalding it with sufficient boiling water to make a thick dough. This was made out in small cakes and fried to a golden brown in hot fat. These fried cakes were commonly called "corn dodgers" or, in the Deep South, were sometimes known as "hush puppies." Larger cakes of corn meal were sometimes baked in a Dutch oven. This form of bread was originally called "journey cake" because the housewife would bake a supply of it for her husband to take with him if he must go on a journey. This term was later corrupted into "johnny-cake." Baked in the ashes, or on a hot stone or hoe, the bread was known as "ashcake" or "hoe-cake."

Mush was made by stirring meal in boiling water which had been lightly salted. It was eaten with milk, and "mush and milk" were articles of frontier diet almost as well known as "hog and hominy." Any mush left over was poured into a bowl and the following morning was cut into thick slices and fried in hot fat for breakfast. It was usually eaten with syrup or honey, as were also the corn griddle cakes. When milk was available, corn bread was made with sour milk and soda and baked in a Dutch oven or, after the coming of cookstoves, in long, black pans. People in the North often put sugar in corn bread, a practice the Southerners have always asserted was one of the primary causes of the Civil War!

Despite the almost universal use of corn bread on the frontier, virtually every family kept at least a small supply of flour on hand and had wheat bread at times. The ratio of wheat to corn bread used, however, varied widely. Some people, especially in the upland South, were satisfied with biscuits for Sunday morning breakfast and upon such other occasions as they might have guests at a meal. Others demanded wheat bread, usually biscuits, for breakfast every morning, while still others insisted upon it at least twice a day. In some sections of the North, and particularly in the prairie West where wheat was the staple crop, bread made from wheat flour was the standard type and corn bread was served only once or twice a week.

Throughout the South, biscuits formed the standard staff of life, and bread made with yeast, commonly called "light bread," was very exceptional. The "beaten biscuits" of Virginia and some other parts of the Old South were, however, seldom seen on the frontier. Ordinarily biscuits were made with sour milk and soda. At their best, when baked to a rich brown, with crisp crust and flaky interior, "buttermilk biscuits" were almost the last word in food. Unfortunately they were often tough, pale blue in color, and streaked with soda. In such cases, when a plate of them was said to "look like a gang of terrapins a-comin'," they were about as poor a makeshift for bread as could be imagined. Every housewife was known by her biscuits, which probably had a wider degree of individuality than any other article of food. Baking powder, commonly called "yeast powders," came into use comparatively late and was never popular, since biscuits made from it were not thought to be healthful as a regular diet.

The cow country and some other sections of the frontier specialized in the sour-dough biscuits. Biscuits were not common, however, in the northern zone of frontier settlement. Here the staple food was yeast bread, usually baked two or three times a week. Packages of dry yeast cakes could sometimes be bought at the country store but many housewives preferred to make their own. This was done by boiling dry hops purchased at the store and adding to the water two or three boiled potatoes well mashed, a cake of yeast from the last batch made, and sufficient corn meal to make a thick dough. This was rolled out about half an inch thick and cut into round cakes which were dried slowly in the shade. When hops were lacking, peach-tree leaves might be used as a substitute.

Bread was made by dissolving one of these yeast cakes in warm water and adding flour to make a very thick batter or sponge. This was allowed to rise overnight and flour was then added to make a dough which was well kneaded and set in a warm place to rise. It was then "worked down" and made into loaves which were placed in pans and allowed to rise again before baking. Some housewives made salt-rising bread, and its peculiar fragrance always hung about their kitchens. Other forms of food made from wheat flour, especially in the North, were griddle cakes, muffins, doughnuts, fritters, and popovers. Buckwheat cakes were also common and nearly every housewife had her own particular recipe.

One of the first tasks of virtually every frontier settler was to plan and plant a garden in order to furnish his family with an ample supply of vegetables. These were of many kinds, including beans, peas, squashes, pumpkins, radishes, mustard, lettuce, carrots, beets, onions, turnips, cabbage, potatoes, sweet potatoes, cucumbers, melons, and several others. Tomatoes, formerly called "love apples," were in early days thought to be poisonous but were occasionally grown as ornamental plants because of the bright red fruit. It was some years before it was learned that they are a wholesome article of food and they became a commonly grown vegetable on the American frontier.

Pending the growth of a garden, the pioneer settler must depend upon such native products as were available for fresh vegetable food, but these were often of considerable variety. The Indians consumed quantities of wild onions of which they were very fond, but these were seldom eaten by the white settlers. Yet there were many wild products which were widely utilized, including several kinds of "wild greens" such as lamb's quarter, "poke salad," dandelions, and two or three varieties of dock. Boiled with a piece of salt pork, any of these furnished a tasty and satisfying food and, while the pioneers had never heard of vitamins, such wild pottage was regarded as conducive to good health and in addition furnished a welcome change from the dry or salt food which had been the ordinary diet of the winter months.

Once garden vegetables were available the pioneer usually had an ample supply of fresh vegetable food throughout the summer and early autumn. Mustard, spinach, turnip tops, cabbage, and collards took the place of the "wild greens." Green peas, commonly called "English peas," were boiled with new potatoes with the addition of a lump of butter and half a cup of milk into which had been stirred a spoonful of flour. String beans and potatoes were also boiled together with a slab of salt pork.

Potatoes were cooked in a variety of ways and sweet potatoes were roasted in the ashes or boiled. In some cases, raw sweet potatoes were cut in thick slices and fried for breakfast. Squashes were baked in the shell or cut into pieces and stewed with the addition of a little sugar. Turnips and cabbages were boiled with salt pork. Radishes, lettuce, and spring onions were eaten raw and mature onions fried in butter or pork fat. Also onions, boiled beets, and raw cucumbers were sliced and covered with vinegar, and boiled beets were often sliced and buttered.

The pioneer settlers usually put away large quantities of vegetables for winter use. Green corn was boiled, cut from the cob, and dried in the sun. Beans and peas were shelled when dry and put in sacks to be hung from the rafters of the smokehouse. Potatoes, sweet potatoes, turnips, beets, cabbage, and pumpkins were stored in a "root cellar" or merely piled up in heaps in the field or garden and covered, first with hay, then with a thick layer of earth to prevent their freezing. Slices of peeled pumpkin were commonly dried in the sun and long strings of onions hung up in the smokehouse, shed room, or cellar. Remote from markets, and with virtually no "money crop," the pioneer could concentrate each summer on the problem of providing an adequate supply of food for his family during the coming winter.

Lack of fruit proved a considerable hardship to many pioneer settlers, especially on the western prairies, though this was true to a somewhat lesser degree even in the wooded regions of the earlier frontier. Orchards and vineyards are of comparatively slow growth, usually requiring some years to come into full bearing. In the meantime, the settler must depend upon wild fruits and berries, or such fruit substitutes as could be grown in a single season. In the forested area, wild grapes and plums of several varieties were abundant. In addition, there were often blackberries, dewberries, strawberries, raspberries, gooseberries, currants, papaws, and persimmons. These were eaten fresh, stewed, or made into pies and cobblers during the time they were in season, and made into preserves, jams, or jellies for winter use if sugar or even syrup could be had, but the supply of sugar was often very scanty. The wild berry bushes or vines were also dug up and transplanted to a plot of ground in the garden to form a "berry patch." In addition, virtually every settler sought to "put out an orchard" just as soon as possible. Peach seeds were brought from the old home, planted thickly in rows, and when the young trees were a year old they were transplanted to the ground set aside for the orchard. Some men were adept at grafting or budding better varieties of fruit upon these original stocks though many seedling peaches were excellent in quality. A few young apple, pear, plum, or cherry trees were sometimes brought from the old homeland in the original migration, the roots packed in moist earth and carefully wrapped in coarse cloth on which water was poured each night during the journey. If the settler did not find it possible to take a few fruit trees with him to the West, he might order some through the traveling agent of some nursery in the East or select them from a catalogue and order by mail. Difficulties of shipment were frequently great, however, and moreover, few pioneer settlers had enough money to purchase very many trees, so the orchards usually remained small for several years.

There is the classic folk tale of "Johnny Appleseed," an old itinerant who traveled about throughout the American frontier, stopping for the night with pioneer families and claiming a "right of purveyance" by virtue of little packages of apple seeds which he dispensed freely in a thousand households. A generation ago some apple trees still to be seen in the Middle West were said to have been grown from seed furnished by this half-legendary character.

Substitutes for orchard fruits were melons, rhubarb, tomatoes, after they came into general use, pumpkins, and, on the far western prairies, several varieties of vines producing yellow globular fruits known as "pomegranates," or "poor man's apples." Quantities of delicious watermelons were grown. From the rinds were made preserves, and sweet pickles, and if the garden did not afford cucumbers a substitute was found in tiny green melons pickled in vinegar. "Pumpkin butter" was a fair substitute for apple butter, and a marmalade was sometimes made from the flesh of cantaloupes or muskmelons. Citron melons and pie melons were used both for pies and preserves. Tomato preserves were also common, and rhubarb was used in lieu of apples both for pies and sauce. Once the orchards came into bearing, ample fruit was usually available for every purpose and a supply of peaches and apples was dried in the sun for winter use.

With the coming of the so-called "self-sealing" glass fruit jars every family sought to can a quantity of fruit each season. These jars were too expensive, however, for the average frontier householder to be able to afford more than a few dozen at most. It is an interesting commentary on the size of pioneer families that every frontier housewife insisted upon half-gallon jars, asserting that the quart size did not hold enough to go more than halfway around in serving her family. Yet, the modern housewife virtually always demands either pint or quart jars, usually the former, and the half-gallon size has almost disappeared from the market except in a few localities.

While the various vegetable foods that have been mentioned were all fairly common on some portion of the frontier, it must not be assumed that the pioneer settler was in any sense a vegetarian. America has always been a nation of meat eaters, and it is doubtful if any section of our country has ever consumed a greater quantity of animal food per capita of population than did the western frontier. The American colonists brought domestic animals and poultry from England very early and these increased rapidly under the favorable conditions of range and climate. As settlement advanced westward, most pioneers took with them cattle, hogs, chickens, and in some cases sheep or goats, though neither of the last named were numerous on the greater part of the American frontier, especially in the South, until the Far West had been reached. In the wooded areas, fields and gardens were enclosed, at first with brush and later with rail fences, and cattle and hogs ranged outside. While the number of such animals was not large at first, the increase, particularly of hogs, was very rapid, six to ten pigs in a litter being the usual number. In consequence, it was not long until virtually every settler had an ample number of hogs to supply his family with meat and lard, and enough cows to provide sufficient milk and butter.

Pending this time, however, the pioneer must secure a meat supply from the forest. This was seldom very difficult. In the early stages of settlement, game was usually abundant on most parts of the American frontier. This consisted of deer, turkeys, squirrels, rabbits, wild pigeons, grouse, quail, ducks and geese in some localities, and in the Far West antelope and elk. The countless buffalo which roamed the Great Plains had largely been destroyed before the coming of actual settlers to that region and so did not figure in the food supply of many people, except the Indians, trappers, mountain men, and other vanguards of the Far Western frontier region.

Virtually every pioneer settler was more or less a hunter, and the same was true of all his sons above the age of ten or twelve years. Venison was often a staple article of food in the frontier home, and deer hams were hung up and cured for winter use. Fried quail, rabbit, and squirrel commonly appeared on the table, as did squirrel stew, pigeon or quail pot-pie, and roast duck, goose, or turkey. Gradually the game disappeared, however, due to the ever-growing influx of settlers; but by the time it had become scarce the domestic animals had increased sufficiently to provide an ample supply of meat. After this, hunting declined as a serious business and became more of a sport or avocation. Yet in the absence of fresh meat during the greater part of the year, an occasional mess of quails, or squirrels, or a wild turkey made a most acceptable addition to the pioneer's ordinary fare. After the first few years, however, the staple meat of the frontier settler and his family was pork and its various products as ham, bacon, and sausage.

Pigs were "earmarked" when quite young so that each man might distinguish his own animals from those of his neighbors. Ranging at large in the woods, they fattened largely on the "mast" which was the general term for nuts and acorns. Perhaps this took a long time, but in the language of the Arkansas settler: "What is time to a hog?" It was customary, however, if at all possible, to call them up each evening and feed them a little corn or slops from the kitchen. This was designed, in the frontier vernacular, to "ha'nt 'em home" or attach them to the dwelling of their owner. This enabled him to see them each day, and also the additional food kept them growing faster and in a thriving condition. If sufficient corn had been grown, those designated for slaughter were confined in a pen for six weeks or more in the autumn and fed liberally on grain until they were fat enough to be butchered.

Hog-killing time, usually late in November, was a more or less gala occasion, especially for the children of the family. The meat was cut into hams, shoulders, and "middlings" or sides. These were carefully trimmed and "salted down" in barrels or large wooden boxes. The scraps trimmed away were ground into sausage which was seasoned with salt, pepper, and sage, and stuffed into long narrow sacks made of cloth to be hung in the smokehouse. Some preferred to pack the sausage in stone jars and pour melted lard on top of it. Others made the sausage into cakes which were fried, packed in jars, and covered with melted lard. The more usual method, however, was to pack it in sacks, but in the absence of material to make them it might be wrapped in cornhusks and hung in the smokehouse or "shed room." Hog killing also involved "rendering out" the lard, and making of "souse," or head cheese. The liver, heart, backbones, and spareribs were eaten fresh and were often shared with some of the neighbors. Since people killed hogs at different times, this mutual exchange of a surplus usually provided everyone in the community with fresh pork at intervals during a period of several weeks.

Methods of cooking fresh pork varied. Backbones were usually boiled, spareribs cut across three or four times and either fried or sprinkled with salt, pepper, and flour and baked in the oven. Pigs' feet were cleaned and boiled until very tender. They were then cut in two and either pickled in hot vinegar to which spices had been added, or dipped in batter and fried in hot fat. Sausage would keep for weeks or months. It was sliced in thick round slices or made into cakes and fried for breakfast. Many a man reared on the frontier can still remember the savory "sagey" odor of frying sausage which greeted him upon awakening in the morning and which proved the chief incentive to his rolling out of his warm bed into the icy cold of his sleeping quarters in the upstairs of a frontier farm home.

After some weeks, when the pork packed in barrels or boxes had thoroughly "taken salt," it was removed, and surplus salt was washed off, and the cut sides of the hams and shoulders rubbed with a mixture of black pepper and molasses. The meat was then hung up in the smokehouse and thoroughly smoked with hickory wood or chips. Sometimes the "side meat" was smoked to form bacon, but a part of it was often left in salt to be used as dry salt pork. The cured hams and shoulders would keep indefinitely, though the bacon or "middlings" sometimes tended to get strong before the end of the following summer.

Salt pork or bacon was fried, boiled with beans, greens, or cabbage, or in the North, baked with beans. Ham or shoulder was fried, boiled, or baked, but the hams were likely to be reserved largely for "company" or for Sunday dinners and other special occasions unless a sufficient number of hogs had been killed to make it possible to sell some of the "side meat" and retain the extra hams and shoulders for use at home.

Except during the hog-killing season, fresh meat was more or less a rarity in most frontier homes, though someone in the community would occasionally kill a beef and "peddle out" the meat among his neighbors. Scientific methods of meat cutting were unknown. It was merely cut into chunks and sold, the hindquarter usually being one cent a pound higher than the forequarter. "How much do you get for your beef?" was the first question asked when a peddler's wagon appeared. "Six and seven cents" was likely to be the answer, though at times it might be as high as seven and eight or as low as three and four cents a pound.

On the frontier, beefsteak was almost never broiled. It was cut in slices, pounded with a mallet or the edge of a heavy plate or saucer, and then rolled in flour and fried in hot suet. Large cuts containing some bone were boiled, or sprinkled with flour and baked in the oven. After being served at one meal, what was left was sliced and served cold, or cut into small pieces and stewed with chopped potatoes and onions to form Irish stew or hash. With such an abundant supply of pork, ham, and bacon, together with some fresh beef from time to time, and the occasional use of game, it is not surprising that meat constituted a large part of the diet of the average pioneer settler. In fact, so much was consumed as to give rise to the old folk tale of the illiterate Irishman who had newly come to America and asked a friend to write a letter for him to send to his family in the Old Country. "Tell them," said he, "that here in America we have meat three times a week." "Why not say three times a day?" asked his friend. "Faith, no! It's no use to tell them that," was the answer. "They wouldn't believe it but would swear I was lyin'. Make it three times a week and maybe they might believe me."

Few frontier families considered a dessert necessary to the completion of a meal, except on Sunday or in case "company" was present. At other times the syrup pitcher was placed on the table three times a day and each meal was likely to be "topped off" with sorghum or some other form of syrup. Sorghum mills were usually more numerous than gristmills, and many settlers would grow a patch of sorghum which, when ripe, was cut and hauled to the mill to be crushed and the juice boiled down into sorghum "on the shares."

Despite the frequent absence of any form of dessert, the average pioneer housewife was skilled in making pies, cakes, and gingerbread. Cobblers were also made from peaches, blackberries, or sweet potatoes, and fried pies known in the North as "turnovers" were common during the winter season. These were made by lining a saucer with "pie dough" and placing dried apples or peaches, which had been stewed and crushed to a pulp, on one side. The edge of the dough was then moistened all around so that the edges would stick together and the flap of dough folded over the fruit and the edges firmly pressed together. These half-moon–shaped "pies" were then fried to a rich brown in deep fat and served hot. Properly made, they were delicious even if a somewhat heavy food. Children were usually

very fond of them and were happy when one or two were placed
in their lunch baskets or the "dinner buckets" that they carried
to school.

In most frontier homes Sunday dinner, especially "company"
occasions, was an event to be long remembered. Fried chicken
with cream gravy, or stewed chicken with dumplings was likely
to be the central dish. Moreover, the chicken was not a "cold
storage corpse" but was likely to have been running about on
foot only a few hours before being served at the table. At some
dinners, fried ham with red gravy might take the place of
chicken. In any case there were likely to be three or four fresh
vegetables in addition to radishes and green onions, hot biscuits,
corn bread, pie or cobbler, coffee, buttermilk (which had been
cooled in the spring or by lowering a jug of it into the well by
means of a long rope), jelly, preserves, freshly churned butter,
and perhaps several other dishes. Many an old-timer looks back
to such dinners with a wistful feeling of regret and is willing to
swear that they were far better than any he ever ate in a fash-
ionable restaurant or hotel.

Despite the ability of the average frontier housewife, in times
of plenty, to place before her family and guests a sumptuous
feast, not a few of them had a facility, amounting almost to
genius, for preparing, in times of stress, tasty and satisfying
meals from the most meager resources. This could not have been
easy, for there was far less differentiation between the three
daily meals than is true at present. The midday meal, always
known as "dinner," was usually the most substantial of the three,
but all must be heavy. Orange juice, toast, and coffee is no sort of
breakfast for the man who must split rails, or follow a plow from
sunup until noon. The pioneer settler demanded at least hot
biscuits, meat, fried potatoes, gravy, syrup, and coffee.

In the most lean periods, however, his wife was generally
equal to every emergency. Salt pork was often parboiled, rolled
in flour, and fried to give a welcome change from the ordinary
side meat. Gravy was made by stirring a spoonful of flour into
a little hot bacon grease, adding milk, and boiling until it was
thick and creamy. It was a staple not only at breakfast for it often

appeared on the table at other meals as well. Made in the fat in which chicken or beefsteak had been fried, it had a delicious flavor, but in any case it had nearly all the elements of a perfect food. Commonly called "hush puppy gravy" it was an almost universal article of diet among the pioneers. Thousands of children grew to manhood and womanhood and always remained strong and healthy on a diet consisting very largely of corn bread, bacon, gravy, syrup, and buttermilk, with fresh vegetables from the garden in season.

Faced with the necessity of improvising, the frontier housewife often showed rare ingenuity in matters of food. Lacking fruit, she baked a vinegar pie. This was made by mixing half a cupful of vinegar with a pint of water and adding sugar to taste. A lump of butter the size of an egg was then melted in a pan and a heaping tablespoonful of flour stirred into it. To this was added the tangy vinegar mixture, a little at a time, stirring it vigorously all the while until it had boiled sufficiently long to begin to thicken. The mixture was then poured into a piepan lined with a rich crust and additional strips of dough were "crisscrossed" over the top. Bits of butter were sprinkled over these crossbars, and the pie was then baked in a hot oven. It came out with the crust a deep brown and the filling reduced to the consistency of jelly. To serve a considerable number of persons the quantity of the mixture was merely increased and baked in a long pan. This formed something in the nature of a fruit cobbler and was sometimes called "vinegarone."

"Butter roll" was made of a rich biscuit dough which was rolled thin and sprinkled thickly with sugar and small lumps of butter. It was then rolled up and baked to a rich brown in a hot oven. Pies were also made from rhubarb, pie melons, squash, pumpkin, green tomatoes, green grapes, and even the fleshy acid leaves of the wild sheep sorrel. Nearly always, however, the housewife was faced with the problem of a shortage of sugar and, in many cases, honey, sorghum, or some other form of syrup, must be used as a substitute. Fortunately, there was usually an ample supply of milk, butter, and eggs and these

helped vastly in preparing good meals even when other resources were pitifully scanty.

In few parts of America did frontier conditions persist for
more than one or two generations. With the steady growth of
population, the trails over which the pioneer emigrants journeyed west were widened to broad highways. Attractive farm
homes replaced the former log cabins or sod houses. Towns and
cities grew up. Differentiations in the social classes began to
appear. Gradually the old order disappeared, and in its place
came civilization, and the sophistication that is associated with
urban life, while new frontier regions appeared farther west.
One by one these too disappeared until about the dawn of the
present century we came to the end of a great historic movement, and the frontier and pioneer conditions in America vanished forever. Only in a few remote areas among the hills and
mountains, or in regions too rough and rocky to support any considerable population, may still be found a life strongly reminiscent of that of generations past.

VII

We couldn't buy entertainment,
It was simply not to be had,
So we alone must provide our own
And we did not think it so bad.
There were socials, dances, and parties
Where we played the age-old games
Though people today would doubtless say
They had most astonishing names.

There was "Coffee Grows on White Oak Trees"
And "Little Brass Wagon" too,
Or "Miller Boy" we'd all enjoy
And likewise "Skip to My Lou."
"Eighteen Pounds of Meat a Week"
And "Chase the Buffalo"—
They all were fun for everyone,
The games of the long ago.

The Play Party

VII

The Social Homesteader

OF THE VANGUARDS of the frontier Kipling once wrote:

> He shall desire loneliness
> And his desire shall bring
> Hard on his heels a thousand wheels
> A people and a King.

True as this may have been of the hunter, trapper, prospector, and ranchman, it was not true of the homeseekers who followed them, few of whom "desired loneliness." They had left their old friends with deep regret and eagerly sought to acquire new ones.

They began at once to visit their neighbors and form social contacts with them. The younger people, quickly finding that entertainment was not a purchasable commodity, provided their own in the form of dances, socials, box suppers, and literary or debating societies. In an area peopled by native-born Americans from every part of the country, and many German, Scandinavian, and Czech emigrants from Europe, the final result was to break down old-time prejudices and make the community a social unit.

IN 1862 AMID THE TURMOIL of civil war, the Congress of the United States passed the Homestead Act. This granted 160 acres of land from the public domain to every person 21 years of age or the head of a family who was a citizen of the United States or had declared his intention of becoming a citizen and who did not already own more than 160 acres of land elsewhere. During the stress of war no large number of persons took advantage of this but immediately after the close of the conflict, and the return of so many thousands of soldiers to civil life, there was a great outpouring of eager homeseekers to the Prairie West. By 1870 this movement had gathered enormous momentum and during the next two decades the increase of population in most states forming the second tier west of the Mississippi River was truly startling. During the next decade the increase continued and Oklahoma Territory's population grew from 61,000 in 1890 to 400,000 in 1900. Montana, Wyoming, Colorado, and New Mexico show a similar trend.

Regardless of the state or the region in which the homesteader settled, his first desire was to become acquainted with his neighbors. He was above all eager to know what sort of people these were among whom he had cast his lot. Were some of them natives of his own state or members of his own church? How many children were in the community who might be brought into a school or Sunday School? Were these nearby settlers a kindly and hospitable people who would make good neighbors, and among whom he could live on friendly terms and with mutual respect and confidence? On the answer to these questions depended to a great extent the future happiness and well being of the new homesteader and his family.

He soon discovered that neighboring settlers were asking themselves exactly the same questions about him. In a new country co-operation and the development of a community consciousness is most important. The answers to such questions were, moreover, in most cases satisfactory. The people who came to these new prairie regions did so to make homes for themselves and their families. They were for the most part an honest, industrious, God-fearing folk eager to succeed and to build up a stable society in a raw and untamed land. Any members of the rougher element that had drifted in soon found themselves so far outnumbered that they departed in search of more congenial associates and an environment more suited to their tastes.

Much has been written of the never-ending labor of the American pioneer. It is true that the settlers of the timbered regions always had a job. The idea, however, that the homesteader on the wide prairies farther west faced unremitting toil is largely a myth. The women were, as a rule, kept very busy, but not so the men. Located on a prairie claim forty to sixty miles from the nearest railroad, the settler, once he had made his first improvements of the homestead, found himself the possessor of abundant leisure. The distance to the railroad was too great to make it possible to market there any surplus farm or garden products even if the little frontier railway towns had furnished any considerable market, which in most cases they did not. Also drought, hot winds, and grasshoppers often kept the quantity of any such surplus very low.

Under such circumstances the pioneer settler fell back upon subsistence farming which in most cases had been the form of agriculture to which he had been accustomed in his old home. He felt that farming was not a business to be carried on for profit. It was a way of life and was the only way he knew as well as the only one he wanted to know and pursue. Enough wheat, corn, or kafir corn could easily be raised to provide bread for the family. This was ground at a small mill in the community. He had two or three milk cows to provide milk and butter and three or four pigs to furnish the winter's supply of meat. The garden afforded vegetables, and wild plums or grapes could be gathered from the sand hills along the rivers. Sorghum could be grown and syrup made at a neighborhood sorghum mill. A few chickens supplied the family with eggs and occasionally with roast or fried chicken. As for money it was largely nonexistent. In times of stress he could leave the family and journey east for a few months' work at seasonal labor and so earn enough to provide his wife and children clothing and shoes for the winter with something left over to buy sugar and coffee.

As for securing profitable employment in the homestead region itself, the very thought of it was absurd. All of the neighbors were in the same situation as himself. None had any money with which to hire labor or any profitable labor to be done. A census of the unemployed rural persons in western Oklahoma, Kansas or Nebraska in the early nineties would have included, except for ranchmen and cowboys, virtually the entire population. The new farm supplied a living of sorts, but no money, and for such crops as were grown there was no cost of production. Any labor expended in farm work had no value. The pioneer raised his own help just as he raised his own meat, bread, and vegetables. With four or five big, strong boys who needed to be taught to work, the settler often had to figure ways and means to keep them employed at useful tasks, especially since the school term was seldom more than three or four months.

Under such a regime there was abundant time for social contacts with the neighbors and new-found friends. Such contacts in the earliest days of homestead life often took the form of "visiting." These were not the formal calls to which a later generation has become accustomed, but an all-day visit of the entire family. On Sunday morning the father would hitch the mules to the big farm wagon while the mother gathered her brood about her, scrubbed their faces, and dressed them in their Sunday best. The entire family then piled into the wagon and drove four or five miles to the home of a friend where they always received a warm welcome. During the forenoon the men sat beneath the brush arbor in front of the sod home, if it were during warm weather, and smoked while they talked of politics, religion, and the future of the community. Inside, the women bustled about preparing dinner and visiting at the same time, while the children ran wild on the prairie or played such games as "town ball," "prisoner's base" and "black man."

When dinner was announced the adults gathered about the table while the children had to wait, since there was neither room nor dishes enough for all. No matter how meager the weekday fare might be, the Sunday dinner in which guests shared seldom left anything to be desired. Chicken and dumplings, hot biscuits with butter, three or four vegetables from the garden, hot coffee, cool buttermilk, and vinegar pie were attacked with enthusiastic vigor. After what seemed to the youngsters an interminable time, the elders finished, the dishes were washed and the table laid afresh. Sometimes the visiting lady would insist that it was not necessary to wash a plate for her son since he "could eat off his paw's plate," but the hostess in virtually every case declared that it was no trouble and that no child should be called upon to eat from a soiled plate. In most cases the lad had long since passed the stage of being unduly particular.

After the children had eaten, and the dishes had been washed a second time and put away, the "visiting" was resumed. The men walked about over the farm, inspected the crops and livestock, the children went back to their games and the women compared fancy work or engaged in small talk until the declining sun warned the visitors that it was time to go home.

At first such visits provided almost the only social diversion for older people but it was not long until the young men and women began to plan more active and colorful forms of amusement. The old-time square dances, common to the cow country, were often taboo in this new social order, especially in the southern zone of settlement, though they were sometimes popular farther north. Even in the Southern Plains region they were fairly common in those communities where some ranching still existed and were shared in by the wilder or more rowdy elements of the neighborhood. Dancing, as a rule, however, lies at the two extremes of civilization. The primitive and the sophisticated both dance but the in-betweens will have none of it. Such scruples, however, did not extend to socials and play parties. These began to be held quite often and older people often came to share in the fun. All such events were noninvitation affairs. A couple of young men eager for "something to go to" would ride over to a settler's home and ask the good housewife if a party might be held at her home on a certain evening. Having by earnest urging secured her permission, they then made the rounds of the community announcing that there would be a party at the home of Mr. and Mrs. Smith next Saturday with "everybody invited, nobody slighted."

Such parties assumed various forms. One of the commonest was the "social" sometimes locally known as the "set to." At this, seats were arranged around the wall and, as the young people assembled, they were seated in couples by a young woman known as the "hostess." After a man had talked to a girl for ten or fifteen minutes, it was the duty of the hostess to bring up another man, pluck the first one away, and give his place to the newcomer. The first man would then be seated by some other girl, and so the people were shifted about until every man had been introduced to every girl and had talked with her for at least a few minutes. When the number of boys greatly exceeded that of the girls, a man might be left out in the cold to chat with his male friends for a time, but eventually he was once more put back into circulation. The success of such a party depended a great deal upon the fairness and wisdom of a hostess who would play no favorites, but used reasonable discretion in shifting couples that were not congenial and in allowing those who seemed to be having a good time to prolong their conversation beyond the limit ordinarily allowed.

Refreshments were usually served about the middle of the evening, but, owing to the meager abilities of the average household to provide them, the guests often brought their own. Such an affair was called a "pound party" since each young man had been instructed to bring a pound of some delicacy to help out the good cheer of the occasion. If the home boasted two or more rooms, a long table, usually made of rough boards, was set up in one room. Here the packages were unwrapped, the cans or jars opened, and their contents put in dishes and strung along the table. The result was sometimes a bit startling. Pounds of candy, crackers, apples, cookies, figs, dates, nuts, canned fruits, and various other things were scattered about over the table and five or six couples came out at a time and chose what they wanted.

For the more boisterous young people and those who had formerly danced and perhaps still would, were it not contrary to public opinion and the rules of the church, the play party was a favorite diversion. The procedure of "getting it up" was exactly the same as for the social, but at such an affair "singing games" were played instead of merely devoting the evening to conversation. The play party was perhaps imported directly from the hills of Missouri or Arkansas or the timbered regions of Texas. Favorite games were "We'll all go down to Rowser's," "Coffee Grows on White Oak Trees," "Chase the Buffalo," "Little Brass Wagon," "Old Dan Tucker," and a multitude of others. Some members of a community, especially those who would have liked to dance, viewed such games askance and declared they were "only dancing with the best part of it, the music, left out." Certainly the steps and figures were more or less reminiscent of the old-fashioned squares, and yet many older persons who thought dancing an invention of the devil viewed the games of the play party with entire approbation. The words sung were often sheer drivel, but the tunes were catchy and the figures danced sometimes quite intricate. Note these words of a popular favorite:

> Then come on, my dearest dear
> And present to me your paw
> For I know you've got tobaccer
> And I'm bound to have a chaw.
> I'm bound to have a chaw.
> And I'm bound to have a chaw.
> For I know you've got tobaccer
> And I'm bound to have a chaw.
>
> Then come on, my dearest dear
> And we all will fight and scratch
> For we'll all root together
> In the sweet potato patch.
> The sweet potato patch,
> The sweet potato patch.
> For we'll all root together
> In the sweet potato patch.

Another less common was as follows:

> Eighteen pounds of meat a week
> Whiskey here to sell
> How can the boys stay at home
> When the girls all look so well
> When the girls all look so well.
>
> If I had a scolding wife
> I'd whip her sure as she's born
> I'd take her down to New Orleans
> And trade her off for corn.
> And trade her off for corn.

As the words were sung with spirit and sometimes a good deal of harmony, the couples on the floor went through an elaborate dance figure with all the movements of swing, dos-à-dos, promenade, and various others. Other more childish games such as "snap," "marching 'round the levee," "miller boy," and "hunt the thimble" were sometimes played.

If some home had a cottage organ, the young people of the community would sometimes assemble there for an evening of singing. Hymns were usually sung, though other songs, particularly those of a humorous nature, were also common. Even those people who cared little for music and knew even less about it, would come to a "singing" merely for the opportunity it gave to meet friends and form new social contacts.

The early settlers of the prairie frontier had an almost fanatical belief in education. Almost the first community enterprise in every neighborhood was the erection of a school building and the establishment of a little school. Once this was done, the opportunities for social life were greatly increased. The schoolhouse, no matter how small or rude, soon became something of a social center. To it were transferred many of the community "singings." A Sunday School was quickly organized and arrangements made to have church services at least once or twice a month. The school itself was, moreover, a matter of general interest. Visitors dropped in on Friday afternoon to hear the children "speak their pieces" that were usually given at that time or to enjoy the spelling and ciphering matches.

A literary and debating society to meet twice a month was usually formed. This was in most cases held every other Friday evening and a program committee worked hard to see that each meeting was an unqualified success. Here recitations and declamations were delivered, most of them old selections chosen from McGuffey's Readers or from some special "speech book." "Spartacus to the Gladiators," "Curfew Must Not Ring Tonight" and "Lips That Touch Liquor Must Never Touch Mine" were prime favorites. Quartets and soloists rendered numbers, dialogues were presented, and debaters, with more fire than grammar, thundered forth their views as to which is the more destructive element, fire or water, or as to whether there is more pleasure in pursuit or possession.

Box suppers to provide funds for an organ for the schoolhouse or some other laudable enterprise were common and well attended. Every woman and girl in the community packed a choice supper for two in a pasteboard box which was frequently covered with tin foil or gay tissue paper and decorated with artificial flowers. When all had assembled at the schoolhouse, these were sold at auction, the purchaser of a box having the privilege of eating supper with the lady who had prepared it. Whether you should eat a square meal at the usual time before leaving home or merely take a light snack to hold body and soul together until the boxes were opened at about nine-thirty was a question which each individual had to decide for himself.

After the boxes had all been sold and supper eaten, a cake was sometimes presented to the most popular young lady as a means of raising additional funds. Votes were usually one cent each and in most cases there were but two leading candidates. One represented the churchgoing element and was usually a girl who taught a Sunday School class, sang in the church services, and was known to be good "to wait on the sick." The other in all probability represented the more frivolous and wilder element. She made all the play parties, dressed in showy fashion, and was commonly considered "good company," whatever that might mean!

The two girls were usually led to the end of the room and seated near the teacher's desk where everyone might appraise the charms of his favorite candidate. Then the voting began, and as the money came in, the number of votes was checked up on the blackboard. Sometimes the election was quite spirited and became more than a friendly contest between two personable young women. It was a struggle between two sets of ideals, a battle of two types of society.

Other forms of entertainment flourished throughout the community and other types of social events became common. All-day singings were held at the schoolhouse. A singing school lasting two weeks or more was taught by some itinerant music master.

The young people for miles around attended each evening, paying a small fee for the privilege. A difference of opinion usually arose at first as to whether song books with round notes or with "shape notes" should be used, but after this had been settled, things went smoothly enough. Perhaps they learned little of the music, but the singing school was invaluable as a means of becoming better acquainted with one's young neighbors and often had some of the attributes of a matrimonial agency.

As time went on, the number and variety of social events increased. Candy breakings, taffy pullings, fruit suppers, and pie suppers became common. Fish fries and picnics were often held, the latter varying from the small Sunday School picnic which had nothing more exciting to offer than a basket dinner, foot races, and a ball game, to a two- or three-day affair which people traveled long distances to attend. At these, concessions were granted for lemonade stands, a merry-go-round, and other attractions. Political speeches were in order and rival schools brought glee clubs or drill teams. The protracted meetings held under an arbor in summer often had quite as much of a social as they did a spiritual aspect. Oratorical contests and religious debates were popular, as were Sunday School conventions, and at times, private theatricals.

The growing importance and complexity of social life in a region that had never heard of telephones created some more or less grave problems. If a young man wanted to take a girl to a party or the literary society, how should he proceed in order to make the necessary arrangements? This was an important question since the men usually greatly outnumbered the girls and competition was in consequence quite keen. But the resourcefulness of the frontier was equal to the occasion. The ordinary procedure was for a young man to send the young lady a note by one of his friends and await her answer with whatever patience he was able to muster.

Having determined to ask for a date, he brushed the dust off the family ink bottle, sought out a pen and "ink tablet" and carefully and painstakingly indited a brief epistle. This was a difficult and delicate task. Should he say "Dear Miss Smith" or "My dear

Miss Smith"? Might not the latter salutation indicate a spurious claim to ownership that was quite unwarranted? Perhaps "Dear Miss Mary" would be better even though slightly informal. Having settled this weighty question with some qualms as to whether or not the word "Dear" should be used at all, he got down to the body of his communication. "May I have the pleasure, or honor, of accompanying you, or of your company, to the party tomorrow night?" Then there was another struggle over the conclusion. Should it be "respectfully" or "very respectfully yours," "sincerely," or "very sincerely yours," or "yours very respectfully, or sincerely"? All this having been decided upon, the note, commonly called a "compliment," though nobody seems to know why, was folded carefully and addressed to "Miss Mary Smith, at Home."

One corner of the note was folded down, again for no known reason, and a friend was asked to deliver it. This he did, stopping long enough on the way to read it in hope of learning something that would be helpful to his own technique in preparing similar missives. He always waited for the girl to write an answer, which she did with the same painstaking care shown by the boy friend. Once this had been delivered, the transaction was complete.

On the evening appointed, the young man appeared at the girl's home in his buggy if he had one. If he did not and the young woman owned a horse and side saddle, he merely rode over early enough to catch and saddle her pony and they were ready to start.

During the lean years of the frontier's early settlement, the problem of clothing a family was a serious one. Many tragic instances might be given of an attractive young woman who was frequently denied the opportunity of attending a social event because she lacked a good pair of shoes or a suitable dress. Young men were also hard put at times to find the money for a "Sunday suit" and must stay at home because they had nothing to wear but their working clothes. Such experiences were among the minor tragedies of frontier life perhaps, but they could hardly have seemed minor at the time to the young people concerned.

In the abundant leisure that was theirs, the prairie pioneers naturally celebrated with enthusiasm virtually every holiday. Thanksgiving was seldom shown much attention except by those settlers from the North who had acquired something of the spirit of the day from New England. Eggs were colored for the children at Easter, however, and the big picnic of the summer was usually planned to include the Fourth of July as its most important day. The greatest holiday of the entire year, however, was Christmas.

Usually two or three weeks before Christmas a mass meeting would be held at the schoolhouse to make plans for a community Christmas tree. At this meeting the various committees were appointed and their duties outlined. One of these was the committee to provide the tree. This consisted of three or four stalwart young men since it was often necessary to drive ten or fifteen miles to some mountain or canyon to find a suitable cedar tree. This must be cut down, loaded on the wagon, and brought to the schoolhouse and then set up at the end of the room.

The next committee was the one to dress the tree. Its chairman was usually some elderly lady famous for her patchwork quilts and crocheted tidies. Then came a committee on program, usually headed by the school teacher, and finally a committee to provide something for the "poor children" of the community! If this last committee had taken the words "poor children" literally, it would have been forced to provide for the entire junior population of the neighborhood, but there are degrees of poverty even on the frontier.

With its duties definitely assigned, each committee set to work with amazing energy. A tree was brought and set up at the schoolhouse and the teacher prepared a program of drills, songs, and recitations, keeping her young charges long after the ordinary dismissal hour in order to practice. The committee to provide for the poor solicited gifts of money or presents, and the group chosen to dress the tree worked hardest of all. Christmas tree ornaments were quite unknown but popcorn was strung by the yard and by the rod and looped in gay festoons upon the green branches. Nuts were gilded, and stars and crosses made of pasteboard were covered with tin foil from between layers of plug tobacco. Golden oranges, big red apples, and bags of candy, made of mosquito netting so the candy could be seen, were distributed over the tree under the critical eyes of the artistic chairman. Last of all came the presents proper!

The drug store in the little frontier town had always laid in a stock of Christmas goods and these were purchased with a reckless abandon limited only by the extreme scarcity of money. A dressing case which consisted of a red or green plush box containing a comb, brush, and mirror could be bought for a couple of dollars or less and was considered an ideal, though lavish gift. A manicure set with the same type of box containing scissors, nail file, tweezers and other accessories cost about the same. There were other less expensive gifts, however, in abundance. Mustache cups, shaving mugs, "fascinators," celluloid glove boxes, collar boxes, gold-washed jewelry, and scores of other articles were sent down, carefully tagged with the name of the recipient, to be hung on the tree by the harassed committee.

A shaving set was a wonderful though expensive gift for a man. For children there were all kinds of toys, fruit, candy, mittens, and sweaters. An autograph album was a gift of which any girl was certain to be proud. It was usually bound in plush or in pink celluloid, or sometimes in leather. If the giver had the education and finesse to write a sentiment on the first page, the value of the gift was greatly enhanced. Such a sentiment might be as follows:

> When the golden sun is setting
> And your mind from care is free
> When of others you are thinking,
> Won't you sometimes think of me?

Or one equally fetching might read:

> Forget me not, forget me never
> Till yonder sun shall set forever
> And when it sets to rise no more,
> Forget me then and not before.

Such a worthy and altogether reasonable request could hardly fail to touch the heart of a girl and give her a very warm feeling toward one who accompanied his Christmas gift with such a beautiful sentiment.

Perhaps the most popular present of all was a photograph album. A large one bound in red plush set with a small mirror, or in celluloid painted with a spray of forget-me-nots, was an ideal gift. It always contained spaces for two sizes of pictures—"cabinet size" and tintypes—and few people knew that any other dimensions for a photograph were possible. Once in a while a very expensive album would have a small music box enclosed in the cover which, when wound, played "Home, Sweet Home" when the book was opened.

A photograph album was not only a beautiful gift but a very useful one as well. Kept on the little table in the front room, it could be used by a girl as an excellent source of entertainment for a young man. Filled with all the family pictures, it could be turned through slowly, and names, relationship, and general status of all the relatives explained in detail to every caller. Solemn-eyed babies, plain-faced aunts, long-whiskered uncles, and always Aunt Jane's wedding picture, were viewed in turn. For a visitor to show indifference was the height of rudeness. He was expected to manifest an interest in each portrait, ask questions and comment favorably upon the dress and appearance of every individual pictured. With the proper technique, an hour or two could be spent in looking through an album. It was a pleasant pastime and in the words of Kin Hubbard: "You can make fun of the old family photograph album all you please, but it *did* give a young fellow a pretty good idea of the gang he was marryin' into."

When Christmas Eve at last came and the presents were on the tree, virtually all the people living within a radius of several miles assembled at the schoolhouse. Usually they filled the room to overflowing. The teacher gave her program, bringing the children out and putting them through their paces. Then when the last one had "spoken his piece" and the applause had died down, there came a great jingle of bells outside and Santa Claus came through the door, bowing and scraping and shouting greetings, while the pop-eyed children screamed with delight. Making his way to the tree he began to take down presents, read off the names, and willing hands passed them back to the one for whom they were intended. His running fire of jokes and comments kept the crowd laughing, and happy little squeals of joy from various parts of the room as the gift packages were opened only served to increase the general merriment.

Altogether it was a wholly joyous occasion and yet a thoughtful onlooker might have seen there a note of pathos too. Rough, bearded men proudly fingered white-handled razors that would never shave, celluloid collar-and-cuff boxes, or pairs of gilt cuff buttons certain to turn green far sooner than would the brown prairie, no matter how early spring might come! A wife with face as faded and worn as her own calico dress fondled lovingly with toil-roughened hands a foolish little jewel case or pink celluloid glove box, and looked up with misty eyes at the big, rough-featured, self-conscious man by her side. Perhaps among people who so desperately needed the bare essentials of life, the very uselessness of the gift made it even more dear, when she considered that her husband had denied himself something that was a real need in order to please her.

Eventually the last gift had been taken from the tree and the apples, oranges, and bags of candy and nuts distributed to the poor children of the neighborhood. Then Santa Claus bowed himself out, the sleepy babies too young to enter into the spirit of the occasion were bundled up, the older children helped into coats and jackets, and the happy crowd poured from the building and climbed into wagons for the drive home. The next day came a good Christmas dinner and life settled down into normal channels. Christmas was over until next year.

It was not many years until the character of frontier society began to change. The coming of railroads made markets readily available. Farming for profit instead of merely "holding down a claim" became the rule. This brought more money and less leisure. The region became more thickly peopled. The store and a blacksmith shop grew to a small town, the town to a thriving little city. The dugout or shanty was replaced by a commodious farmhouse and the straw-covered shed by a big red barn. The straggling little fruit trees grew to an orchard. Another room or more was added to the schoolhouse. Good roads, rural mail delivery, and eventually telephones, became common.

With changed conditions came changes in the social order. People became so numerous that society tended to form itself into groups. Invitation affairs took the place of the old "free for all" social gatherings. With a greater sophistication came formal calls, dances and bridge parties to take the place of the old time socials, box suppers, and candy breakings. The old order was passing. No doubt it is better so, and yet there are people in the West today who look back upon the pioneer years with a certain feeling of regret. They have many happy memories of their social life in a far different West and feel that with the passing of the old-time ways and customs, there passed away something fine and beautiful which we will never see again, in quite the same form at least.

VIII

He taught them to read and write and spell,
This teacher of earlier years,
And bound up hurts of the younger fry
And wiped away their tears.
The knotholes in the schoolhouse walls
Let in the wintry air,
But tobacco-chewing lads all felt
That Providence put them there!
But in "educating the whole child"
This teacher knew when to begin
When any obstreperous youngster
Committed some minor sin!

The Pioneer Teacher

VIII

Teaching on the Prairie Plains
1890-1900

TEACHING A RURAL SCHOOL during the last decade of the nineteenth century might be said to constitute a liberal education. The teacher's responsibilities were multitudinous and meeting them required both diplomacy and wisdom. He had little with which to work except his pupils, plus a blackboard, crayon, and a map or two, and usually knew nothing of educational methods or child psychology. Yet under his direction the children learned the fundamental subjects surprisingly fast. It must also be confessed that he usually commanded more respect in the community than does the average teacher today. It now seems that the one-room rural school will eventually disappear. Many distinguished men and women who began their education in such a school, however, feel that it had something to commend it and will view its passing with nostalgic memories closely akin to regret.

DURING THE LAST QUARTER of the nineteenth century there was a great outpouring of population to the Prairie Plains. Most of these settlers journeyed west with their families in covered wagons attracted by the lure of free or cheap lands upon which to establish homes, though a few located and established some form of business in the little towns that sprang up mushroomlike throughout the area. For a long period of time, however, most of these towns remained small, for they were only commercial centers to supply the needs of the settlers living within the limits of the town's so-called "trade territory," most of whom had little to sell and little money with which to buy goods. On the whole, the economy of the Prairie Plains area during the pioneer period was a rural economy, and any discussion of education in the region must be largely devoted to rural schools which employed perhaps 80 to 90 per cent of the teachers and enrolled an equal percentage of all children who attended school.

Many of the men and nearly all of the women who left their old homes to seek new ones in the Prairie West began the journey with one great, haunting fear in their hearts. This fear was that on this new frontier their children would have little opportunity for schooling and so might grow up in ignorance. They fully realized that it takes time to establish adequate schools and they knew all too well how quickly healthy boys and girls grow to the stature of men and women. In consequence, once a tract of land had been occupied and the first crude home erected to shelter his family, the average settler was likely to be discussing with his neighbors ways and means of providing a school for the children of the community.

Fortunately, during the period under consideration, there was a state or territorial government in operation under which these pioneer settlers were to live. These governments had almost immediately after their formation set up a system of public education. Usually this provided for a territorial, or state, superintendent of schools, elected by the people, who was *ex officio* a member of the board of education, consisting ordinarily of five or seven members. In addition there was a county superintendent of schools in each county elected by the voters. He, as a rule, was assisted in giving teachers' examinations by two persons appointed by himself, the three forming the county board of education. The laws also provided for the formation of school districts in each county upon presentation to the county superintendent of a petition signed by a certain percentage of the voters within the limits of the proposed district. School matters within a district were under the control of a board of trustees chosen by the voters.

The fact that a legal machinery existed for the creation of local schools meant little to the first settlers of a new community on the Prairie Plains. True, a school district could be established, bonds voted for the erection of a building, and taxes levied for school purposes but such bonds could sometimes not be sold at any price. Moreover, it was impossible to raise any considerable sum of money by taxation. Homestead land was not taxable until final proof had been made and a patent issued, which in most cases was not until after the expiration of a five-year period of residence. In the meantime only the improvements and personal property of the homesteader could be taxed and the average settler had very little of either.

Few persons who have lived on the prairie frontier of a generation ago will deny that the eagerness of these early settlers to provide education for their children was little short of pathetic. Many of these people had themselves grown up as children under pioneer conditions in the region farther east and had been caught in the trough of educational depression which was likely to characterize the occupation of each successive frontier. Lacking much education themselves they were determined that their children should not suffer the same fate. Others fortunate enough to secure a reasonably good education were determined that their boys and girls should have even more.

Yet lack of money for public education seemed to present an almost insuperable handicap. Unwilling to wait until bonds could be voted for a school building and sufficient taxes collected to pay a teacher's salary, the first settlers of many a community set to work to provide a school through their own efforts. Despite the scarcity of money enough could usually be raised by popular subscription to provide doors, windows, and lumber for a floor. Labor constituted little problem since there was usually abundant leisure. In consequence, the able-bodied men assembled and, on an acre of land donated by some public-spirited citizen, they proceeded to erect a sod schoolhouse. In some instances a large dugout might suffice, in others there was building stone available to construct a small stone school building, while in still others sufficient timber could be cut from some ravine or canyon to build a structure of logs. Once a building was made available some rough benches were provided and a local girl or young man employed to conduct a "subscription school" at a charge of about one dollar a month per pupil.

This, however, was regarded as only a temporary expedient. As soon as possible application was made for the creation of a school district, trustees were elected, taxes levied, and bonds voted to provide for a more adequate and permanent building. This was usually a frame wooden structure about twenty by thirty feet. It was furnished with a table and chair for the teacher, and ten or twelve long benches for the pupils. Near the center was a large stove, often of sheet iron, which kept the room reasonably comfortable in winter. There was a blackboard but seldom any maps, charts, or other teaching aids. Sometimes an enterprising teacher would provide a few pictures for the walls or three or four mottoes proclaiming such worthy sentiments as *Education Is Wealth*, or *Knowledge Is Power*. Outside was a large pile of wood, replenished from time to time by some philanthropic citizen, and an axe and chopping block. Big boys vied with one another for the privilege of cutting and bringing in wood or carrying water from the nearest well, while the larger girls a great deal more reluctantly took turns at sweeping the room during the noon hour or after school. It was in this type of school that the average budding young educator on the Prairie Plains secured his first experience in teaching.

While graduates of the normal schools were ordinarily granted a life certificate to teach in the state or territory, virtually all teachers had only what was known as a county certificate issued by the county superintendent and his board of education upon the applicant's passing successfully an examination in the subjects required. Such examinations were held quarterly at the county seat and certificates were of three grades—first, second, and third. To secure a third-grade certificate in Oklahoma it was necessary to pass an examination in eleven subjects. These included the ordinary common school branches and pedagogy, or methods of teaching. An average of 70 per cent was required in all of these, with not less than 50 per cent in any one branch. For a second-grade certificate civics was added and the required average was 80 per cent, with not less than 60 in any subject, while for one of first grade, one must make an average of 90 per cent and not fall below 70 in any one branch. Third-grade certificates were issued for only one year and the holder was not required to have had any teaching experience, while those of second grade were valid for two years but were issued only to persons with at least three months' teaching experience. First-grade certificates were good for three years but the holder must have taught for at least three terms, or a total of twelve months, and an examination must be passed on bookkeeping and physics in addition to those subjects required for a certificate of second grade.

Such qualifications seem quite low at present even in theory, but they were even lower in practice. It was commonly asserted that anyone who had successfully passed an examination for graduation from the eighth grade could secure a third-grade certificate if he were willing to devote some time to the study of educational methods. It was necessary that the requirements for teaching be made not too high since persons regarded as competent who were willing to teach were not too plentiful. Salaries were extremely low and school terms, short. In 1874, thirteen years after statehood, the average length of all school terms in Kansas was only five and a half months, and men received an average salary of $37.24 and women $28.69 a month. By the end of the century teachers' salaries were considerably higher in Kansas but in 1900 the average school term in Oklahoma Territory was less than five months and teachers with a third-grade certificate received $29.40 a month. Those with second-grade certificates were paid an average of $32.33 a month while first-grade teachers drew an average monthly salary of $38.08. In that year, however, only 128 first-grade certificates were issued in the Territory as compared with 642 second- and 708 third-grade certificates. It is clear, therefore, that over 90 per cent of the teachers held either third- or second-grade certificates and that the income of most teachers was not great.

To make matters worse, teachers were often paid in district warrants which must be discounted from 10 to 25 per cent at the local banks. Even so the teacher frequently had more money in his pocket than did most of the settlers, many of whom were almost unbelievably poor. The purchasing power of money must also be considered. The custom of "boarding around"—common a generation earlier in the states farther east—does not seem ever to have prevailed to any considerable extent on the prairie frontier, but the teacher usually paid only from six to eight dollars a month for bed and board and in some cases could hardly tell which was which!

In spite of short terms and low salaries most teachers took their work very seriously and sought diligently to improve their methods and cultivate a professional attitude. Virtually every county had a flourishing county teachers' association with a full quota of officers who arranged for a two-day meeting or "convention" usually at least twice a year, which every little town in the county was eager to secure. The committee on local arrangements secured free room and board for the visiting teachers at the homes of generous citizens, and made provisions for certain entertainment features, often a play or a program of songs and speeches by the older pupils of the local school. To attend such a meeting, many a teacher would drive from 15 to 30 miles over rough, bumpy roads. At the meeting itself papers were read and eagerly discussed, a luncheon would be served by the ladies of one of the churches, and frequently the territorial or state superintendent, or the president of the university or normal school might be prevailed upon to come and address the teachers.

Very few teachers had ever attended college or normal school or had received the slightest professional training. Most of them had learned all they knew about teaching by trial-and-error methods. In order to supply this deficiency and at the same time provide an opportunity to prepare for the examination for a certificate every county superintendent sought to provide each summer, usually in August, a four-week school for teachers commonly called the County Institute or Summer Normal. The State or Territorial Board of Education issued to those who could pass a suitable examination a certificate authorizing the holder to conduct such an institute or to give instruction in one.

Toward the end of the school year the county superintendent employed someone holding a conductor's certificate to take charge of the County Normal and if the county was populous, he might also employ an instructor to aid him, or authorize the conductor to employ his own. This County Institute was usually held at the county seat. It was well advertised among the teachers, and the citizens of the little town were urged to open their homes to them and provide room and board at reasonable rates. The county superintendent had a small sum of money for the Institute allocated to him from state or county funds, and this was eked out by the three-dollar fee paid by each teacher who enrolled.

If the session was to begin on the first Monday in August, the teachers or prospective teachers usually appeared in town on the Saturday or Sunday before in order to make the necessary arrangements for room and board. Each brought necessary clothing and all of his school books. On Monday morning at nine o'clock they assembled at the school building and were likely first of all to listen to an address of welcome by the county superintendent. They were then enrolled by the conductor, lessons were assigned, and class work began immediately. Each student received a small pamphlet issued by the State or Territorial Board of Education containing some twenty lessons in each subject required for a certificate. If the conductor must operate alone, he usually chose one or two of the older and more experienced teachers to hear at least a few of the classes. If he had an instructor to assist him, the two divided the classes between them, perhaps alternating work occasionally in order that their students might have the benefit of the ideas of both. Work was continued from nine until twelve and was resumed about one-thirty and continued until four.

Since these teacher-students came from various states of the Union, their textbooks were of great variety and classes were frequently enlivened by differences of opinion due to divergent backgrounds and training. Geography, spelling, physiology, and some other subjects offered little opportunity for such differences, but American history, especially when the Civil War period was reached, was likely to provoke violent controversies. Opinions also varied as to the best methods of solving certain problems in arithmetic—a subject likely to be something of a bugbear to many young teachers, particularly those on the distaff side of the profession. It was in the grammar class, however, that flaming arguments, usually generating far more heat than light, were most likely to develop. The student brought up in the nurture and admonition of Harvey, Reed and Kellogg, Holbrook, or some other author of a text in that field had often developed fixations very difficult to shake. "How do you diagram the sentence, 'The clock is about to strike'? Or 'My wife is not yet ready to go'?" "How do you define *gerund, gerundive,* or the subjunctive mode?" Answers to such questions often revealed a shocking diversity of ideas or, in some cases, an entire lack of ideas with respect to the English language.

Life during the weeks of the Summer Normal, however, was not wholly made up of study and classes. A debate was usually held sometime during the session either between some local lawyer and the ablest orator the teachers could muster from their ranks or between two rival teams from the Institute itself. A picnic was nearly certain to be arranged in some shady grove, if one could be found, where a huge basket dinner was served and the afternoon given over to foot races, pitching horse shoes, and various other sports including, perhaps, a game of baseball.

Old friendships were renewed, new ones formed, and romances developed. Most teachers who attended a County Institute later remembered the four weeks spent in it with much pleasure. It is doubtful if the young people who had never taught, but only hoped to become teachers, learned much of educational methods in the class in pedagogy, but they did profit a great deal by their close contact for an entire month with mature and experienced teachers. Moreover, their chief purpose in attending was not so much to receive teacher training as it was to review the subjects required for a certificate so they would not fail the examination.

The weeks slipped by and at last came the final one, the last two days of which were devoted to the examination for certificates. The State or Territorial Board of Education had prepared the questions on each subject and sent them out to the county superintendent well in advance in sealed envelopes marked "to be opened only in the presence of the teachers." On the fateful first morning everyone appeared early at the school building equipped with pencils and paper. For two days they labored diligently over arithmetic problems or questions in orthography, physiology, geography, and history, while the perspiration rolled down their faces and dropped on the paper before them, mingled sometimes with the tears of a few of the more nervous young women. In the meantime the members of the County Board, sometimes assisted by the conductor, toiled with equal diligence at grading the papers.

There were seldom many failures. Teachers were scarce and the examiners usually tempered justice with mercy and over-looked minor vagaries and even some major ones, doubtless reasoning that after all this applicant would never have to teach any pupils beyond the fifth or sixth grade. One young man in a county of western Oklahoma has related that he was once wrestling an examination in bookkeeping. On his chief problem his books failed to balance by $37.50. He tried in vain to discover his error but time was running short and at last in desperation he wrote on the short side, "Cash to balance—$37.50." Probably the board member who graded his paper was growing too tired to be discriminating. At any rate the young man's paper was returned to him marked 100 per cent, which served to lift a heavy load off his mind.

Safe home with his treasured certificate the prospective teacher must next find a job. Those of experience might already know where they were going to teach, but the young beginner must canvass possibilities and then call on the school board of any district that he might learn was still lacking a teacher. The wise young man or woman realized that in these United States committees or boards of three members usually consist of one voice and two echoes. He therefore sought to determine which one of the three possessed the voice and called upon him. Failing to find him at home he visited some other member of the board, frequently finding him plowing in the field.

Often this board member told him to see the other two trustees and whatever they said would be all right with him. It was there-

fore necessary to seek out the remaining school directors and in-
terview them. After some days, marked by a considerable
amount of buck-passing on the part of the board members, they
at last got together, rendered a decision, and notified the applicant that the school was his. A date was set for the opening of
school and the future teacher paid another visit to the community in order to arrange for room and board. This was not
usually too difficult since it was regarded as a distinct privilege
"to board the teacher." It was considered very good for the children of the household to have an educated person in the home
and besides, the seven or eight dollars a month added to its
income was very important to the average family.

It must be confessed, however, that not much could be offered
in the way of accommodations. The average settler's home consisted of not more than two or three rooms. In consequence, the
teacher if a young woman must room with one or more of the
older daughters of the household, or if a man must sleep upstairs
or in the shedroom with the boys. If the house had only one large
room, which was sometimes the case, it was only by a discreet
use of curtains hung from the ceiling that even the smallest degree of privacy could be insured. Reading or the grading of
papers done in the evening must be by the light of a kerosene
lamp, and in cold weather the entire family must sit huddled
about the stove or fireplace. It might be supposed that people
living so close together would inevitably get on one another's
nerves but this was seldom true. Adults and children alike
treated the teacher with an exaggerated respect, and the behavior of the family was usually characterized by the utmost
courtesy and a modesty that was truly Victorian in type. The
teacher's position in the household was that of an honored guest
or rich relative—not one rich in money but in things which the
parents desired far more for their children—education, culture,
and good manners. Not infrequently a close and enduring friendship amounting to real affection grew up between a teacher and
the family with whom he lived during a school term.

The day before school was to begin the teacher appeared at
his boarding place, always receiving a warm welcome. On the

following morning he reached the schoolhouse early in order to see that everything was neat and clean by the time the first pupils arrived. The doors were never locked, for the schoolhouse on the prairie frontier was in every sense a public building. Church was held there every Sunday morning and evening when a preacher was available, and it was used during the week for prayer meetings, box suppers, political rallies, funerals, and various other gatherings. Travelers frequently camped on the school grounds, kindling their little campfires on the sheltered side of the building at a safe distance and sleeping inside on pallet beds spread down on the floor if the night happened to be cold or rainy. In consequence, the fact that the room was in perfect order late in the evening was no guarantee that it would be so the following morning.

By eight-thirty the children began to arrive and after depositing their books and dinner pails hurried outside to play. At nine o'clock the teacher rang the bell vigorously and they all came trooping in more or less ready for the first day's work. Then began the task of securing names, ages, degree of proficiency in various subjects, and the assigning of seats and lessons.

By noon this was usually completed, a program for each day's work was on the blackboard, and the teacher was ready to call classes and hear recitations. A couple of long benches on which each reciting class was to sit were placed as far forward as possible, usually just in front of the teacher's desk in order to interfere as little as possible with the study of the pupils farther back in the room. It was customary to hear classes of the younger pupils first since they could not be expected to study very much anyhow, thus giving the older ones a chance to prepare their lessons while their small brothers and sisters were engaged in reciting.

Some teachers laid down the first day an elaborate set of rules as to what pupils must or must not do. Others deemed it better merely to tell the youngsters to behave themselves and then deal with every example of misconduct on an individual basis. Fortunately, the problem of discipline was not often an important one. There were exceptions, of course, particularly in those regions where the transformation from ranching to crop growing was not yet complete. Here a few big boys whose chief ambition in life seemed to be to wear boots and spurs, ride broncos, smoke cigarettes, and chew tobacco might band together and make trouble. There were always a few districts in every county that were notorious because of the incorrigible nature of the older pupils and where respect for the teacher was largely measured by the weight of his hand, but these were quite exceptional. Usually country children on the Prairie Plains were shy but obedient, studious, and very eager to learn.

Before the end of the first week the pupils had taken the measure of their teacher and vice versa, a regular routine had been established, and work was in full progress. Intermissions of fifteen minutes each were given in the mid-morning and afternoon, commonly called "morning and evening recess," while a full hour was allowed at noon. Since most of the pupils must walk from one to three miles to school, virtually every child, or family of children, brought a lunch usually in a five- or ten-pound lard pail called a "dinner bucket." The teacher usually did the same since it was as a rule too far for him to return to his boarding place for lunch, and besides, he did not like to leave the children unsupervised during the noon hour.

The good housewife almost invariably took great pains to provide the teacher with a good lunch, though her resources were often extremely meager. The contents of the children's dinner buckets, however, varied as widely as did the children themselves. Some contained only slabs of corn bread or large blue biscuits split in two with a slice of bacon between the halves and perhaps a teacup filled with sorghum molasses. Distributed among the others might be sandwiches, fried chicken, hard-boiled eggs, gingerbread, doughnuts, turnovers or pieces of pie, and slices of pound cake. As a rule every "dinner bucket" was packed with an ample supply of good nourishing food, though a professional dietitian would probably regard it with horror as a meal for growing children.

The children usually bolted their food as rapidly as possible and then hurried outside to spend the remainder of the hour in such games as "black man," "town ball," marbles, or the spinning of tops. The teacher, if a young man, frequently joined in these sports while the lady teacher usually remained inside to chat with the older girls, supervise the sweeping, or read a little, turning aside at times to tie up a cut finger or dry the tears of some younger member of the school who had fallen or received a minor bump at play.

Despite the lack of teaching aids the children often learned surprisingly fast. Tots six or seven years old who did not know A from Z on the first day of school were in many cases able to read fluently at the end of four months and to spell every word in the primer and first reader. Other youngsters ten or eleven years old who had never before had an opportunity to go to school, and in consequence barely knew their letters, after three sessions aggregating twelve to fourteen months, were the equals of pupils in the sixth to the eighth grade today in such fundamental subjects as reading, writing, spelling, arithmetic, and geography. School was regarded as a serious business; there were no picture shows and few other distracting influences; extra-curricular activities were lacking; and the children almost invariably had every possible encouragement from their parents.

The interest shown in the school by the older people of the community sometimes proved embarrassing to the teacher. Invitations to "come home with the children and spend the night" were frequent and at times so insistent that they could not be refused. Moreover, parents or older brothers and sisters of the pupils often visited the school, normally choosing the worst possible time, which was Friday following the afternoon recess.

Every teacher soon discovered that his position imposed upon him many duties and responsibilities quite apart from hearing classes and maintaining discipline. He was expected to go to church with reasonable regularity, teach a class in the Sunday School if one were organized, keep out of neighborhood rows if any developed, encourage all worthwhile activities, and be a guide, philosopher, and friend to everyone in the community who manifested an interest in cultural things. He must by example and precept seek to develop neatness, courtesy, and a love of learning on the part of his pupils and strive to keep on study at least a part of the mind of some larger boy who in the spring-time found his fancy turning more or less lightly to thoughts of what the big girls had been thinking about all winter! It is not surprising that the able, intelligent young teacher at the close of his first term of school often felt that he had learned far more than even the brightest and most diligent of his pupils.

The last day of school usually was largely given over to closing exercises participated in by pupils and their parents alike. A dinner might be brought in by the older people and the entire day devoted to speeches, drills, and dialogues. In any case the teacher was nearly certain to buy ten or fifteen pounds of candy and perhaps a box or two of apples and give the children a treat. Then good-byes were said, often accompanied by tears and sticky kisses from the smaller members of the flock, and the teacher returned home to devise ways and means of living until the first pay check of the next session six or eight months in the future.

During the early years of the twentieth century, life was rapidly changing on the Prairie Plains with corresponding changes in education and teaching. With the coming of many new settlers with their families, and the younger children of the old-timers reaching school age, most districts soon had too many pupils for one teacher. Another room was added to the school-house and a man employed as principal to teach the older children, with a young woman as his assistant to instruct the little ones. He was the principal while to the young men of the com-munity his assistant was the interest, and interest rates were always high on the frontier! As a matter of fact most young women teachers married out of the profession in three or four years and many did not last more than one or two sessions. One who continued to teach for nine or ten years was commonly regarded as sunk and usually was!

The increase in school population eventually made even two rooms and teachers insufficient but by this time the movement for consolidation was sweeping the plains area like a prairie fire. Oklahoma, which on its admission to the Union in 1907 had only two consolidated schools in the entire state, within a dozen years had in some counties merged all of the small districts into twenty or more large units each with a commodious brick building housing a modern graded school offering at least two years of high-school work. The little towns were also growing in astonishing fashion and virtually all of these erected new high-school buildings, employed a staff of specialists, and offered a full four-year high-school course. Automobiles, good roads, and above all the great increase in the value of taxable property had all combined to make this possible. Homesteads, once patents had been issued, automatically went on the tax rolls, and the value of improvements and personal property also rapidly increased.

Faced with the necessity of giving high-school subjects, teachers with little formal schooling beyond the eighth grade hurried away to the state normal schools to enroll as students. Here they were placed in what they felt was very aptly called "the Sub-Normal Department"! After a year or so they got out of the Sub-Normal Department into the Normal Department, eventually graduated, and then entered the University and in time secured bachelor's and master's degrees.

With changing conditions came longer terms of schools and higher monthly salaries for teachers. All of these changes were due in part to better methods of financing public education. In earlier years the district schools were supported almost entirely by local taxes. The state and county school fund, derived from the leasing of school lands and fines or license fees, seldom amounted to more than a dollar or so per pupil. Such a system brought gross inequalities. The school district crossed by a railroad might have funds for an eight or nine months school while an adjoining district with no railroad property to tax found it difficult to maintain one for even three or four months.

Such a situation was intolerable. Gradually the idea grew that the state owes to every child within its boundaries the opportunity to attend school for nine months each year; the principle was accepted by the legislature and a large sum appropriated for state aid to weak schools. In time many schools derived their chief support from such funds and teachers were no longer without employment for six to eight months of every year. This made it far easier to attend summer sessions of the normal schools, teachers' colleges, or the state university. State certificates were secured by most teachers, and the old-time summer normal, and even county certificates, largely passed into the limbo of forgotten things.

The movement for consolidated schools was much more popular in some states or certain areas than in others. That there are still many one-room rural schools throughout the prairie states is, of course, apparent but most of them have nine-month terms, and are conducted by reasonably well-trained teachers whose work and lives are quite unlike those of the teachers of a generation ago.

Many people can be found today who are quite willing to assert that teaching a rural school on the prairie frontier, despite the hardships and lack of facilities, was a rich and interesting experience which served to develop personality, resourcefulness, and other qualities of great value. Certainly the number of city superintendents, high-school principals, and college teachers who did their first teaching in such a school seems to indicate that this is true. Not a few persons even declare that the old-time country school with the close personal relationship between teacher and pupil, and which placed chief emphasis upon only a few fundamental subjects, was not without distinct advantages. Again it may be pointed out that the many successful men and women whose early education was secured in this type of school furnish some proof of the truth of such a statement.

Everyone must agree that education has made an enormous advancement in the past half century. Nevertheless, a few old timers with a nostalgic longing for the past still insist that not every change in teaching and educational methods has been progress but in some instances has been only change. Regardless of how much opinions may differ on such matters, however, few will deny that the pioneer teacher on the Prairie Plains of half a century ago was the most important factor in the promotion of those cultural and spiritual values without which any society must be poor indeed.

IX

To socials, parties, and dances
All of us liked to go,
But we figgered they didn't learn us much
Of things we'd ought to know.
So we formed a society literary
Down on Cottonwood Creek
To meet at the schoolhouse Friday nights
Of every other week.
We had dialogues and speeches
And always wanted some more
Like "Curfew Must Not Ring Tonight"
Or "The Face on the Barroom Floor"
Or "Little Orphant Annie," and always a big debate,
And it was certainly lots of fun to hear those chaps orate.
But one of them now is in Congress
Who first stood up to speak
In a literary meeting we had
Down on Cottonwood Creek.

                              Frontier Intellectuals

The Frontier Literary Society

THE LITERARY AND DEBATING SOCIETIES of the frontier may have had their roots in the New England town meetings and the political debates between rival candidates for office. Yet they would probably have been created without any such stimulus. In every pioneer community there were always a few bookish individuals who felt that the eager desire of young people for social life might be partially satisfied by organizations designed to promote intellectual and cultural values. These would to some extent replace the dances, socials, and box suppers. It was such persons who took the lead in the formation of literary and debating societies.

THE PIONEER SETTLERS who poured westward in the decades following the Civil War to occupy homesteads on the prairies of Nebraska, the Dakotas, Kansas, and western Oklahoma were in their own language a "sociable" people. It had been with deep regret that they left old friends and neighbors of their former homeland. Once established in new homes on the western prairies these settlers eagerly sought to form new ties with the people about them.

The first social contacts usually took the form of visiting with the families on the adjoining or nearby homesteads. Most people were so poor that they had little else to spend so could only spend the day! Such visits, together with shorter ones for an evening or afternoon were for a time almost the only social diversion of the older people of the new community.

It was not long, however, until the young unmarried people

began to demand something a trifle more exciting than friendly visits. What they wanted was "something to go to." This may seem strange to many of us today who must live in the midst of the bustle and hurry of a more sophisticated society. What we prefer is "something to stay away from"!

In virtually every community, however, there were at least a few persons of scholarly tastes and literary leanings who felt that while parties, taffy pullings, hayrides, and similar frivolous activities were harmless enough, they should not be allowed to absorb the entire social activity of the neighborhood. What they felt was needed was some organization of an educational nature which would provide intellectual stimulus for the entire community. Obviously, it should be something with activities in which both young and old could participate and which would not only furnish entertainment but promote the cultural growth of all who attended its meetings. The formation of a literary society seemed the ideal way to meet this need.

The origin of the literary society in America seems lost in the mists of antiquity. Certainly it appears very early in our nation's history and in some instances may have been formed as a sort of artificial substitute for the New England town meeting. In the Prairie West the organization of such a society appears, in some instances, to have been suggested by the Friday afternoon exercises of the rural school.

The country school teacher was usually keenly alive to the fact that his salary was paid by the people he served. In consequence, with grave forebodings in his heart and fingers discreetly crossed, he hospitably invited his patrons to visit the school at any time they might feel so inclined. A people starved for entertainment usually accepted his invitation in considerable numbers. Almost invariably they chose Friday following the afternoon recess. At that particular hour the youngsters, eagerly looking forward to the two whole days of freedom, seemed possessed of the devil, while the teacher, with nerves worn to a frazzle by a hard week's work, always appeared at his worst.

To get past this "graveyard shift," the period was often given over to exercises by the children. These might take the form of a spelling match or "ciphering match," but more often consisted of the "speaking of pieces." Then it was that "Mary Had a Little Lamb," "Twinkle, Twinkle, Little Star," "The Boy Stood on the Burning Deck," "The Widder Spriggins' Daughter," and all the other old-time favorites were given. Sometimes they were presented haltingly and at others with express-train speed, apparently with the objective of getting it over with as soon as possible, making a bow, and getting back to the safe haven of a seat.

To the "frontier intellectuals" these Friday afternoon exercises suggested the formation of a literary society in which children and adults alike could share. Some had belonged to such an organization in the region from which they had come and so had acquired a body of experience that would prove useful in the establishment of another. Once the suggestion was made it was received with enthusiasm. In typical American fashion, a meeting was held at the schoolhouse, a constitution and by-laws framed and adopted, officers elected, and committees appointed.

The most important of these was the program committee of which the school teacher, as the educational leader of the community, was usually a member. With commendable zeal this committee set to work to canvass the neighborhood for persons willing to give a reading, sing a song, or take part in a debate. Talent, like gold, is where you find it, and the diligent committee members often found it in most unexpected places. Sometimes a near illiterate would be discovered who could play the banjo or guitar like a real artist, or who had an excellent voice and a large repertoire of popular songs. A shy young girl might be revealed as a surprisingly good reader, or as having great ability in playing the leading role in a dialogue or short play. Men never suspected of any knowledge of public speaking sometimes proved to be clever debaters, delivering speeches that were wise, witty, and convincing. It was the task of the program committee to seek out all this talent and put it to work and at the same time to encourage the backward and help the inexperienced to improve and gain greater confidence.

In addition it was necessary to make a diligent search for materials that might be presented. Poems suitable for reading might be found in old school books or magazines. One or two "speech books" or collections of dialogues were likely to be unearthed, and in some instances others were ordered from publishers in the East. A small library was often assembled by securing donations of books and occasionally by purchasing a few volumes. These were kept at the schoolhouse and checked out by the librarian at the close of each meeting.

Meetings were usually held twice a month, though in some cases they might be weekly—usually on Friday night. If the schoolroom did not have a stage one was constructed of rough lumber. A wire was stretched from wall to wall in front of this stage from which curtains of dark calico were hung by small rings so that they could be slid back and forth by two willing volunteers from the ranks of the older boys of the school. Since people often came three or four miles to attend the meetings, the schoolhouse was usually filled to overflowing by a little after dark. The program consisted of recitations, or readings, interspersed with drills, musical numbers, and dialogues. Readings included such ancient classics as "Rienzi to the Romans," "Curfew Must Not Ring Tonight," "Whistling in Heaven," and many more of a dramatic nature. Some in a lighter vein were "How Ruby Played," "Darius Green and His Flying Machine," "How We Tried to Lick the Teacher," and many others chosen with due regard to the age and ability of the reader.

The dialogues were as varied as the readings. Popular ones, to be given by three or four persons, were "Arabella's Poor Relations," "Sam and the Postman," and "The Train to Mauro." Usually they were of a humorous nature but as was to be expected of a generation brought up in the tradition of the McGuffey Readers, most of them sought to point a moral or teach a good lesson. Drills by school children were often held since a large number could take part. This was good psychology on the part of the officials of the society for the larger the number that participated in the program, the greater would be the interest of the community. A favorite drill was called the "Choice of Trades." Each child was given a tool or other object typical of a trade or profession. Carrying it with him he came out and gave a few lines of verse describing how he expected to carry on his life work. After each had spoken they all marched about the stage, each reciting his verse. For example a lad with the medicine case of a doctor would appear and deliver the following:

When I am a man a man I'll be
I'll be a doctor if I can and I can
My pills and powders will be nice and sweet
And you can have just what you want to eat
When I am a man.

Others would express in verse their preference for the role of a farmer, carpenter, blacksmith, cowboy, lawyer, or teacher. A dozen youngsters presenting such a number were nearly certain to mean the presence at the program of a dozen fond fathers and mothers to view the whole proceeding with beaming approbation.

After the recitations, dialogues, drills, and musical numbers had been presented it was customary to have a brief recess followed by a debate. Subjects were frequently of an abstract or philosophical nature as: "Resolved, that fear of punishment has a greater influence over human conduct than does the hope of reward." Other subjects dealt with historical questions or current political issues. Sometimes, but not often, the subject chosen would be of a humorous or frivolous type, as: "Resolved, that a clean cross woman makes a better wife than a dirty good-natured woman." Such a subject was unusual, for the debate was in most cases a serious affair. Those participating planned their speeches with great care, practiced them diligently, and delivered them with as much fire and vigor as though the destiny of nations hung upon their words.

The organization and carrying on of a successful literary society might become a major activity for a large number of people. Children must be drilled on their speeches and songs, reluctant individuals persuaded to share in the programs, and rehearsals held by the characters in the dialogues. This was all preliminary to the actual presentation of the program. Yet the latter also had its problems. Stage properties had to be brought in and arranged. The curtain sometimes stuck at most inopportune times or youngsters forgot their speeches and had to be prompted. Characters in dialogues might easily forget their lines or garble them in fantastic fashion.

Slips of the tongue were sometimes made with tragic results. At a literary society meeting in a rural schoolhouse in central Kansas a young woman gave the favorite old reading, "Curfew Must Not Ring Tonight." She moved along beautifully and had the audience almost in tears as she described how Bessie climbed to the belfry and clung to the clapper of the swinging bell the tolling of which was to be the signal for the execution of her lover. When she came to the final lines, however, detailing the maiden's appeal to Cromwell and his promise of pardon for the young man, disaster struck. She meant to say: " 'Go, your lover lives,' cried Cromwell, 'curfew shall not ring tonight.' " Frightened and nervous, she said: " 'Go, your liver loves,' " which nearly broke up the meeting and caused the girl to flee from the stage weeping bitter tears of humiliation.

Scarcity of suitable materials also sometimes caused the selection of a reading not suited to the appearance and personality of the one who gave it. Joe Williams, a former Oklahoma cowhand, has related that he once rode ten miles to attend a literary society at Valley View Schoolhouse. The third number was a reading given by a girl about seventeen years old. He described her as tall, lean, and cross-eyed, with stringy red hair, freckled face, and projecting front teeth. But the subject of her reading and the refrain closing each stanza was this: "Lips That Touch Liquor Must Never Touch Mine." Joe said it was a good speech but no temperance argument at all!

No doubt literary societies flourished in many rural communities of Nebraska and other Western Prairie states during the last quarter of the nineteenth century but most of them kept no records. The minutes of one very interesting one, however, have been preserved. These are significant, not only for what they say, but for what can be read between the lines. The organi-

zation was established in the Rock Creek community, about
sixteen miles northeast of Lincoln, Nebraska, sometime prior to
1880. It was first known as the Mutual Improvement Society
and as such met every Friday evening during the autumn and
winter months for nearly three years. It seems to have lapsed
for a time after 1882 but was reorganized in October, 1884, as
the Rock Creek Literary Society. Under this name it was carried
on, with some lapses and reorganizations, until 1895. Possibly
it was continued after that date, but if so the minutes have not
been found, the last entry being for March 8, 1895. The change
of name made in 1884 is apparently meaningless, for the membership rolls show that the same persons were officials and
members, in some cases for the entire period of fifteen years.
The objectives of the Rock Creek Literary Society are revealed
by the following constitution and by-laws:

CONSTITUTION AND BY-LAWS OF THE ROCK CREEK LITERARY SOCIETY

I

This society shall be known as the Rock Creek Literary Society.

II

The object of this society is to promote the intellectual and social
interests of its members; to encourage the study of subjects literary,
scientific, philosophical, amusing, musical.

III

This society shall be governed by Cushing's Manual and the following by-laws, which may be amended as the occasion demands.

1

A membership fee of five cents for each person over fifteen years of
age shall be charged to defray incidental expenses.

2

The officers of this society shall consist of a President, Vice-President, Secretary, Treasurer and Sergeant-at-Arms.

3

The duties of the officers shall be as follows:

The President shall preside at all meetings of the society, call extra meetings, decide points of order, appoint committees, levy all fines, and with the assistance of the Sergeant-at-Arms, preserve order.

The Vice-President shall preside in the absence of the president and perform all the duties of that office upon such occasions.

The Secretary shall keep an accurate record of all meetings of this society, call the roll, and read the program.

The Treasurer shall collect all fines and dues, keep an exact account of all moneys received and paid out, and report each month to the society.

The Sergeant-at-Arms shall clean the lamps, build the fires, sweep the floor, cut a dog-wood club and preserve order in the hindermost parts of the house and such other parts as may require his services; he shall also perform all other duties not herein mentioned that may arise from time to time.

4

The members of this society shall be cheerfully governed by the officers, and respond promptly to duties assigned them, and work first, last, and all the time for the best interests of this society.

5

All members failing to respond or to furnish an acceptable substitute shall be fined five cents (cases of sickness only excused) for every failure.

6

The regular meetings of this society shall be held on Friday evening of each week.

7

The officers of this society shall be elected every fourth meeting.

8

Nine members shall constitute a quorum for the transaction of business.

9

The order of business shall be as follows:
1. Call to order.

2. Reading of the minutes of the last meeting.
3. Roll call.
4. Reports of committees.
5. Unfinished business.
6. New business.
7. Exercises of the evening.
8. Reading of program for next meeting.
9. Adjournment.

The society could hardly be called a wealthy one. The minutes of the meeting for November 12, 1880, show the following entry: "The question of making the sergeant-at-arms a saleried [*sic*] office was brought before the house and it was voted to pay the holder of that office 40 cts. a month." On March 10, 1882, it was voted "to pay the Sergeant 20 cts. for building fires and 10 cts. for lamp chimney." On November 5, 1884, the treasurer rendered a report showing "total on hand $1.94. Expended as follows. Lamp .60, paper .25, lamp wick .05, coal oil .25. Total $1.15. Remainder on hand $0.79." Clearly the duties of the treasurer were not too onerous and it is plain that there was no reason for bonding that official.

The unusual provisions for electing officers every fourth meeting was probably designed to stimulate interest in the society by giving a large number of members an opportunity to serve as officials. Also it gave many persons experience in presiding over meetings and conducting the work of the organization. In view of the duties outlined for him it is not surprising that the office of sergeant-at-arms should have been made a "saleried" office or that one member should have protested that he had not been legally elected since the individual nominating him "had failed to rise and address the chair before making the nomination."

Early presidents of the society were Obadiah Hull, P. S. Galley, Warren Clark, Charles Post, William Armstrong, James Bixby, I. F. Dale, C. A. Rogers, J. R. Speck, James Parks, William Folger, J. M. Armstrong, L. A. Price, and Paul E. Clark. Some of these, including Obadiah Hull, Warren Clark, and I. F. Dale, served repeatedly over a long period of years. Secretaries in-

cluded Emily Birdsall, H. P. Dale, James Bixby, I. F. Dale,
I. E. Ormsby, Ida Bixby, Emma Core, Lulu Burnett, John Armstrong, Jessie Galley, M. H. Jeffery, Mattie Hall, Ella Jeffery,
Minnie Armstrong, and Ethel Birdsall. Emily Birdsall served repeatedly for several years.

The society had a library of nearly forty volumes. These were
probably largely donated and were constantly checked out by
the members of the organization, probably to be used in many
cases in assembling information for the debates. Such debates
were a regular feature of nearly every program, the first part of
which consisted of readings, songs, and dialogues. A short recess
was then held and the debate, with two speakers on each side,
was the concluding feature of the evening. Occasionally there
were three speakers for each side and in some instances only
one. Since the decision of most judges is unconsciously influenced by their own views, the results of the discussion of
current questions may give some index as to the political
opinions of the people of this part of Nebraska during these
years.

Space does not permit giving all subjects debated by the
society but the following list gives the questions discussed during the period from 1880 to 1882, together with the decision of
the judges.

1880

1. February 6, 1880: Resolved that the use of intoxicating liquor
has destroyed more lives than war. Dec. for aff.
2. February 13, 1880: Resolved that U. S. Grant should be our next
President. Dec. for aff.
3. March 5, 1880: Resolved that corporal punishment should be
abolished in our schools. Two judges for aff., one neg.
4. March 12, 1880: Resolved that Chinese Immigration should be
prohibited by law. Dec. for aff.
5. November 12, 1880: Resolved that railway rates should be regu-
lated by law. Dec. for aff.
6. November 19, 1880: Resolved that the reading of works of fiction is beneficial. Dec. for aff.

7. November 23, 1880: Resolved that the Irish agitators should be prosecuted. Dec. for neg.

8. December 3, 1880: Resolved that commerce has done more to civilize the world than all other agencies combined. Dec. for neg.

1881

9. January 14: Resolved that Nebraska should have a prohibitory liquor law. Dec. for neg.

10. January 28: Resolved that women should be allowed to vote. Dec. for neg.

11. February 11: Resolved that U. S. Grant should be placed upon the retired list of the army with the rank and pay of general. Dec. for neg.

12. February 18: Resolved that science contradicts the Bible. Dec. for aff.

13. February 25: Resolved that the United States should have control of all of North America. Dec. for neg.

14. March 8: Resolved that married men are more useful to the community than bachelors. Dec. for aff.

15. October 28: Resolved that it would be to the interest of the U.S. and also the Negroes that the colored people of the U.S. be colonized. Dec. for neg.

16. November 4: Resolved that the Indian Territory be opened for settlement. Dec. for neg.

17. November 25: Resolved that the treatment of her Irish citizens by the British government has been disgraceful. Dec. for aff.

18. December 2: Resolved that greater honor is due Washington for defending America than Columbus for discovering it. Dec. for neg.

19. December 9: Resolved that Guiteau should be hanged for shooting President James A. Garfield. Dec. for aff.

20. December 16: Resolved that the right of suffrage should be extended to women. Dec. for aff. [reversed earlier decision on same topic].

21. December 30: Resolved that the cultivation of a talent for poetry is detrimental to success in life. Dec. for aff. Society voted to meet Pleasant Ridge society at Waverly in debate on January 13. Warren Clark, Obadiah Hull, I. F. Dale and H. P. Dale to be speakers.

1882

22. January 5: Resolved that it would have been better for the Negroes and for the states of the South had the enfranchisement of the colored men been gradual instead of immediate. Dec. for neg.

23. January 20: Resolved that conscience is an innate faculty of the soul. Dec. for aff.

24. January 27: Resolved that lawyers are a public nuisance. Dec. two for neg. one aff.

25. February 3: Resolved that no man who cannot read and write should be allowed the elective franchise. Dec. for neg.

26. [n.d.]: Resolved that ignorance has caused more suffering than ambition. Dec. two for aff. one for neg.

27. November 3: Resolved that the use of tobacco should be prohibited by law. Dec. for neg.

28. November 24: Resolved that the United States should adopt the policy of a tariff for revenue only. Dec. for aff.

The above list includes all subjects debated during the period indicated. While the debate was sometimes postponed, due to the length of the program, or the failure of one or more of the scheduled speakers to appear, it was apparently designed to be a regular feature of most meetings.

The rolls of the society during this period show 41 members in 1880, 51 in 1881, and 45 in 1882. Of these, however, only twelve men and one woman, Miss Ida Bixby, participated in any of the debates. Miss Bixby appeared in but one—the question as to the relative honors due Washington and Columbus. On the other hand Obadiah Hull was one of the speakers in 24 out of the total of 28 debates while I. F. Dale spoke in 20 and his brother H. P. Dale in 19 of them. The remaining nine participants shared in from two or three to nine or ten of the discussions. When it is considered that the membership of the society included many women and at least some children it seems that the number who took part in the debates was as large as could be expected. With meetings held weekly a few of the debaters must have devoted a fair share of their waking hours to studying the questions and preparing their speeches.

Apparently nearly all of the other members of the organization shared in the earlier part of the programs which consisted of recitations, musical numbers, and dialogues. A special dialogue committee was appointed and seems to have been very active. At the close of each meeting the critic rendered a report freely dispensing praise and blame wherever they were felt to be due.

After the reorganization of the society in 1884 the debate does not seem to have formed so prominent a part of the programs as formerly. Yet it was by no means abandoned and various new questions were discussed and some of the older ones brought up again. In the case of the latter, however, the decision of the judges seldom varied from the one given before. On November 12, 1884, the society voted to have a "paper" prepared and read at the meeting on November 26 instead of holding a debate. An editor and assistant were appointed and until the organization closed its year's work the following March the "paper," called *The Rock Creek Astonisher,* seems to have been a regular feature of nearly every meeting.

It is unfortunate that no copy of *The Rock Creek Astonisher* seems to have been preserved. Probably it was not unlike most other literary society papers which have come down to us, or that can be largely restored from the memories of a few older people who in their youth edited them. These "community organs" usually gave news items of the neighborhood but this was only preliminary to the main feature which was the good natured "ribbing" of the local belles and beaux. Special attention was always given to budding romances of the young people. Typical gibes and quips might be as follows:

"No, that is not the rising sun you see in the east. It is Hank Smith's new red-wheeled buggy headed in the direction of Mary Johnson's house." "Mrs. Simson says that Ed Adams and Sam Williams come so often that she 'can't throw out a pan of water without throwing it on one of them boys.'" "When Bill Jones told Bessie Jenkins that he was going to hang himself if she wouldn't marry him Bessie said: 'Well, my dad says you'll sure have to do it at home because he's not going to have you hanging around here!'" "Bonnie Phillips says that Earl Wilson's new mustache reminds her of a baseball game—nine on a side."

Seven wonders of our own little world.

1. Wonder who's going to keep that new house Joe Thompson is building.

2. Wonder if Amy Bixby means to take her a boy to raise.

3. Wonder why Bob Carter always has to go by Ethel Holt's house when he goes any place.

4. Wonder why Mr. and Mrs. Hilton's dogs bark at everybody except Jack Hall.

5. Wonder why Della Walton has to go to the post office every day.

6. Wonder if Johnnie Burton's sprucing up so here lately means anything.

7. Wonder if Buck Rainey got those two hound pups to help him catch a Fox.

Such joking always brought a laugh and resulted in the persons whose names were mentioned receiving a good deal of chaffing from their friends in the community.

The Rock Creek Literary Society was a type. Similar organizations existed not only all over Nebraska in the pioneer era but in virtually every other Western state, and their influence upon the cultural development of the communities in which they were held must have been very great. Members read widely in seeking materials for the programs or in preparing speeches for the debates. Poems and dialogues were memorized and current questions to be discussed studied. The historical or philosophical subjects debated also required wide reading and diligent study by the speakers. The information which they had thus acquired was then passed on to an eager audience. Confidence as well as skill in public speaking was gained by all who participated in the programs. No doubt many lawyers, legislators, members of Congress, and other public officials received their first training in public speaking in the frontier literary and debating societies. For example Obadiah Hull served in the 1895 and 1897 sessions of the Nebraska legislature.

The educational influence of such an organization also must have been very important for the children of a community. Youngsters not old enough to participate in the activities of the Rock Creek Literary Society when it was first formed grew to young manhood and womanhood during the fifteen years of its existence. From observing the work of their elders in the organization they were stimulated to participate in its programs themselves as soon as they were old enough. In consequence they literally grew up with the institution having an important influence upon their lives. The literary society created and sustained an interest in history, literature, and public speaking. It affected the cultural growth of children in the same fashion that the church and Sunday School influenced spiritual development.

In a newly settled region the literary society was also a powerful factor in bringing people more closely together, in the creation of friendships, and the establishment of a community consciousness. In 1897 the people of the Timber Creek community in western Oklahoma established a literary society. The settlers had come from many states of the Union and most of them had occupied their homesteads in the past twelve months. At the conclusion of the first meeting of the society the newly elected president who was from a northeastern state made a brief speech. In closing he said:

I am very proud of the honor you have bestowed upon me by electing me President of the Timber Creek Literary Society. We have all come here within the past year to settle and make our homes in this new country. We have come from many regions. I happen to be from the Northeast while many of you are from the South or the West. But we must not let this influence our feeling toward one another. In the future we want no North, South, East, or West in our thoughts, but only Timber Creek. Let us forget everything except that we are all friends and neighbors working together in this society to advance the cultural and educational development of the Timber Creek Community.

X

If anyone ever enjoyed poor health
It must have been old Aunt Jane
For she always knew just what to do
To relieve every ache or pain.
There was hardly a back in the neighborhood
But had known her plasters and salve,
And her tonics and pills could cure all ills
That anyone happened to have.
She left us only the other day
The glories of Heaven to share
But once she is sure there is no one to cure
She'll not be contented up there.

The Medicine Woman

X

Frontier Medical Practices

AMONG PRIMITIVE PEOPLES the cure of disease has always been closely associated with the priesthood. While the frontier settlers had no medicine men or witch doctors, as did the American Indians and the natives of Africa, virtually every community had one or two persons reputed to have extraordinary skill in healing the sick. The treatment recommended by these was in many cases more than a little tinged with superstition. This chapter is a brief account of how the pioneers, remote from physicians and hospitals, relied first upon home remedies often prescribed by these self-appointed guardians of public health. Later they began a wholesale use of proprietary medicines still widely advertised and sold although they have to a considerable extent been replaced by doctors' prescriptions.

MANY PERSONS NOW PAST, or approaching, the age of the threescore and ten years traditionally allotted to man, and who grew up on the American frontier, will assert that in the old days sickness was quite rare. They seem to remember that in their youth they had no aches or pains but were always strong and healthy and even declare that all other people in their home communities were the same.

Such people must either be afflicted with acute amnesia or have what the late Professor Edward Channing once referred to as "a constructive memory." While it is quite true that the American pioneers were a vigorous and hardy breed, partly because the weaklings did not live long under the conditions of frontier life, they were, nevertheless, human animals and as such were subject to most diseases and ailments which afflict people today plus some additional ones that were the result of their manner of living and their lack of knowledge of the most elementary principles of hygiene and sanitation.

The practices herein described were as common in such states as Indiana, Illinois, Kentucky, and Tennessee between 1840 and 1870 as they were in the trans-Mississippi Valley down to the end of the nineteenth century. In fact, traces of them may still be found in the more remote and backward communities of the southern and central portions of the United States.

In the pioneer West an entire family lived in a log cabin, sod house, dugout, or structure of rough lumber usually consisting of not more than three rooms and often of one or two. Even though the great majority of these frontiersmen were comparatively young people, there were often three or four children and in some cases as many as six or seven or even more. Such a small house meant crowded quarters for five to eight or nine people. In winter it was cold and draughty and yet ventilation was often poor. The family slept two or three in a bed with the windows tightly closed just as they had been throughout the day. It has been said that "the air is pure in the country because country people always sleep with the windows closed!" Certainly that was the custom in the frontier communities because in the prairie region fuel was scarce and even in the wooded areas the pioneer found it easier to close the windows than to chop more wood.

Screens for the doors and windows were unknown and flies were a perpetual plague in summer by day and in many places mosquitoes a great source of annoyance by night. A child was frequently given a leafy branch and assigned the task of "minding flies off the table" when company was present, but the guests usually felt that it was only courteous to assert that this was unnecessary and that everyone should be expected to "mind his own flies." That disease germs were frequently carried to food by flies was of course certain. A sheet of mosquito bar was frequently spread over a cradle to keep flies off a sleeping baby but many were likely to find their way beneath it. The same material was also used to prevent the entrance of mosquitoes, but few householders had a sufficient quantity to cover all windows and a "smudge" was sometimes kindled to discourage these pestiferous insects.

The water for household use came, in most cases, from a nearby spring or stream or was drawn from a shallow well. It was not always pure and in many instances must have been contaminated by the presence of colon bacilli or other germs of disease. The whole family drank from a common cup, gourd, or tin dipper, washed in a single pan, and dried their hands and faces on the same towel. The crossroads store always had a shelf in the rear equipped with a pail of water with a tin cup hanging on a nearby nail from which thirsty customers drank freely, undisturbed by any thought of the unsanitary nature of such a practice. The country school had a single water pail to accommodate thirty or forty youngsters who seemed to the teacher perpetually thirsty. The little hotel or tavern had similar drinking arrangements and guests, after washing their hands and faces in a common basin, dried them on a "roller towel," the more fastidious ones rolling it up or down often in a vain effort to find a reasonably clean and dry spot.

Visitors to a home drank from the common dipper and used the same wash basin as did the family, with the hostess making no concession except to put out a clean towel. The small son of the household filled a basin half full of water, and he and his little playmate alternately snorted into it a couple of times, dabbling a little water on the more central portions of their faces, and sometimes chanting the little couplet: "Wash together, Friends forever."

Bathing facilities were extremely meager. In summer the settler and his sons swam in the creek or pond, and in winter a washtub was filled with water every Saturday night and the children placed in it by strong-arm methods.

Every family had a single comb and brush which was used by all of its members. Toothbrushes were unknown unless a hackberry root with one end chewed sufficiently to form a small mop could be so designated. It was dipped in salt and used to rub the teeth lightly or they might be polished a bit with one corner of the towel. Some men carried a gold-plated toothpick, or one made of deer bone, and used it to remove particles of food from between the teeth after every meal. Chewing gum, commonly called "wax" in the South, was scarce and a single chew was passed about from mouth to mouth of three or four children sometimes for days.

When a number of boys assembled to play ball one hot Sunday afternoon at the edge of the Cross Timbers of North Texas, one of the four Dye brothers eagerly besought his younger brother to go to the nearest well a quarter of a mile away and bring a pail of water for the benefit of the sweating, thirsty players. "Now, Walter," he pleaded earnestly, "if you'll take the bucket and bring us a bucket of nice cool water from Mr. Clark's well, I'll let you chew the wax! Monroe is chewin' it now but his hour is about up and it's my time to chew it next. Now you do that, Walter, like a good boy, and I'll skip my turn and let you chew the wax!" Unable to resist the promise of such a reward, Walter seized the water pail and started in a lope for Mr. Clark's well.

Under such conditions, it is not strange that when any person acquired a communicable disease, it was not only likely to be transmitted to all other members of the family but to sweep through the entire community. Colds, flu, measles, mumps, whooping cough, scabies, sore eyes, and other contagious or infectious diseases were very common among the American pioneers. Smallpox was usually regarded as serious enough to demand the isolation of the patient though it, too, might occasionally reach epidemic proportions. Venereal disease was uncommon among rural settlers but by no means unknown, and tuberculosis must have taken a considerable toll of lives. Trachoma undoubtedly existed but was not known by that name but as "granulated lids." The treatment of any of the diseases named was, moreover, usually crude and quite unscientific.

The food of the average pioneer settler was abundant and substantial and of a type calculated to enable him to swing a heavy axe, hoe, or maul for hours but it leaned heavily towards fats and starches. Meat was plentiful but, except in the early years of the settlement of a region where game was abundant, it was usually salt pork, bacon, or ham. Fresh meat was rare in summer or, in fact, at any other season except "hog-killing time" in the late autumn, or upon those occasions when a neighbor killed a beef. At such times, children, who had subsisted largely on strong "side meat" for many months, ate "not wisely but too well," often with disastrous results. Refrigeration and ice were, of course, unknown and food frequently spoiled in warm weather. If the family had a spring house, milk, butter, and other perishable foods were kept in it. Otherwise milk was strained into large shallow stone "crocks" and placed on a table in the cellar, along with butter wrapped in a wet cloth. A jug of buttermilk was often tied to the end of a long rope and "hung in the well" in much the same fashion as was "the moss-covered bucket." Nearly every kitchen had a cupboard with sides made of wire screen or perforated tin to allow a free circulation of air without admitting flies. Dishes and food were kept in this cabinet, which was commonly known as a "safe." With a number of perpetually hungry children about, the term was something of a misnomer so far as food was concerned.

During the winter months there was a lamentable lack of fresh fruits and green vegetables. As a result many impatient youngsters could not wait for fruit to ripen but often ate green apples or watermelons. Even later when fruit was ripe they stuffed themselves to repletion with plums, peaches, berries, and grapes, as well as green corn and various types of vegetables. The result was often grave disturbance of the digestive system commonly referred to as "summer complaint." Milk was abundant in some areas but very scarce in others where even small children drank strong black coffee.

Knowledge of what constitutes a proper diet for young children was almost wholly lacking. Babes in arms were fed mashed potatoes, cabbage, spinach, squash, pie, cake, and cookies. While so young that they had only their natural food, they usually remained reasonably healthy, but once they began to be fed such things as would tax the digestion of an adult laborer, it frequently became another story. The type of solid food given to them was probably largely responsible for the widely prevailing belief that the most dangerous period for every baby was "the second summer." In the light of modern medical science it is not surprising that infant mortality was shockingly high, but that so many children lived to maturity. As a matter of fact while only the strong and healthy survived, one who lived to the sixth or seventh year was likely not only to reach manhood or womanhood but to achieve a ripe old age.

Since hospitals were unknown, all babies were brought into the world in the primitive homes often without the benefit of any further medical skill or attention than such as could be furnished by some ancient midwife, commonly known as a "granny woman." Under such circumstances childbearing was a frightful ordeal accompanied by much suffering and grave danger. The cemeteries scattered about the region that was frontier half a century or more ago have many grave stones inscribed "mother and infant" which tell a tragic story.

The manner of life of the pioneer settler was such that he and the members of his family suffered many minor injuries such as cuts, burns, bruises, and abrasions. The children cut their fingers or stepped on nails, thorns, or bits of broken glass. They were stung by bees, wasps, or scorpions, bitten by spiders, or occasionally by a snake, or developed boils and felons, or acquired stone bruises. A foot was sometimes cut open by an axe. Chidren were hurt at play, and there is the old story of the small boy who came running in to tell his mother that: "Oscar got hit in the back of the head by the ball and the bawl came out of his mouth!"

Such injuries were usually of minor importance, but there were some that were serious, and proper methods of treating them were seldom employed. Common baking soda was put on a sting or bite of an insect, while the turpentine bottle was to be found in every household and was brought out upon numerous occasions. Turpentine was applied to bruises or aching joints and sometimes was mixed with lard and rubbed on a sore throat or chest. Other common remedies for bruises or abrasions or to reduce swelling and inflammation were goose grease, mutton tallow, gizzard oil, or snake oil. Some of these were mixed with turpentine or camphor to insure greater potency.

In addition there were poultices of infinite variety. These were made of bread and milk, onions, flaxseed, scraped beef-steak, hot salt, mustard, poke root, and a host of other substances. They were applied to a boil or "felon" to "draw it to a head" or to any wound, bruise, or sore spot. Mustard plasters were designed to relieve a soreness in the chest. A small chicken was split in halves and one half of the warm, quivering flesh applied to a spider bite to "draw out the poison." A snake bite was usually treated by administering a stiff drink of whisky and cutting the wound to make it bleed freely. It was then sometimes cauterized with a hot iron or by pouring a little gunpowder on it which was then ignited with a match or flaming splinter. If a child were bitten on the foot, the entire member was sometimes placed in a pail filled with kerosene.

In addition to these home remedies, there were various types of liniments and salves purchased at the local drug store. These were of great variety and included many preparations known by the name of their manufacturer and recommended as "good for man or beast and a sure cure for aches, pains, cuts, bruises, old sores, or burns." Also there were eye salves, eye water, "red precipity," used as a cure for itch, arnica salve, and ointments of many kinds. Axle grease or tar was sometimes applied to cracked hands, and glycerine to chapped lips, while sweet cream was used to relieve sunburn or skin eruptions due to poison ivy.

Most pioneers had a marked fear of hydrophobia and every community sooner or later had its "mad-dog scare." Rumors that a rabid dog had appeared in the community created intense excitement and were carried by the "grapevine telegraph" to everyone in the neighborhood. The men promptly armed themselves with rifles or shotguns loaded with buckshot and tramped the fields and woods in search of the animal, their steps guided by reports of its having been seen at various places in the community. Most of the searchers declared that they would be less alarmed by the knowledge that a ferocious lion was loose in the neighborhood. In the meantime, the women remained close at home and tried to keep the children indoors, regaling one another with horrid tales of someone of whom they had once heard who had been bitten and some days later had gone raving mad. The victim was alleged to have had convulsions, accompanied by foaming at the mouth and an insane desire to bite anyone who came near. In his lucid moments, he was said to have earnestly begged to be put out of his misery, but, nobody caring to accommodate him, the unfortunate person had suffered frightfully for two or three days and at last died in great agony. The popeyed children who listened to such frightful stories were usually not difficult to keep inside the house. Few of them could have been induced to step outside even for a moment.

When the animal had at last been tracked down and dispatched, the entire community heaved a sigh of relief. Even then, however, the incident was not closed. There still remained the task of slaughtering all dogs that had been bitten or that were even suspected of having been bitten. In consequence faithful old Rover was likely to be sent to the happy hunting ground by a charge of buckshot, secretly if possible, to avoid the tears and lamentations of the younger members of the household.

If by chance some person had been bitten by the rabid animal, which was seldom the case, he was immediately rushed to a "madstone" if one could be found in a radius of twenty or thirty miles. The stone which was said to have been taken from the body of a white deer was applied to the wound and if it refused to stick, it meant that there was no poison in the wound and so no cause for worry. On the other hand, if it stuck, there was no doubt but that the deadly germs of hydrophobia were present. When the faithful madstone had decided to call it a day and refused to cling longer to the wound despite repeated applications, it was regarded as *prima facie* evidence that a complete cure had been effected. The madstone was then placed in a bowl of sweet milk and lurid stories were related of how the milk curdled and became green in color from the poison that it had drawn from the wound. In any case, the patient felt safe and returned home relieved of any further concern.

Other animals than dogs were alleged to have hydrophobia in some instances and there were hair-raising stories of experiences with rabid wolves and "hydrophobia cows." The bite of the small striped skunk, sometimes known as a "hydrophobia cat," was alleged always to produce hydrophobia. They were dreaded even more than rattlesnakes and any person bitten by one must rush to a madstone immediately. If such a cure was not available, it was commonly believed that he might as well make his will, arrange his worldly affairs, and, in the words of the old story, start making a preferential list of those he expected to bite when he became mad!

The superstition with respect to the madstone was common on the frontier but was only one of many that related to the prevention or cure of ailments. A man sometimes carried a buckeye in his pocket to ward off rheumatism. A mole's foot was attached to a string and tied about a baby's neck to make cutting teeth easier. Also a small bag of asafetida was worn on a string around the neck of a child to keep away disease germs. Probably there was some justification for this practice since no one cared to go close enough to a child so equipped to transmit any germs to him! The same reasoning may have been responsible for the idea that eating large quantities of onions would prevent taking a cold.

On the frontier the use of internal medicine was quite as prevalent as was the application of salves, ointments, liniments, and plasters to relieve pain or heal minor injuries. There were some attempts to practice preventive medicine, though most of the many concoctions taken to ward off disease apparently had little or no value. In the early months of spring, children were given a mixture of sulphur, molasses, and cream of tartar to purify the blood. Also they were dosed with sassafras tea to thin the blood and so make them fit to face the heat of summer. Tonics were of infinite variety. A quart of whisky would be put into a jug and some wild cherry bark, prickly ash berries, and sarsaparilla roots added, and the mixture allowed to stand for several days or until the medicinal properties of the various other elements had become merged with the whisky. A swallow of this taken night and morning was said to prevent malaria, tone up the system, and improve the appetite. Other forms of bitters were made of a brew of sarsaparilla roots, bitter apple, and various additional roots and herbs in order to stimulate the appetite and improve digestion. Rusty nails were put into a bottle of water and a sip of the liquid taken every day to insure plenty of iron in the blood.

As already suggested, digestive disturbances due to improper food or excessive eating were very common especially among children. A tea made by boiling the roots of a plant known as "red root," which grew abundantly in the Southwest, was often given as a remedy for diarrhea, dysentery, or "summer complaint." In fact "teas" were of as wide variety as poultices. In addition to those already named there were sage tea, pennyroyal tea, ginger tea, sarsaparilla tea, beef tea, rhubarb tea, horehound tea, and teas made from blackberry roots, oak bark, or sheep droppings. They were ladled out to children not only for digestive disorders, but also for colds, fever, or general "puniness" and a "run down condition." Commercial tea called "store tea" was widely used in some parts of the North as a beverage but on the Southern frontier it seldom appeared except in cases of sickness. The same was true of lemons, rice, and oranges which in many pioneer communities were seldom purchased unless some member of the household was ill.

On the frontier, as today, children attacked by colic due to overloading the stomach with more or less indigestible foods were liberally dosed with castor oil. Appendicitis must have been fairly common but the name was unknown, and it was commonly called "inflammation of the bowels." Typhoid fever, usually known as "slow fever," was also prevalent, in most cases being acquired from drinking contaminated water from shallow wells. It was treated by giving the patient calomel or "blue mass" and sometimes quinine and limiting his diet to soup and soft foods.

In winter, coughs, colds, bronchitis, sore throat, and pleurisy were widespread and pneumonia was by no means uncommon. Every person had his own remedy for a cold which is not too different from the situation today. Soaking the patient's feet in hot water and requiring him to drink a hot lemonade or a large cup of hot ginger tea before going to bed was almost universally regarded as the proper treatment. The masculine members of a household usually regarded a "hot whisky stew" as more effective than either the lemonade or ginger tea but in any case the patient must retire immediately and be covered with heavy blankets so that he might perspire profusely and so "sweat the cold out of his system." A favorite remedy for coughs and colds was whisky in which had been dissolved a considerable quantity of rock candy. In addition there were cough syrups of various types, but the most common was made by making a strong tea of horehound leaves, adding sugar, and boiling it until a thick syrup was formed. A teaspoonful of this three or four times a day was regarded as a sure cure for a cough.

Malaria was common on nearly every part of the frontier except the high arid plains. This is not surprising, with no screens on the doors and windows of the homes, which were often near a stream or pond that produced myriads of mosquitoes. The cause of malaria, commonly called "chills and fever," was, however, quite unknown. Some asserted that "chills" were due to eating green watermelons, excessive swimming in the creek, or merely to "being out in the night air." Just what air you were expected to be out in after dark if not "night air" nobody took the trouble to explain. The term *malaria* obviously means "bad air," but tradition rather than the word was responsible for the pioneer's fear. The remedy was quinine but since gelatine capsules had not yet been invented, it was hard to get it down the youngsters. Sometimes it was dissolved in coffee, or more often wrapped in a piece of soft stewed fruit and gulped down with the hope that the wrapping did not slip while it was still in the mouth. Often a quantity would be added to a quart of whisky and the mixture shaken up and a swallow taken night and morning in chill season as "preventive medicine."

In some sections of the Southern frontier chills were accepted almost as an inevitable part of life and the man who was virtually "shaking the bark off the trees" with a chill in the late afternoon would be going about his work the following morning singing, whistling, and apparently in the best of health and spirits. In fact one individual, with that trend toward exaggeration characteristic of most pioneers, declared that in his community a man who did not have a chill every other day and an addition to his family every year would hurry to a doctor to find out what was wrong with him!

In addition to quinine, there were on the market numerous "chill tonics" some alleged to be "tasteless" which was usually another example of exaggeration. As a matter of fact, the average pioneer settler, in addition to the use of home remedies, spent an astonishingly large percentage of his meager income for medicines both for external and internal use. The local drug store sold huge quantities of "liver regulator," "black draught," liver pills, or "bile beans," all advertised as a sure cure for "biliousness." Of the so-called "patent medicines" there was an infinite variety, some of which are still sold. They included: Peruna; Swamp Root; Golden Medical Discovery; Vegetable Compound; Stomach Bitters; Wine of Cardui; Beef, Iron and Wine; Ozomulsion; and a host of others. Some were recommended for a single disease while others were real "omnibus remedies" alleged to be a sure cure for any or all of a dozen ailments. For infants and young children there was a wide assortment of soothing syrups, cordials, and of course, paregoric and Castoria.

Makers of patent medicines advertised their wares widely in the weekly papers and especially in the monthly or semi-monthly household journals. Such advertisements sometimes showed the picture of a dejected-looking individual labeled "before taking" and a stalwart physical specimen tagged "after taking." Testimonials from grateful users of the remedy were often printed as: "I was run down and life was a burden but after taking only five bottles of your wonderful medicine, I am now entirely recovered." Occasionally an advertisement writer essayed verse, asserting that

Used outward or inward it never does harm
As sure as you're faithful it works like a charm.

One knowing the virtue, or lack of it, of most charms and amulets worn by primitive peoples to ward off disease would probably agree that the statement was correct. Another widely circulated bit of verse designed to promote the sale of a popular child remedy was as follows:

When Baby was sick, we gave her Castoria,
When she was a Child, she cried for Castoria,
When she became Miss, she clung to Castoria,
When she had Children, she gave them Castoria.

The constant repetition of the name could hardly fail to impress it upon the reader and fix in his mind the perennial value of the medicine though on one occasion an over-particular Victorian was heard to remark that some mention of a change in "Baby's" marital status should have been indicated prior to the last line!

Other makers of patent medicines also essayed verse in bringing their wares to the attention of the ailing public, such as the following:

Little spells of fever
Little chills so bland
Make the mighty graveyard
And the angel band.
A little Cheatham's Chill Tonic
Taken now and then
Makes the handsome women
And the healthy men.

There is some evidence that manufacturers of so-called "patent medicines" made an earnest and concerted effort in the eighties and nineties to induce people to substitute such preparations for the old-time home remedies of earlier years. Certainly the volume of advertising increased enormously, no doubt owing in part to the fact that the number of newspaper readers grew rapidly as many additional periodicals were established and the older ones greatly increased their circulation. Makers of numerous proprietary medicines advertised in virtually all of these local newspapers, so almost any one of them is typical of a hundred others, all of which carried the same advertising matter. The Fort Smith *Elevator*, a four-page weekly periodical, in its issue of July 15, 1887, carried nineteen advertisements for as many different remedies, including two on the front page. Among these medicines were Castoria, Ague Busters, Ayers Sarsaparilla, Prickly Ash Bitters, Dr. King's New Discovery (for consumption), Botanic Blood Balm, Dromgoole's English Female Bitters, Merrell's Penetrating Oil, Tansy Capsules, Shiloh's Vitalizer, and Spark's Blackberry Balsam.

Several of these had disappeared from the pages of this newspaper two years later but there were many new ones, including Malarion, Arkansaw's Own Famous Liver Remedy, Morley's T-X-S Ague Tonic, Dr. Haine's Golden Specific to cure the liquor habit, Hunt's Cure for Itch, Clarke's Flax Salve, Syrup of Figs, and some others. Some six years later the names of most of these had vanished from the pages of the *Elevator* and had been replaced by a whole crop of new ones.

The issues of 1895 each usually carried about twenty-five patent medicine advertisements, including those for Dr. Pierce's Golden Medical Discovery, Brown's Iron Bitters, Ozmantis Oriental Pills, Mother's Friend, Plantation Chill Cure, Dr. Green's Onion Syrup, Herbine, Nerve Seeds, Dr. Miles Heart Cure, Karl's Clover Root, Shiloh's Catarrh Remedy, Electric Bitters, Ballard's Horehound Syrup, and Solalium Carolinense for the cure of fits. These ads together with those of doctors and dentists occupy approximately one-fourth of some pages of the paper.

It was not only in the small-town weeklies, however, that vendors of remedies and medical appliances advertised their wares. The St. Louis *Globe Democrat* carried on its front page advertisements of Nerve Beans, Swayne's Ointment, Bile Beans, and Dr. Owen's Electric Belt and Suspensory. The last named was a contraption consisting of a number of metal disks strung on a leather strap. It was worn about the waist next to the skin and was alleged to "cure rheumatic complaints, lumbago, general and nervous debility, kidney disease, nervousness, trembling, wasting of the body, etc." The electric belt proved so popular that an enterprising manufacturer designed and placed on sale an "electric ring" which when worn on the finger was guaranteed to have the same curative properties as did the cumbersome and uncomfortable belt, which was probably true. *Harper's Weekly* also advertised proprietary medicines, including Dr. Scott's Electric Plaster described as "combining electromagnetism with all of the best features of standard porous and other plasters." It was said to cure colds, coughs, chest pains; nervous, muscular and rheumatic pains; stomach, kidney, and liver pains; dyspeptic, malarial and other pains; rheumatism, gout, and inflammation, and the advertiser asserted that

> They who suffer ache and pain,
> Need suffer never more again.

Even trade and technical journals of the 1890's carried advertisements of proprietary medicines. The monthly *National Detective and Police Review* published at Indianapolis advertised Carter's Relief for Women, Cancer Cure, and Rupture Cure. Many of the medical preparations so widely advertised were made in New York but others were manufactured in Indianapolis, Buffalo, St. Louis, Chattanooga, and various other cities, and a few were made in smaller cities and had a considerable local sale.

Most manufacturers of the patent medicines most widely distributed realized that a large part of the frontier population did not in their own language "take a paper." This was especially true of the less literate people to whom the purveyors of such preparations looked for a large part of their customers. In consequence, many such manufacturers published an almanac for distribution through the mails or local drug stores. These were of the type of the *Old Farmer's Almanac* established in 1793 by Robert B. Thomas and published in recent years by Little, Brown and Company of Boston. Like their ancestor, these almanacs contained a calendar, astronomical calculations, the names and characters of the signs of the Zodiac, the dates of holidays, and much miscellaneous material, including household hints, weather forecasts, recipes, advice to farmers, and jokes and anecdotes. On every page, however, the virtues of the remedy were proclaimed in type that could hardly fail to catch the reader's eye. Advertising was yet in its infancy and modern techniques of making the product offered only incidental to the picture of a dizzy blonde in abbreviated costume had not been discovered. The cover of the almanac carried a picture but it was always one designed to fix the attention of the reader upon the remedy. Sometimes it depicted St. George, plainly labeled as the medicine, slaying the dragon of disease. Among the pioneers the belief was common that the Indians had much medical lore, especially with respect to the curative properties of certain roots and herbs. The cover of one popular almanac pictured an Indian woman pointing to a growing plant and exclaiming to her white sister bowed down with suffering, "The Great Spirit planted it!"

Doctors, except in the towns, were few and far between and most of them had little to recommend them except imposing whiskers and an impressive bedside manner. Yet they made up for their lack of medical skill and scientific knowledge by an enormous energy and conscientious devotion to duty. In subzero weather, often through sleet and snow, they traveled many miles in open buggies or on horseback to relieve suffering and minister to those in need of help. They brought to many a household comfort and hope and uncomplainingly made enormous sacrifices and endured frightful hardships to give their poor best to suffering humanity. To them the people of America owe a heavy debt of gratitude.

This scarcity of physicians was obviously responsible for the rapid increase in the sale of proprietary remedies or "mail order" medical treatment. It was also responsible for the early appearance of the traveling doctor with his "medicine show," an institution which was continued well down into the twentieth century. Usually he was a somewhat corpulent individual in striped trousers, a Prince Albert coat, white shirt, and black string tie, who appeared on the streets of a Western village just after sundown in a large flat truck drawn by two white horses with silver-mounted harness. Sitting in chairs on the truck were two or three black-faced comedians vigorously playing a violin and a banjo, guitar, or accordion. Stopping at the most prominent street corner, these black-faced boys would burst into song and continue until a considerable crowd had gathered. Then the "Doctor" would stand and in a deep, sonorous voice begin his speech:

"Ladies and Gentlemen: I am traveling about over the country trying to bring aid to suffering humanity. We have not come out here this evening to try to sell you anything but only that we may all have a good time—" "Yum, yum," would interpose one of the comedians, "Ain't we a-gwine hab a *good time!*" "Shut up, Sam," the doctor would exclaim. "Now, folks, we are not interested in making money or selling you something but only in helping you to feel better and in curing any ailments you may have. I look at you men standing there and I can see that some of you have a dull ache in the back, and twinges of pain in your shoulders and legs." The village blacksmith who had worked at a forge all day sharpening plows, or shoeing horses, and the farmer who had hoed corn since sunrise and then dropped over to town to do an errand would look at one another and nod knowingly. It took no great stretch of imagination to make them feel the dull aches and twinges so aptly described by the wise doctor. Having planted the seed, the doctor proceeded to cultivate the crop, certain of a reasonably bountiful harvest. "Now, men," he would continue, "in my laboratories at home I've worked for years hoping to find a preparation that would cure cases just like yours and at last I found it. Here it is, gentlemen, Dr. X's Marvelous Elixir. Take one tablespoonful and that dull ache will vanish as if by magic and if you'll take a dose night and morning for three weeks, I'll guarantee that it will never come back. You'll have a better appetite, feel better than ever before in your life, and be able to do a full day's work without that rundown, wornout feeling you now have. Only a dollar a bottle for anybody that wants one and you'll say it's the biggest dollar's worth you ever saw in your lives. Step right up, gentlemen, who'll be first?"

After one or two had stepped forward and rather sheepishly tendered a dollar, the contagion grew and there was likely to be a rush to exchange dollars for bottles of the Elixir. When sales began to fall off, a brief recess was held and the black-face boys played again and sang more songs while others joined the little crowd. Then sales were resumed and continued until all customers had been supplied, after which one of the boys mounted to the driver's seat and, with the others gaily singing and playing, the truck was driven to the camping place that had been selected just beyond the edge of town.

There were of course many variations. Some proprietors of medicine shows dispensed several remedies, including liniments, salves, an "inhaler" for catarrh and colds in the head, or soap "made from the roots of the Mexican yucca." There were also traveling "corn doctors" who usually displayed a large box of corns and calluses taken from the feet of former customers. It is doubtful if the preparations sold by these itinerant shows had any curative effects but they at least gave to those who "enjoyed poor health" a new remedy to try and the entertainment features brought a little color and excitement to drab and monotonous lives.

Dentists were even more rare on the frontier than were general practitioners, though one or two could usually be found at the more important towns. They advertised extensively in the local newspapers, offering their services at prices that would shock present-day members of the profession. "A fine set of false teeth" was offered for eight dollars, and teeth would be extracted "without pain" at twenty-five cents each. Outside the larger towns, however, people paid virtually no attention to their teeth unless one began to ache. Then a hot poultice would be applied to the jaw or a cavity stuffed with a bit of cotton soaked in laudanum or some form of "toothache drops." The loose milk tooth of a child was pulled by the father or mother with the fingers or yanked out by looping a bit of thread about it and giving a quick jerk or tying one end of the thread to the open door and suddenly closing it. The youngster was always told that if he did not put his tongue into the vacant space a gold tooth would grow there but never found it possible to test the truth of this assertion. If an adult's aching tooth could not be eased by poultices or medicated cotton, it was sometimes knocked out with a chisel or screwdriver and hammer, or pulled by means of a pair of bullet molds in the hands of a husky neighbor.

A traveling dentist equipped with a small case of tools of his craft would sometimes appear in a community but he seldom did more than pull bad teeth and give some advice as to the care of those left. When an individual had very few teeth left, eating became a serious problem but many managed to struggle along with surprisingly few. There is an ancient story to the effect that one old lady at an experience meeting expressed her thanks to the Lord that she still had "two teeth left and they hit."

When false teeth became absolutely necessary, a trip was made to the nearest dentist, which sometimes required a journey of two or three days. Once there, impressions were made and the patient returned home to receive his teeth two or three weeks later by mail. Naturally they seldom fitted well and were usually worn in a pocket most of the time and placed in the mouth only when required for eating or when visitors appeared.

In addition to traveling doctors and dentists, spectacle salesmen also peddled their wares throughout many frontier areas, and persons with failing eyesight fitted themselves with glasses by the simple method of trying on a number of pairs and choosing the one with which they could see best. There is an old story to the effect that one such salesman stopped at a country store in the Ozark Mountain region on a Saturday afternoon and, observing that nearly every man of the considerable number of loafers assembled there had a red mark across the bridge of his nose, was very hopeful of doing a big business. To his disappointment, however, he was solemnly informed that none of these men had ever worn glasses but had acquired these marks in drinking corn whisky out of a fruit jar!

While physicians and dentists were very few on the frontier, it was usually possible to obtain the services of either if the emergency were sufficiently grave but often only after considerable delay. Trained nurses, however, were unknown. Sometimes there might be found in a community a woman who would care for sick people for hire but this was unusual. Such a woman would today be called a "practical nurse" but it must be admitted that if one of these could be found on the frontier, she was as a rule, to paraphrase Voltaire, "neither practical nor a nurse." At best she was only a person with considerable experience in the sickroom who was willing to come into a home and work on a twenty-four hour shift for the duration of the emergency, getting what sleep or recreation she could when relieved by relatives or friends of the patient.

Of professional nursing, however, there was virtually none. A sick person was cared for by members of his family and kindly neighbors who were always ready and willing to lend assistance. "Sitting up with the sick" was regarded as the plain duty of everyone if the need arose and some persons achieved a local reputation as humanitarians by virtue of being "so good to wait on the sick." If anyone in the community became seriously ill, it was expected that his family would notify the neighbors, and any failure to do so was regarded almost as an affront. It was only necessary to pass on the word of illness in a family to a very few. The grapevine functioned with amazing efficiency and kindly persons hastened to call to bring special dainties to tempt the patient's appetite and to offer their services to "sit up" or to aid in any other possible fashion. Usually two or three would come in each evening and do some quiet visiting as they watched from an adjoining room. During the day there were likely to be many visitors to inquire about the situation and to sit and talk with the patient unless the latter were so ill that it was deemed inadvisable to admit any "company" to the sick room.

It must be confessed that an occasional visitor to the sick might be characterized as a "Job's comforter" whose influence was far from salutary. Such a person would come in on tiptoe, seat himself by the bed, and after a long survey of the patient would shake his head sorrowfully and remark: "You must be pretty bad, Bill; I don't like your color. You look a lot like my uncle Joe did just before he passed on." If the patient protested that he felt much better than he had the day before, the visitor would again shake his head and continue: "Yes, Uncle Joe did, too. He rallied a little right at the last and then all at once went out just like a light." By the time the pessimistic individual had at last departed, the patient was likely to be in a cold sweat of fear and to feel that at any minute he might begin "picking at the cover," which among pioneer peoples was regarded as a sure sign of impending death.

Fortunately such gloomy visitors were very few. Most persons who came to call upon the sick brought not only food and flowers, and help to the overburdened family but something even more important—cheerfulness and sunshine and a breath of the pure air of the world outside. Among a people who lacked all modern facilities for the care of the suffering the kindly helpfulness of friends and neighbors robbed illness of much of its terror for the patient and his family alike. Many a person at last rose from a sick bed with a heart filled with gratitude for many favors and a spirit humbled and chastened by the knowledge that so many whom he had formerly regarded with indifference had, in his hour of need, proved themselves true and devoted friends. Undoubtedly illness often served to strengthen the bonds of friendship and helped to promote that neighborly feeling and community consciousness so characteristic of the American pioneers.

With the passing of the years, the old frontier days and ways began to disappear. Manners and customs were changing and this was as apparent in medical practices as in everything else. The coming of railroads brought in a larger population, towns grew up, and with economic advancement more physicians came in to open offices and begin a medical practice. They were, moreover, men of far more training and skill, in most cases, than had been the old-time frontier doctors. Hospitals supplied with modern equipment were established. Graduate nurses became available. The old home remedies gave way to the prescriptions of physicians and even the rage for patent medicines began to abate as scientific investigations were made proving many of them worthless. Some standard remedies are still sold but many preparations disappeared from the market and the sale of others was far less than formerly, though weekly and daily newspapers still advertise some proprietary medicines and television has, in recent years, become a very important medium. New remedies appeared on the shelves of the pharmacies and new treatments of disease were evolved. In addition many of the ailments that had formerly afflicted the pioneers have largely disappeared.

Only in a few backward communities do the old medical practices still persist in the nature of customs that half a century or more ago were virtually universal, at least in the rural districts of most states west of the Mississippi River, and in many east of that stream. A long and intensive study of the medical practices of the American people in the West during the past three quarters of a century and of how they have changed would undoubtedly produce a worthwhile contribution to the field of social history.

XI

The neighbors all assembled
And we built our house of God
With a decent floor of lumber
And the walls and roof of sod.
But we put us in some windows
And built some benches rude
And a pulpit made of boxes
Which perhaps was very crude.

The preacher was no scholar
But he surely preached the Word
And the voices of the women
Were the sweetest ever heard.
As they sang the hymns of yesterday
About the Promised Land
It seemed that God was closer there
Than in churches fine and grand.
                              The Sod Church

XI
The Old-Time Religion

THE GREAT MAJORITY of the pioneer settlers who removed westward to establish new homes on the frontier were a deeply religious people. There were exceptions it is true, yet the Bible was read daily in many of these humble homes, and family worship each evening was by no means uncommon. In fact, it was only a deep spiritual faith which enabled many men and women to endure the loneliness and hardships of life in a strange new land.

It is hoped that no reader will regard the description of the revival meeting as unduly flippant or frivolous. It was written in all reverence with a full realization that in such meetings many persons turned their feet into paths of righteousness which they steadfastly followed to the end of their lives. Some humorous incidents and remarks, however, were common to every revival and these must be recorded by any writer who seeks to give a true picture of an institution which was a great influence for good and so vitally affected the lives of so many persons.

WITH RESPECT TO THE RELIGIOUS BELIEFS of the prairie pioneers of fifty years ago, it is difficult to generalize. In the northern zone of settlement were found many communities of South German Catholics, and others of North German or Scandinavian Lutherans. Some Presbyterians, Episcopalians, and Congregationalists might be found everywhere, but the settlers from Missouri, Arkansas, and eastern Texas who occupied the Southern and Central Plains region largely belonged to the Baptist, Methodist, Presbyterian, or some branch of the Christian Church. Their religion was in many cases of the "emotional type," and their ministers were, on the whole, characterized more by devotion and sincerity than by education or special training, since comparatively few were graduates of a college or theological seminary. Many of them professed to have received a "call" to preach the Gospel and had responded to it with a fervor that sometimes bordered upon the fanatical.

Regardless of church or creed, however, most of these pioneer people were deeply religious. It was one of their most pronounced traits. Religion was to them far more than an abstract conception of a relationship with the Divine. It was a vital, moving thing, an ever-present light to their feet, a solace in time of trouble. In prosperity and adversity alike this deep religious faith led them on: "a pillar of cloud by day and a pillar of fire by night."

The hardships and privations of a crude and primitive life no doubt had its influence in the promotion of a strong spiritual faith. In a modern, sophisticated society, we can do so many things for ourselves that it seems many people at times develop a self-sufficiency which tends to make them unmindful of any Higher Power. With furnace heat and electric fans or air conditioning, we can banish from our homes much of the discomfort of icy or torrid weather. The pioneer had no such resources. The bitter cold of winter or the sweltering heat of summer had to be faced as they came with a prayer to Him "who tempers the wind to the shorn lamb." In a modern urban society if someone is hurt or ill, it is quite easy to step to the telephone and call an ambulance to take the suffering one to a hospital where he may have all the care that the resources of present-day science can give.

The prairie pioneers were in a far different situation. They had no telephones, ambulances, or hospitals. In many cases no doctors and even no medicines were available. Under such circumstances if a loved child fell ill, what was the pioneer mother to do? She could only administer such home remedies as she might be able to devise and, in the last extremity, put her trust in "that Great Physician who can heal all diseases." This very helplessness in time of sickness or trouble was a powerful factor in promoting the simple, childlike faith so characteristic of most people in a primitive stage of society and which was especially apparent among the permanent settlers of the American frontier.

It is true that among these people were found many still "living in sin," as their state was commonly called. Frequently they never did anything worse than indulge in a bit of mild profanity when things went wrong, or sometimes take a drink, or join in a social game of cards. Even if they did none of these, however, but had never "professed religion" and joined the church, they were still "sinners" in the eyes of the good church people, who felt it their duty to labor earnestly to bring these erring ones into the fold. In fact, a man noted for high moral character, strict honesty, and kindly, unselfish nature, particularly if he were fairly prosperous, was sometimes regarded as more dangerous than was the irresponsible, worthless rascal. The latter had no influence, and youths would never pattern their own lives by his, while the former was an influential citizen whom young people might choose as a model, thereby entirely ignoring religion as a necessary factor in human life and behavior.

Contrary to the idea expressed by many writers of fiction, ministers of the Gospel were seldom lacking among the settlers of the prairie frontier, and almost the first assemblies were for the purpose of public worship. Church services were often held among the Boomers who settled Oklahoma, the emigrants to California and Oregon, and the early homesteaders of every prairie state or territory. At times the difficulty was not in finding someone to preach, but rather in choosing one from three or four, all willing and even eager to "preach the Word" to an interested and appreciative congregation. When a considerable number of persons were traveling together, or encamped in a group for a few days to rest their livestock, or waiting for the flood waters of a river to subside, church services were common. They were held under the trees, on the open prairie beside the wagons, or in a large tent. Once the end of the journey had been reached and homesteads selected, the settlers assembled for worship under a rude brush arbor or in the newly built home of one of their number.

This was neither comfortable nor convenient, however, except during the warm days of summer, and as soon as a schoolhouse had been constructed, it also became a place for religious worship. A Sunday School was promptly organized and arrangements made for church services as often as possible.

This meant, of course, that church organizations must be formed. The leading spirits of some particular denomination would invite a minister of their faith to come on the following Sunday to preach. All members or former members of that church would be urged to attend and at the close of services a "church" would be formed and given a distinctive name, as the "Bethel" or "Valley View" Methodist Church. Officials would be chosen, such as stewards or deacons, and letters of honorable dismissal from the church in the old home to which members had formerly belonged were presented. Those who had neglected to secure letters agreed to write for them, and a membership was thus formed. It might receive additions upon a profession of faith and baptism.

The church so formed proceeded at once to seek a minister. He was usually an itinerant preacher or "circuit rider," who agreed to come and preach upon one designated Sunday in each month. Further plans might also be made for the Sunday School and Wednesday night prayer meeting, though these were at first sometimes "union services" in which all denominations joined in order to insure a larger attendance and carry on the work more efficiently. A Ladies Aid or some similar organization of women might also be formed.

Encouraged by the success of the first church group, the members of some other faith would also organize in a similar manner. Before a year had passed, it was common for each community to have at least one or two churches organized and in operation, each having services once a month. Thus the Methodists might have preaching the first Sunday in each month, the Baptists the second, the Presbyterians the third, and the Christian church on the fourth.

It was unusual, however, to have in a single community enough people of each of these creeds to form a church. Ordinarily, if two churches were organized and services held at the same schoolhouse regularly twice a month, the people of a neighborhood felt themselves fortunate. The members of other denominations would in most cases attend these services with considerable regularity, however, and seek to have a minister of their own faith occasionally come to preach to them. Sometimes more members of their own church were to be found in the adjoining community or in one not too far away. There a church of their creed would be organized, and members would travel long distances to attend its monthly meetings. People who in modern times find it a considerable hardship to attend church during bad weather, even though it is only a few blocks away, have difficulty in understanding the religious enthusiasm of these hardy pioneers. Some would drive or ride thirty to fifty miles to attend services of the church of their choice, starting early Saturday morning and returning home on Monday. Saturday and Sunday night were spent with one of the "brethren" and his family, kindly, hospitable souls who gladly slept on a "Baptist pallet" of quilts spread on the sod-house floor in order that the visitors might have comfortable beds.

The ministers who served these little churches were literally "traveling salesmen of spiritual wares." They rode thousands of miles every year in heat or cold, through rain and snow with a Bible and a hymn book in their saddle pockets in order to "meet their appointments" at the various schoolhouses included in their circuits.

"I'll be at your house on Friday night if not Providentially hindered, or Saturday morning anyhow," an elderly preacher was accustomed to tell some member of his far-flung flock; and considering the bitter weather in which he often rode to keep an appointment, it seemed sometimes that he meant exactly what he said.

It was little enough return for all the hardships endured, that these devout ministers were gladly accorded the "right of purveyance" not only by members of their faith, but by virtually everyone. The moment the preacher arrived, one young son of the household was given the task of stabling and feeding his horse while another was sent to run down and kill a chicken for supper. The best bed was made ready for him, and the housewife busied herself with preparing the most tasty meal that could possibly be evolved from her meager resources. One of the cherished jars of canned fruit was brought up from the cellar and opened, a white tablecloth was spread on the table in lieu of the usual oilcloth, and if anything seemed to be lacking, a child was dispatched to the home of one of the neighbors to borrow it.

Such activity was at times a trifle puzzling to the children of some households whose members seldom attended church or entertained a minister. An early settler's wife relates with great glee that one evening a neighbor's small boy appeared at her door saying: "Mother wants to borrow a cup of sugar because Jesus Christ has come to our house and is going to stay all night with us."

Despite the fact that the pioneer preacher was usually himself a homesteader who mixed tilling his farm with his spiritual labors, he always found time for a multitude of duties other than preaching the Gospel. He conducted family worship in the homes where he spent the night, assisted in the Sunday School, led the singing, baptized repentant sinners, visited the sick, married lovelorn couples, and "preached the funerals" of those who died. In addition he advised people about their problems, spiritual or otherwise, helped to adjust domestic difficulties or disputes between neighbors, visited schools and talked to the children, and brought to the bereaved words of consolation and hope. His pay was meager, but even in the little time left for labor on the farm he was able, with the help of his wife and children, to wring something from its soil and so managed somehow to get along.

Just as the school had its social as well as educational aspects, so did the frontier church speedily become a social as well as a spiritual institution. In fact, many older people, except for friendly visits with neighbors, found attendance at church and Sunday School their nearest approach to any form of social activity. Here they met and talked with their friends before and after services. Here the weary wife and mother and her husband sat on their hard benches and relaxed from the toil of the busy week as they listened to the sermon, noting at the same time the new clothes and hats of their neighbors, the behavior of the children, and the demeanor of the young people. For all but a very few people, Sunday was a day of rest and worship. Every man must shave, put on a clean shirt and his "Sunday suit." The children must be scrubbed and dressed in their best, and the mother likewise donned her best dress. People who failed to do so and merely loafed about home in their everyday clothes were regarded as "trash" who would never help build up a new country or prove worthy citizens. Even the "trashiest" seldom worked in the fields on Sunday, however, since in many areas such working was contrary to law as well as custom. To make no concession to the day, except to rest, was in the eyes of many something not to be considered by decent, self-respecting persons. If no church services were available, it was still everyone's duty to "dress up" to go visiting or to be prepared to receive visitors who might come to spend the day.

On Sunday when there was preaching at the schoolhouse, however, nearly everyone in the community was certain to attend. Realizing that the sermon would in all probability be long, most women with babies or very small children carried with them a small satchel containing a few sugar cookies and perhaps a small bottle of milk and "other essentials." First in the service came two or three hymns in which everyone joined with enthusiasm, and in most cases there would be one old lady in the congregation who invariably sang off key and whose shrill voice seemed to dominate all the others. After the sermon had been delivered and the benediction pronounced, it was customary to linger a few minutes to visit with neighbors and invite them to "go home with us to dinner." Half a dozen or more guests must

have meant a busy Sunday for the housewife, even though many
of the preparations for dinner had been made on Saturday. Yet,
the table must be laid and vegetables prepared for cooking Sunday morning before time to start to church. When to these tasks
were added those of getting the children ready, making the
beds, washing the breakfast dishes, and putting the house in
order for company, the woman must have been almost too tired
to get the most from the sermon. If the family was large, however, as was the rule, the older children washed and dressed the
little ones and helped with the other work as much as possible.
Upon returning from church with an extra family or two for dinner, the only thing which saved the reason of the hostess was
that the visiting lady or ladies, according to custom, followed
her to the kitchen and helped in the preparations for the meal
and the dishwashing that followed it.

   In addition to the social features of the Sunday services, the
Sabbath School, and the midweek prayer meeting, many purely
social events were sponsored and carried out by the frontier
church organizations. The membership would from time to time
arrange a donation party for the minister, or, in their own language, to "pound the preacher." This was usually a surprise
party, the church members agreeing that they would all go to
the minister's home on a certain evening, each bringing a donation. This was mostly food, but was seldom a single pound unless
it happened to be a gift of coffee, tea, or some other fairly costly
commodity. More often one person would bring a ham, another
half a bushel of potatoes, still others bags of flour or sugar. Some
would bring canned or preserved fruit, others a jug of syrup, two
or three pumpkins, a sack of meal, or a large piece of beef or
pork. Occasionally, three or four women would piece a quilt and
bring it as their offering, or present a gift of hand-embroidered
towels, tea towels, or aprons. Having presented their donations,
the group would spend the evening with the minister and his
wife, sometimes popping corn, making candy, engaging in group
singing, or in some cases merely "visiting."

   The church as an organization also looked after the welfare
of its members. If a man was hurt or ill and his crop needed

work, the membership would assemble at his home, bringing food which the women prepared for dinner while the men worked in the fields. Many hands made light work, and even after stopping for an hour or so in the middle of the day to enjoy the good dinner prepared for them, the men would have the crops cultivated and every weed destroyed long before nightfall. All then returned to their homes, everyone having had a good time while helping a neighbor in time of need.

The church, in addition, arranged many social affairs at the schoolhouse. Money was often needed to buy song books, to make a payment on the organ, to add to the minister's salary, or to help support a missionary enterprise. To raise needed funds, a pie supper, an oyster supper—for which canned oysters were used—a church fair, or a social might be arranged. These events were planned with great care and frequently brought in a considerable sum of money as well as providing enjoyable social contacts. The ladies' aid or missionary society also gave the women an opportunity to get together, usually at someone's home, for an afternoon once or twice a month. Here they spent some hours in sewing or knitting, their tongues keeping pace with their busy needles.

One of the most important activities of the church, however, was the revival meeting, generally held in summer after crops had been "laid by" and when everyone had ample leisure. Its avowed purpose was "the saving of souls," but it was not without its social features as well. In fact, it is to be feared that many people thought quite as much of its social aspects as they did of its spiritual significance. Sometimes it was conducted by a single church group, as the Baptist, Methodist, or Nazarene, but in other cases it was a "union meeting" or a co-operative affair in which the membership of the churches of two or three faiths participated. Always the meeting was advertised throughout a large area.

Since no schoolhouse was large enough to hold the crowds expected, the ordinary procedure was to erect near the school building a large arbor covered with brush or hay. The ground beneath was strewn with hay or straw to keep down the dust. A platform was built near one side on which was placed the pulpit, the organ, and seats for the choir or principal singers. The benches were brought out from the schoolhouse and other seats made of rough boards. Lanterns or flaring torchlights were hung up to furnish light, and the song books were assembled and stacked on a bench near the organ to be distributed to the members of the choir and throughout the congregation.

A professional evangelist or "revivalist" was usually employed to conduct the meeting. He was assisted by the local pastor or pastors, and sometimes brought with him an "evangelical singer" to organize the choir and conduct the singing. This might be a member of his family, such as his wife, son, or daughter, or in some cases a young man not related but who had worked with him during many former revivals.

Sometimes two services a day were held, one at eleven o'clock in the morning and the other in the evening. Two were almost too much for any one man, however, and unless there were two evangelists to conduct the meeting, it was more common to have only an evening service each day, beginning "at early candlelight."

Before darkness had fallen on the evening that the revival began, a large crowd had assembled beneath the arbor. In some cases the evangelist then arose and explained the general nature of the services that were to follow and what he expected of the congregation. "I want you mothers to come," he would declare. "Don't worry about your babies. If a baby cries, it will not disturb me in the least. If it is necessary for the mother to leave and take the baby, feel perfectly free to do that; but I want you to watch these 'yearlins' of yours, these two- and three-year-olds, don't let them get loose and run up and down the aisle. If they try it, you take 'em out and administer the good old Presbyterian doctrine of 'laying on of hands.' There are precious souls here to be saved, and the Lord's work must not be interfered with in any way. And I want you all to leave your dogs at home. Tie 'em up, if necessary. We don't want dogs running up and down in this arbor and interfering with the Lord's work." Upon one occasion an elderly deacon piped up and said: "Anyhow, the Bible says to beware of dogs."

"Yes," replied the evangelist, "it does, and believe me I'm 'ware of 'em, too. You leave the dogs at home and take care of these 'yearlins' and the babies won't disturb me the least bit in the world."

Each meeting was begun with a song service in which the entire congregation, led by the choir and its director, sang several old favorites such as the "Glory Song," the "Lost Sheep," "Amazing Grace," and "It Is Better Farther On." The singing was followed by a "testimony meeting," in which the church members, one by one, would rise in their places and say a few words about what God had done for them and what religion meant in their lives. Then more songs would be sung, a fervent prayer delivered, the Scripture read, and the preacher would give his text and begin the sermon.

The themes chosen were generally appropriate: "Sir, we would see Jesus." Pursuing this subject, the revivalist would point out that people all over the world were looking for Jesus in business, in the professions, and in their daily life, and were in many cases finding Him not.

Another appropriate text was "Seek ye first the kingdom of God and His righteousness, and all these things will be added unto you." With this as a starting point, the evangelist would go on to point out how important it is for every man, woman, boy, and girl to put religion first and trust that all else in life will be well. No matter how large the congregation, the thundering, impassioned tones of the minister reached to the most remote parts of the big arbor and even to the little knots of boys or young men lingering outside the circle of light where they could talk and smoke cigarettes.

Concluding his sermon, the revivalist would call upon all of those who wanted to be saved or to ask the prayers of God's people, to come forward, and urged the personal workers to make their appeals to those of their neighbors, friends, and relatives who might be "lost in sin." The organist would start a hymn, and the preacher, clapping his hands from time to time, would interpolate earnest invitations between verses of the song. The hymns were chosen with an almost uncanny insight into human emotions and mass psychology. Usually the first was an invitation:

> Softly and tenderly Jesus is calling,
> Calling for you and for me.
> See, on the portals He's watching and waiting,
> Waiting for you and for me.
> Come home! Come home!
> You who are weary, come home.
> Softly and tenderly Jesus is calling,
> Calling, "O sinner, come home."

Then the choir director would shift to a new hymn:

> Jesus is tenderly calling you home,
> Calling today, calling today.
> Why do you wander, oh, why do you roam
> Farther and farther away?
> Calling today, calling today,
> Jesus is calling,
> Yes, tenderly calling today.

As the throbbing notes of the organ rose and fell and the congregation sang with deep fervor and intense feeling, the preacher would call: "Yes, come! Everybody come! 'The spirit and the bride sayeth come! and whosoever will, let him come and partake of the waters of life freely.'"

Another stanza would be sung, and the preacher's voice would again rise above the clear voices and the moaning organ: "Why do you tarry? Why delay longer? Do not be like that man in the Scripture who said, 'At a more convenient season I will come to Thee.' For remember that the Lord said, 'Thou fool, this night shall thy soul be required of thee.'"

Sobs would begin to be heard throughout the crowded arbor, and two or three weeping girls would rise, move down the aisle, shake hands with the preacher, and seat themselves at the mourners' bench with their handkerchiefs pressed to their eyes.

One or two men would follow. Some elderly woman back in the congregation would lift up her voice in shouting, "Glory Hallelujah! The Lord is mighty to save!" More people would rise and hurry down the aisle to take their places at the mourners' bench, and the personal workers would eagerly urge their sinner friends to go forward and accept salvation.

Perhaps neither the evangelist nor the song leader had ever studied psychology, but with a cleverness little short of genius, they would choose the next hymn, apparently designed to show that God's people had something which the unregenerate lacked:

> Blessed assurance, Jesus is mine,
> Oh, what a foretaste of glory divine,
> Heir of salvation, purchased of God,
> Born of His spirit, washed in His blood.
>
> This is my story, this is my song,
> Praising my Saviour all the day long,
> This is my story, this is my song,
> Praising my Saviour, all the day long.

Others would come forward and again a hymn would be chosen with a view to urging sinners to accept salvation:

> Oh turn, Sinner, turn,
> May the Lord help you turn,
> Oh turn, Sinner, turn,
> Why will you die?

Feeling that perhaps there were some of the seekers who felt themselves unworthy, the next hymn would seek to appeal to these:

> Just as I am, without one plea
> Except Thy blood was shed for me,
> And that Thou bidst me come to Thee,
> O Lamb of God, I come, I come.

Again the minister would add his appeals, and perhaps a girl seated at the mourners' bench would suddenly rise to her feet shouting with joy and with her face shining with a great happiness. She had accepted salvation, or in common parlance "had at last got religion." Her relatives and friends crowded around to embrace and congratulate her, and again someone in the audience would lift his voice in shouting, "Hallelujah! Glory to God!" This gave the cue for the next song:

> 'Tis the old time religion,
> 'Tis the old time religion,
> 'Tis the old time religion,
> And it's good enough for me.

> It was good enough for Father,
> It was good enough for Father,
> It was good enough for Father,
> And it's good enough for me.

The song went on through more stanzas, stating that it was good for Paul and Silas, it was good for the Hebrew children, "and it's good enough for me." Again the minister would shout: "Yes, Brothers and Sisters, it's good enough for all of us; it's the only way of salvation; it's the greatest thing in the world."

Various others at the mourners' bench would "come through," to use the language of the scoffers, and begin to shout that they had been saved. There were always some, however, who were still hesitant, and back in the audience were others who, despite the earnest pleas of the personal workers, refused to come forward and ask for the prayers of the minister. Again, with rare knowledge of human emotions, the preacher would choose another song:

> I've got a mother over yonder,
> I've got a mother over yonder,
> I've got a mother over yonder,
> On the other shore.

> By and by I'll go and see her,
> By and by I'll go and see her,
> By and by I'll go and see her,
> On the other shore.

> Won't that be a happy meeting,
> Won't that be a happy meeting,

Won't that be a happy meeting,
On the other shore?

Punctuated by the sobs of those at the mourners' bench, the occasional shouting of persons in the congregation, the booming voice of the minister urging people to "surrender all" and trust only in the Lord, together with the swelling tones of the organ, the song continued: "I've got a sister over yonder," "I've got a father over yonder," or "I've got children over yonder," with the object of touching the heart of the sinner by naming the exact relationship of the one whom he had "loved and lost."

The first evening the services were usually brought to a close about eleven o'clock, but as the days went by and the excitement mounted, they were often continued until midnight or later. Even then the revivalist would sometimes dismiss the congregation while he and a few of their friends and relatives would remain an hour or more longer to labor with half a dozen seekers after salvation who still sat sobbing at the mourners' bench.

As evening after evening went by and the time for closing the revival drew near, it became apparent that despite the large number of conversions, there were still a few who remained deaf to all pleadings and who chose to remain "buried in sin." Finally, some evening when the excitement was at its height, the evangelist, in the language of the unregenerate, "played his last card." Amid the ringing voices of the congregation and the sobs of those at the "mercy seat," he would suddenly rise and hold up his hand for silence. Then as the wailing notes of the organ died away and a deep hush fell upon the assemblage, he would speak in solemn, vibrant tones: "Brothers and sisters, a strange feeling has all at once come over me which I never had but once before in all my life. It is a feeling that there is someone in this congregation—I do not know who it may be—but there is *someone* who will never again have the opportunity to accept salvation. Three years ago I had this same feeling one evening when I was conducting a revival in Texas. It struck me all at once just as it has done tonight, and I made this same statement, that there was some one person who would never again have the chance to be saved.

"In the congregation there was a young man—a very fine young man in many ways—who had come to the meetings every night. But though his mother and sisters and friends pleaded with him each evening to come forward, he always hardened his heart and refused. The very next day while he was hunting in the woods, he accidentally fell and his gun was discharged, killing him instantly. They found him that evening lying in his blood, cold in death, cut off in his sins without hope of eternal life. I had that feeling then—I have it again tonight. Let me implore you not to be like that young man. We are going to stand and sing one more song, and if there is anyone in this congregation who is willing to surrender his heart to God, let him come forward and give me his hand."

Such an appeal was calculated to freeze the blood and lift the hair on the head of the young sinner, who remembered that he must ride a wild, half-broken young horse home as soon as services had ended. Not infrequently he rose instantly and in a dramatic voice declared that he here and now renounced his sins and accepted the salvation so freely promised him. In many cases his closest friends and comrades followed suit and there was a wholesale stampede for the mourners' bench.

The clever revivalist, recognizing the tendency of youth to form gangs, had in most such instances concentrated his attention upon some one young man whom he believed to be the ringleader. Watching his face closely, the evangelist turned upon him the full force of his eloquence, certain that if he could be made to yield, a number of others would immediately follow his leadership.

The evangelist and his helpers never left anything undone which might facilitate their work in saving souls. In a certain little frontier town in the Southwest there were four men with excellent voices who sometimes sang as a quartet. One was a saloon keeper; the second a gambler who devoted most of his time to dealing monte for the Indians of the nearby reservation; the third, a bronc buster, made his living by breaking wild horses; while the fourth was a cowhand whose personal life certainly left much to be desired.

When the revival meeting started, however, these men began to attend; and the evangelist, discovering their ability, promptly brought them up front to join in the singing. When the excitement would rise to intense heights and a large part of the congregation was singing, shouting, and earnestly laboring personally with unrepentant sinners, these young hellions would improvise words for the hymns in very interesting and ludicrous fashion, purely for their own amusement. In the midst of the hymn,

> The Devil's dead and I am glad,
> Oh Halley, Hallelujah!
> The Devil's dead and I am glad,
> Oh Halley, Hallelujah!

this heathen quartet would sing:

> The Devil's dead and gone to hell
> Oh hally, hally, lujah!
> I hope he's there for quite a spell
> Oh hally, hally, lujah!

As the chorus was sung,

> Shout! Shout! We're gaining ground
> Oh Halley, Hallelujah!
> The love of God is coming down
> Oh Halley, Hallelujah!

the booming voices of the quartet would ring out:

> My uncle had an old red hound
> Oh hally, hally, lujah!
> He chased the rabbits round and round
> Oh hally, hally, lujah!

If they paused for a moment in the singing the minister, never noticing the incongruous words, would wave his hand frantically in their direction urging them to carry on!

As the excitement began to die down after a week or ten days, the evangelist announced the date for the closing of the meeting. Most revivalists preferred to close while there was still great interest and considerable excitement rather than to continue too long, even though by so doing a few more converts might be made. On the last day of the revival it was customary to have baptizing, in which all of those who had professed their faith were baptized into the church. Also a collection was taken for the evangelist, to which everyone contributed to the best of his ability. Life then dropped back into its accustomed channels until the following summer, when another "big meetin'" was held.

By no means all of the pioneer settlers took part in the revival meetings, but usually a large majority did. There were, however, some unbelievers who belonged to no church and made no profession of religion. These often attended the revivals, and in some cases were converted and joined the church. Other persons, who were members of some church, did not believe in the emotional type of religion and objected in principle to the methods of the revival and those responsible for it. Some of them were inclined to scoff at the proceedings of the protracted meeting, which they referred to as the "distracted meeting," and asserted that the conversions were in most cases only examples of nervous hysteria induced by excitement.

Regardless of these opinions, however, or of what many persons today may think of the emotionalism of those who have played a leading part in religious revivals, there can be little doubt of their entire sincerity. Those who sought to lead "sinners to repentance" and who urged the acceptance of religion as the only sure way to peace and happiness, in most cases believed with all their hearts the things they said. Those who declared that they had "felt the Divine Power," that their sins had been forgiven, and they had become children of God, were equally sincere.

Nor is it true, as many people have asserted, that conversions of this kind were always temporary and that the desire to lead a better life and eschew evil soon vanished, leaving the one who experienced these emotions just as he had been before. Perhaps there really are "more things in heaven and earth than are dreamt of in our philosophy." At any rate we have too many examples of young men and women changed overnight through religious experience from frivolous, selfish, and, in some cases dissipated, individuals to earnest, self-sacrificing, temperate men and women, who remained so all their lives, to leave room for doubt that they had really undergone a profound change. This metamorphosis was so complete and so enduring in many cases as to make understandable the phrase "born again." They seemed almost to have experienced a rebirth in nature, ideas, and ideals. It is true that some others seemed to profit little from their religious experience and within a few months had become "backsliders," apparently thinking the same thoughts and leading the same lives as formerly. Enough examples could be given of the first group described, however, to convince most people that individuals do, at times, go through the experience of a spiritual regeneration and become permanently changed.

The social features of the protracted or revival meeting were of great importance. Homesteaders came long distances to attend it, and so new friendships were formed. Also, older ones were renewed between individuals who lived so far apart that they seldom saw each other at any other time. Two families of neighbors would often go together in a single wagon, and during the long drive to and from the meeting would become better acquainted and closer friends. People were also drawn more closely together by the common cause of striving for the conversion of those seeking religion. Interest in reading the Bible, in singing, and in the welfare of others was stimulated. For ten days or two weeks the ordinary activities of life were suspended, or greatly reduced, and the settlers dressed in their best each evening and turned their attention to spiritual matters. Young hearts that, in the words of the preacher, had been "touched and tendered" by religious emotion, remained tender to other forms of emotion. As a result, many budding romances flowered during the revival meeting, and more than one wedding usually followed it within a few weeks or months.

XII

Here on the prairie wide and brown
In years gone by stood a little town
Where could be seen as strange a crew
As any community ever knew.
Big Ed Clark, whose Elk Saloon
Faced the church of Preacher Boone,
Gamblers Johnny, Jake, and Dan,
Old Judge Harlan, remittance man,
Dave, who risked his life each day
Busting broncs for scanty pay.
Painted Indians with braided hair
Came to trade or gamble there.
Former miners gray and old
Roamed the heights in search of gold.
Others came who were just as strange,
Lean brown men from the lean brown range.
Settlers too with their patient wives,
Faded and worn by their toilsome lives,
"Wanted men" from the East back there
And others not wanted anywhere.
These were a few that I used to know
In the little village of Navajoe.

                          The Vanished Town

XII

Old Navajoe

A Typical Frontier Town

IT WAS MY PRIVILEGE to live in or near this remote little village for ten of the some sixteen years of its existence—1886–1902. The only justification for telling its story is that this small town was typical of hundreds of others of the Prairie West during the latter part of the nineteenth century. Yet, the characteristics which differentiated these from other communities of comparable size in the East were in Old Navajoe considerably exaggerated.

ABOUT TEN MILES EAST and three miles north of the little city of Altus, Oklahoma, some seven steep mountain peaks rise abruptly from the level plain to a maximum height of about a thousand feet above the surrounding prairie. They extend north and south across the open end of a horseshoe bend made by the North Fork of Red River as it sweeps eastward and then back in a great loop some four or five miles in diameter. These peaks were formerly called the Navajo Mountains because of the tradition that about the middle of the last century a great battle was fought at their base between a war party of Navajo, who had come east to prey upon the horse herds of the Comanches, and a band of warriors of the latter tribe, in which the Navajo had been completely destroyed.

Perhaps a mile west and slightly north of the highest peak of these mountains, on a low sandy hill, is a little wind-swept cemetery enclosed by a wire fence. No human habitation is near and this grass-grown "God's acre" contains only a hundred or so graves, most of them marked by very modest stones on which are usually carved only the names and dates of the birth and death of those buried there. Here lie the bodies of more than one man who died "with his boots on" before the blazing six gun of an opponent and of others who died peacefully in bed. Here also lie all that is mortal of little children, and of tired pioneer women who came West with their husbands seeking a home on the prairie only to find in its bosom that rest which they had so seldom known in life.

Half a mile south of this small cemetery are cultivated fields where the plowman often turns up bits of glass and broken china or scraps of rusty and corroded metal and, if he is new to the community, he may be deeply puzzled as to their presence here so remote from any dwelling. In such cases inquiry of some old settler may reveal to the curious individual that these fields were once the site of the thriving little town of Navajoe. Nothing remains of Navajoe today. It is one with Nineveh and Tyre, flintlock guns, side saddles, baby golf, and all those other things that lie within the boundaries of the land of Used to Be. Yet in its time Navajoe was a flourishing center of commerce with half a dozen stores and other business establishments and the dwellings of a score or more of families.

Since the nearest railroad point was Vernon, Texas, nearly fifty miles to the south, and there was none to the north, east or west for from eighty to a hundred and twenty-five miles, Navajoe had a vast trade territory and was the southern gateway to a huge though thinly peopled empire. In consequence, it was to some extent both a business and social center for an enormous area. To it came settlers from their prairie claims often many miles away to barter butter and eggs for sugar and coffee or to purchase with their few hard-earned dollars shoes, dry goods, or clothing. Here also at times came the boss of a herd of cattle on the trail running a few miles west of town, bringing the chuck wagon to replenish his stock of provisions before entering upon the long stretch of unsettled lands extending north to Kansas.

In addition there often came a band of Comanche or Kiowa Indians to pitch their round tepees near the north edge of town.

Here they remained for two or three days strolling about from store to store clad in their bright blankets or shawls and moccasins, spending their "grass money" for groceries or red calico, selling in contravention of law their annuity issue of blankets, coats, trousers, and coarse "squaw shoes" for a price determined by their own needs or wants rather than by the value of the articles sold. Above all, the men spent many hours playing monte with the three or four professional gamblers who were permanent residents of the town, dealing out the cards on a blanket spread on the ground inside the tepee while the women looked on or puttered about camp cooking, bringing water from the public well, or busying themselves with other chores.

To Navajoe also came at times young people to attend a dance or party given by some citizens of the little town or a box supper or literary society held at the small unpainted schoolhouse. Among these would-be merrymakers might be included a long-haired, unshaven cowhand from some remote line camp on the nearby Indian reservation. Riding in with his "good clothes" in a sack strapped behind his saddle, he usually put up his horse at the little wagon yard and surreptitiously made his way to the store to buy a white shirt and thence to the barber shop, hoping against hope that he might not meet one of the girls of town until he had been able to make considerable improvement in his personal appearance. Once in the barber shop, he demanded "the works" and emerged an hour later clad in his best raiment with his hair cut, shampooed and "tonicked" and his face shaved, bayrummed, and powdered. In fact, he was so transformed that his partner who had remained in the camp on Sandy, East Otter, or Deep Red, sometimes because of a reluctance to come within easy reach of the long arm of the law, would hardly have been able to recognize him either by sight or smell!

The foundations of Navajoe were laid about 1886 when two brothers-in-law, W. H. Acers and H. P. Dale, established the first general store, no doubt hoping to get some Indian trade, as well as to provision the outfits of trail herds on the way north, and also to supply the needs of settlers that were by this time beginning to come into the area in considerable numbers. Eventually Acers and Dale applied for the establishment of a post office under the name of "Navajo" but the Post Office Department insisted on adding an "e" to the name to avoid possible confusion with another Navajo post office in Arizona, so it was officially recorded as *Navajoe*.

Undoubtedly, the spot for this store was selected largely because of the proximity of the great Kiowa-Comanche Indian reservation whose border was only three miles away and of the cattle trail which passed four miles to the west. In addition it was in the midst of fertile lands and the high mountains furnished a picturesque and convenient landmark for the embryo town. There were in addition the promotional activities of the man who was in some respects the father of Navajoe—the professional booster, J. S. Works.

Navajoe lay within the limits of the area, bounded by the two Red rivers and the hundredth meridian, which was claimed by Texas and had been organized by that state as a county as early as 1860. This claim the government of the United States disputed, asserting that the real Red River was the South Fork of that stream and in consequence Greer County was really outside the limits of Texas and so part of the public domain of the United States.

Joseph S. Works was a typical pioneer of the promoter type. He was a tall, spare individual who always wore a buckskin shirt and his hair in long curls reaching to his shoulders. Because of his peculiar dress he was commonly known as "Buckskin Joe." Apparently he became interested in the Greer County lands about 1887 or possibly earlier. At any rate he came to the site of Navajoe about that time and erected for himself and family a small house of the "half dugout" type which he asserted cost only thirty-five dollars to build. In addition he built a hotel to accommodate land seekers. He was energetic and ambitious, with wide contacts and ample experience in land promotion. His enthusiasm for Greer County, particularly that part of it lying about Navajoe, was boundless. The recently completed Fort Worth and Denver Railroad extending northwest across Texas was only about fifteen miles south of the Red River. It was plain that settlers of Greer County must purchase supplies from merchants of the little towns along the line, sold to the latter by jobbers in Fort Worth. Works accordingly visited that city and told such an alluring tale of the future of Greer County that Texas businessmen supplied the funds for the printing of many thousands of copies of his little publication, *Buckskin Joe's Emigrants' Guide*, which was issued monthly for about a year. In this he extolled the beauty and fertility of Greer County in general and the area about Navajoe in particular.

Perhaps Works had considerable influence in attracting settlers to the region but though he remained at Navajoe for a year or more, he was too restless to stay long in any one place or to devote himself exclusively to any one project. In addition to booming the settlement of Greer County, he also engaged in townsite promotion and diligently sought to develop the town of Oklaunion a few miles east of Vernon, with the object of making it the chief supply point for the Greer County settlers. Doomed to disappointment here, Buckskin Joe, after the construction of the Rock Island Railroad across Oklahoma in 1891, turned his attention to booming the town of Comanche near the western border of the Chickasaw country and to urging the opening of the Kiowa-Comanche Indian reservation to settlement. While his promotional activities never proved too successful, they seem to have netted him a living until 1908, when he was granted a pension by the United States government for his services in the Civil War.

The store built and operated by Acers and Dale was quickly followed by other business establishments. Settlers were coming in, probably stimulated by the activities of Works, and taking claims in the community which they held by squatter's rights despite the warning of the President of the United States that the title to lands in Greer County was clouded and in consequence they might lose their lands. In addition the leasing of the lands of the Kiowa-Comanche Indian reservation to cattlemen gave those Indians considerable sums of "grass money" which they were eager to spend and Navajoe was their nearest trading point. Also the ranchmen purchased supplies for their men as did the foremen of herds on the trail. It was not long until the little town became a considerable center of business as judged by frontier standards.

The creation of the post office helped very considerably. Mail service from Vernon, Texas, was at first tri-weekly, and the periodic rises of Red River caused many local wits to assert that this designation only meant that the carrier went to Vernon one week and "tried to get back the next." Eventually, however, a daily service was maintained, the carrier driving only to Red River, where he met and exchanged mail bags with another coming out from Vernon.

One corner of the establishment of Acers and Dale was partitioned off for the post office, and the arrival of the mail about eight o'clock in the evening usually found most of the male population of the village, together with a number of nearby settlers, and a few cowpunchers, assembled and patiently waiting in the store. Here they sat on the counter, smoked cigarettes, chewed tobacco, and told yarns or indulged in practical jokes while waiting for "the mail to be put up." Once this was accomplished and the window opened each and every one walked up to it and solemnly inquired: "Anything for me?" Few of them ever got any mail; most of them would have been utterly astonished if they ever *had* got any mail; but asking for it was a part of a regular ritual and missing the experience was a near tragedy. All of which seems strange and a little pathetic too. In few cases did anyone in the world care enough for one of these men to write him a letter but they refused to admit it even to themselves.

North of this pioneer store another was soon built by Bennight Brothers, John and Lum. It was a long, red building housing a stock of general merchandise but it did not attract nearly as many of either customers or loafers as did the establishment of Acers and Dale. In addition to his activities as a merchant, John Bennight also served for a time as deputy sheriff.

Beyond this second store was Ed Clark's saloon. It had a long shiny bar extending along the south side complete with brass rail in front and a good-sized mirror on the wall behind it. On this wall also hung a large sign with this legend:

Since man to man has bin so unjust
I scarsely know in hoom to trust
I've trusted meny to my sorrow
So pay today, I'll trust tomorrow.

In addition to the bar, the room had two or three tables where the town's loafers and visiting cowhands sat and played poker, seven-up, or dominoes. The saloon received considerable patronage but the churchgoing element among the settlers regarded it as a den of iniquity and under the local-option laws eventually voted it out, and the town became dry except for individual importations and such patent medicines as Peruna, lemon and ginger, "electric bitters," and other so-called proprietary medicines purchased at the drug store.

This last-named business establishment stood a short distance north of the saloon and was owned and operated by W. H. H. Cranford, who sold drugs, compounded prescriptions, and did a considerable business in notions, cosmetics, and toilet articles. Among other things he sold considerable patent medicine of high alcoholic content to Indians since under the federal laws they could not be supplied with liquor. At the holiday season, he always laid in a considerable stock of Christmas goods consisting of dressing cases, manicure sets, shaving mugs, mustache cups, autograph and photograph albums, and toys. Cranford was in Navajoe but not of it. He was a slightly corpulent individual who always wore a neatly pressed suit, white celluloid collar and four-in-hand tie and was entirely lacking in any sense of humor or interest in what passed for social or civic affairs. In short he was in no sense a frontiersman. He was cold, dignified, and unresponsive, and was alleged to have poisoned marauding cats, which was probably untrue.

At the extreme opposite end of the street from the drug store was the little grocery store of John Brown and his wife. It did little business and Brown spent most of his time in warm weather sitting in a chair in front of his place of business taking his ease, his bright red socks furnishing a brilliant splash of color between the bottoms of his trouser legs and his shoes. Some of the town's loafers offered three boys a pound of candy each if they would go down there, one by one, at twenty minute intervals, call Brown aside and gravely ask what he would take for his red socks but, though the lads talked about it enthusiastically and planned it again and again, they were never able to get up enough courage to carry it through.

All of the buildings named were in a row running north and south, and all faced the east. Most of them had a porch in front with a roof supported by wooden columns and between these pillars was usually placed a long seat made of two-inch lumber, where "gentlemen of leisure" could sit during the long summer afternoons and whittle to their hearts' content. In cold weather they assembled inside about a pot-bellied stove fed with wood hauled, contrary to law, from the nearby Indian reservation. Here they told stories, played checkers, rolled and smoked cigarettes, or chewed tobacco and spat in the general direction of a flat box half filled with sand. Here practical jokes were planned and sometimes executed and the news and gossip of the little community exchanged.

Across the street from the drug store was the home of Dr. H. C. Redding, which also contained his office. Redding was for a time the only doctor of the village and its surrounding country. He was an elderly man with long whiskers, who hated Cranford with an intense hatred because the latter often prescribed and sold medicine when so requested by an ailing settler, thus depriving the doctor of a patient and a fee which he felt should rightfully be his.

South of the doctor's house and directly across from the saloon was a small unpainted church of rough lumber, originally a dance hall and skating rink but bought and transformed through the efforts of the more spiritual members of the community. Church and saloon faced one another like two duelists each battling for a cause, as indeed they were. Here services were held every Sunday when a minister was available and a revival meeting was usually held each summer. Sunday afternoons people also met at the church sometimes to sing, and Christmas festivities with a community tree were usually held there.

With the exception of a little barber shop north of John

Brown's store, these were the only buildings on Navajoe's main street during the earlier years of the town's history. Some two hundred yards southeast of a central point in this row of business houses was the City Hotel, originally built by Buckskin Joe. This was a large, unpainted building displaying a big sign which read: "Meals 25 cents." Near one corner was a tall post crowned by a large bell. Around noon and about six in the evening Aunt Matilda Smith or her husband Uncle Tom, who were proprietors of the establishment, came out and pulled the bell rope vigorously to call their hungry boarders uptown to "come and get it."

Just as pigs leisurely rooting in the woods will at the call of their owner's voice suddenly stop to listen and then with flapping ears race madly for the barn lot, so did every unattached man in town at the first sound of the bell drop whatever he was doing and start in a sort of lope down the path leading to the hotel, gathering speed at every jump until he came to a skidding halt before Aunt Matilda's well-spread table. Despite her low rates, Aunt Matilda always "set a good table" and in a community where beef sold at five or six cents a pound, frying chickens at fifteen cents each, eggs at five or ten cents a dozen, and butter at "a bit" a pound, some profits were derived from meals even at twenty-five cents each. Prices were ridiculously low and money almost unbelievably scarce.

Flour could be purchased at from a dollar to a dollar and a half a hundred pounds and settlers hauled sweet potatoes forty-five miles to the railroad and peddled them out among the residents of Vernon at fifty cents a bushel. As for actual cash, it is doubtful if some men holding down a claim ever saw fifteen dollars in real money at any one time throughout an entire year.

The ranchmen—for example, C. T. Herring, his brother, F. E. Herring, S. B. Burnett, Dan Waggoner and his son, Tom Waggoner, all of whom leased lands for grazing on the Indian reservation—were of course well-to-do, and their cowboys, who drew wages of twenty to thirty dollars a month, usually had a little money, but most settlers were extremely poor. Occasionally one would get a few days' work building fence or plowing fire guards for some cattleman or would sell a rancher a little feed but sums derived from such sources were small. Some raised a small crop of wheat but it had to be hauled forty-five miles to the railroad, where it usually brought only fifty to sixty cents a bushel; and since teams were usually small, and there was the wide sandy river to cross, it was seldom possible to haul more than twenty to twenty-five bushels in a load and the trip consumed three to four days.

In the winter, a few men eked out a small income by poisoning and skinning wolves or from hunting prairie chickens and quail, but coyote skins sold for only fifty cents and prairie chickens and quail only twenty-five and ten cents respectively at the railroad. Two or three young fellows broke horses for the Indians, usually at a price of one dollar for each year of the animal's age, which was anything but easy money.

Even though most people were very poor, however, life at Navajoe and in the surrounding community was colorful and varied. As a rule it was characterized by abundant leisure. Merchants, so called, were seldom kept busy waiting on customers and in consequence had ample time to talk, exchange gossip, and philosophize with one another or with the visitors who frequented their places of business usually only for purely social purposes. The three or four professional gamblers who specialized in playing monte with the Indians, or with an occasional Easterner with money who might be passing through, had long periods of inaction during which they played cards with one another merely for pleasure and to keep in practice, or with the local residents, or two or three cowhands. Every winter three or four cowboys laid off until spring would come to Navajoe and loaf for two or three months, visiting with their friends, playing poker or dominoes in the saloon, "getting up" and attending dances as often as possible, and in general enjoying a little vacation until time for spring work to start, when the boss called them back to riding again. All of these men, together with a few bachelor claim-holders, spent a large share of time sitting around in the stores or saloon, telling jokes or stories, or devoted themselves to arranging dances and candy breakings, courting the few girls, and as a rule enjoyed life hugely.

While in some respects the summer season may have been a bit more dull, it too was not without attractions. Picnic parties to climb the mountain and enjoy the magnificent view from its summit with dinner at some beauty spot at the foot was a favorite diversion. Groups would also make all-day trips to the sand hills along the river to gather wild plums or to Otter or Elk Creek for a fish fry.

Like every other frontier town, Navajoe had its share of unusual and picturesque characters. Among these was Uncle Billy Warren, a small, dried-up old fellow, who had been a scout for the United States Army in earlier days. He spoke the Comanche and Kiowa languages and was regarded as a man of substance, since he drew a pension of thirty dollars a month as he said "just as regular as a goose goes to water." Another interesting character was a gambler known as "Eat 'Em Up Jake" because he was alleged to have once found himself with five aces and when his eagle-eyed opponent demanded a showdown, Jake crumpled and ate the extra card to avoid being caught red-handed.

For a considerable time an elderly remittance man named Harlan lived at Navajoe, boarding at the hotel and spending a good deal of time around the saloon. He seemed to have considerable education and when drunk would talk eloquently, using numerous legal terms, which caused him to be commonly called "Judge." One day the postmaster was much surprised to receive a letter from Justice John Marshall Harlan of the United States Supreme Court inquiring about the welfare of his brother, whom the Justice had learned was now living at Navajoe. The postmaster promptly answered the letter, assuring Justice Harlan that his brother seemed to be in good health, was comfortably situated, and was highly respected when sober and well cared for when drunk, so it was not necessary to feel any uneasiness about him. No reply was ever received, and eventually "Judge" Harlan left Navajoe and drifted away no doubt to some other little frontier town that also had saloons and congenial company.

Still another interesting character was a young man commonly called "Diamond Dick" because he reached Navajoe wearing numerous large diamonds set in rings, shirt studs, cuff links, and a tie pin. Apparently he was the wayward son of a wealthy father somewhere in the East, though he was quite reticent about his family and former home. He did not drink anything like as much as did the old "Judge" but played poker for modest stakes, rode about with the cowpunchers, attended dances, and seemed to have a good time for several months, after which he too departed for some unknown destination.

One day on the mail hack from Vernon came a young man who said that he came from New York City, so he was promptly nicknamed "New York." He established a little store stocked with men's clothing, but he was active in local sporting circles and frankly stated that he had come to the West for the sole purpose of "catching suckers."

Looking about for some means of turning a more-or-less honest dollar, he thought he had found it when two drifting cowpunchers visited him and explained that they wanted to go to New Mexico but had a considerable number of horses which they would sell cheap, as they needed money for the trip. They added that the animals were ranging on the Indian reservation across the river but they would be glad to show them to him. "New York" gladly accompanied the two young fellows, who showed him some fifty head of excellent saddle horses, all bearing what they said was their brand. When a price was named which was clearly only a fraction of their real value, "New York" jumped at the chance of making some easy money and quickly closed the deal. The cowhands gave him a bill of sale, received their money, and departed, but when their new owner rounded up the horses and started for Vernon to sell them, he met a keen-eyed cowboy working for one of the ranchmen grazing cattle on the reservation who noted that every horse bore the well-known brand of his employer. This cowhand notified the deputy sheriff, and "New York" was promptly arrested and lodged in jail where he died a few weeks before the date set for his trial.

Another very interesting character was J. M. Ferris, commonly known as Jim, who lived with his wife and some nine children in a three-room house three quarters of a mile south of town. Ferris had been a Texas Ranger, secret-service man, and deputy sheriff, and so was a professional peace officer trained in that hardest of all schools, the Texas-Mexican border. He became deputy sheriff in that part of the county after the departure of the Bennights and served as the representative of law and order in a wide region. He was a spare, blue-eyed man of medium height, with a gentle, kindly voice, and who always walked, Indian-like, with a soft, catlike tread. Those who knew him best said that when his blue eyes began to shine and his voice fairly dripped sweetness it was time to climb a tree and ask the reason later!

When Tom Anderson, a wild nineteen-year-old boy, shot his employer through the shoulder and fled on foot for the Indian reservation, carrying his Winchester with him, Deputy Jim set out on horseback in pursuit, armed with a long shotgun strapped to his saddle. Ferris overtook the young chap about noon but Tom had his own ideas about submitting to arrest. At two hundred and fifty yards he shot Jim through the thigh, inflicting a bad flesh wound, and would have killed him with the second shot if the deputy had not swung over behind his horse. The lad then took refuge in a thicket and Ferris, leaving a cowpuncher to keep watch at a safe distance, rode home, dressed his wound, and then rode uptown to gather a posse.

It was Saturday afternoon and almost the entire population of the community, masculine, feminine, and canine, had assembled as usual in Navajoe. Every man and boy who could find a horse and any kind of shooting iron followed Jim, and to the number of something like a hundred they bombarded the young outlaw for three hours without scoring a hit. It was not a one-sided battle, however. From a shallow pit he had scooped out in the thicket, the youngster returned the fire with an uncanny skill, putting a bullet through the hat of one of his too inquisitive besiegers and missing two or three more by such a narrow margin as to make them decidedly uncomfortable. Finally, running short of ammunition, he tied a handkerchief to the stock of his rifle and lifting it above the tops of the bushes, came out and surrendered. He was promptly lodged in jail, from which he escaped a month later and disappeared to parts unknown.

The people of the county-seat town of Mangum, thirty-five miles away, took up a collection for the benefit of Deputy Ferris and sent him thirty-five dollars. Jim returned the money the same day, accompanied by a brief note thanking these people for their kindness but asserting that the only expense incurred as a result of his wound had been fifteen cents for a bar of Castile soap and ten cents for a bottle of turpentine. He added that he had been able to pay this himself but if he had not, he was quite sure that some of his nearby neighbors would have been glad to make him a loan. Of such independent stuff were the early Oklahoma pioneers made.

It is impossible to name any considerable number of the many picturesque and colorful individuals who lived for a time in or near Old Navajoe. Among them were two brothers—both physicians—Doctors Joe and Dee Reynolds, who settled in the little town and became for a time competitors of Doctor Redding. None of the three had much practice, for the people of the community were unusually strong and healthy. Any who were not had long before been weeded out. Doctor Joe added to his income by hunting prairie chickens and hanging the birds up on the north side of his house until he had what his wife called "a real good chance of them," when he sent them to Vernon by some passing freight wagon.

In addition there were the elderly Mr. Rusler, who because of his age was always Santa Claus at the community Christmas tree, and the Yeakley Brothers, who grazed seven or eight hundred sheep on the mountains and were the only shepherds in the entire region. There were also John Passmore and Joe Lee Jackson, who eked out a precarious living playing monte or poker with the Indians, Dave Davis, broncbuster extraordinary, and Old Man Fink, who lived for music, and always present when people met to sing, and who had been known to leave his team standing in the field while he hurried to the house and wrote the words of a new song to be sung to the tune of "When the

Roses Come Again"! Some were good, Christian men and others worthless men, but all were generous, unselfish, and kind in their dealings with others. Almost without exception they were hospitable, deeply respectful toward all women, and every man of them would have gladly given the shirt off his back to someone in need, though it must be admitted that no person in his right mind would, as a rule, have wanted the shirt of any one of them!

Tragedy occasionally stalked the town's one street, as when George Gordon shot and killed W. N. Howard. The latter was a one-armed man from the hills of Kentucky who had brought his family to Greer County and settled on a claim about three miles north of Navajoe. The basis of the quarrel between the two men has long been forgotten but both were hot-tempered and dangerous. One afternoon they met on the street, Howard reached for his gun only to discover that he had left it at home, and Gordon shot him. Despite the fact that his opponent was unarmed, Gordon was acquitted on the grounds of self-defense, the jury probably reasoning that a man who sees his adversary reach for his hip is justified in assuming that the latter has a gun and cannot be expected to wait long enough to discover his mistake.

The town had periods of excitement, too. One of these was in 1891 when Chief Polant of the Kiowa tribe was killed a few miles north of Navajoe by a young cowpuncher. The belligerent old chief had left the reservation and crossed the river into Greer County to demand an explanation of why some of his people had been refused a gift of beeves. He emphasized his remarks by drawing his Winchester from its scabbard, whereupon the young cowhand promptly shot him through the head and then made his way to Navajoe to relate what he had done and ask for protection. A large number of Kiowas quickly armed themselves and demanded that the young man be surrendered to them. This was, of course, refused but an Indian war seemed imminent and the nearby settlers hastily brought their wives and children to Navajoe for safety. All the men in the community gathered at town, armed to the teeth and prepared to defend themselves and

their families from the threatened attack. News of the affair
reached Colonel Hugh L. Scott, the Commanding Officer at Fort
Sill, who led his cavalry in a forced march to the Kiowa camp
on Elk Creek and at last persuaded the angry Kiowas that it
would be folly to start a war which could only result in their
own destruction.

Within a few years considerable changes came to the town of
Navajoe. "Buckskin Joe" had departed in search of a more profitable venture in promotion. The opening of the Cheyenne-
Arapaho reservation to settlement on April 19, 1892, took several citizens of Navajoe to that region. Among these were Tom
and Aunt Matilda Smith, who pulled down the hotel, hauled the
lumber to Cordell, and rebuilt it in that newly opened town, and
H. P. Dale, who sold his interest in the store to his partner and
took up a homestead in the "Cheyenne Country." W. H. Acers
operated the store for more than a year, but with the opening of
the Cherokee Outlet on September 16, 1893, he sold it and
drifted up to that region.

The post office was transferred to Cranford's store, and he
then enlarged his place and put in a stock of dry goods and clothing on one side, retaining the shelves on the other side for drugs,
medicines, and notions. He also added a room for the post office
and its lobby and finished up an attic room above the store where
he kept surplus merchandise, empty packing cases, and a stock
of coffins of assorted sizes.

About the middle nineties a wave of outlawry swept over
Greer County and the surrounding region when Red Buck
Weightman, Joe Beckham, and two or three of their comrades
appeared in that area and turned their attention to robbing
stores, stealing horses, and other forms of deviltry. Cranford as
postmaster often had considerable sums of money in his safe,
since there was no bank nearer than Vernon and remittances
were usually made by money order. In consequence he eventually developed an almost morbid fear of being robbed. In an-
ticipation of this he not only buckled on a heavy Colt revolver
the latter part of every afternoon but also installed a bed in the
attic and hired a young man as assistant in the store and post

office, with the provision that he should go armed and sleep in the attic at night among the coffins! In addition, he often talked of installing a wood vise behind the counter beside the opening leading to the rest of the store and clamping a cocked pistol in it when he locked up at night, with a string attached to its trigger, looped around a nail behind it, and stretched across this opening. With such a device prepared, he declared that anyone breaking in who started to go behind the counter would shoot himself through the legs.

Evidently he considered any such protection unnecessary so long as he had a clerk sleeping in the attic, but in 1895 Cranford lost the post office and decided to remove to Cloud Chief in the Cheyenne Country and open a drug store there. Here he fitted up his long-talked-of booby trap for malefactors but unfortunately his wife became suddenly ill one night and he ran hastily down to the store to get some medicine for her and in his excitement completely forgot the product of his own ingenuity. It worked all too well! Cranford shot a leg off and like Peter Stuyvesant of historic fame, was doomed to stump through the remaining years of his life on a wooden leg! Moreover, he lacked even the consolation of the sympathy of his neighbors since no one who knew his story ever felt particularly sorry for him.

As more and more of the first businessmen and residents of Navajoe departed, others came in to take their places. In 1896 the Supreme Court, in the case of the *United States* vs. *Texas*, held that the South Fork of Red River was the principal stream and therefore Greer County was not a part of Texas. This was followed by a special act of Congress attaching the region to Oklahoma Territory. With the cloud removed from land titles, many more settlers came in to take up homesteads and the little town grew in importance as a business center. Bennight Brothers sold their store and returned to Indian Territory. The church-going part of the population voted out the saloon under local-option laws, and Ed Clark returned to his old home state of Kentucky.

George Blalock came from Texas with his family, purchased the claim adjoining the town on the south, and opened a general merchandise store in the building formerly occupied by the establishment of Acers and Dale. W. Z. Peters replaced Cranford as postmaster, and a new hotel was built on the main street of town. John Brown's wife died, and he sold his little stock of groceries and drifted away to parts unknown.

Blalock's store remained the chief business enterprise for some years, but he was eventually elected county sheriff and removed to Mangum, which was the county seat. Other business establishments with new owners followed one another in rapid succession, though a few old-timers remained. Conn and Higgins opened a general merchandise store in the former Cranford building. A hardware store was established by the Martin Brothers which eventually came to be operated by the two Ricks Brothers. Conn and Higgins sold their business, and Blackwell and Akin came in and opened a dry goods and clothing store, followed by Bailey Brothers with a stock of general merchandise. An elderly individual named White operated a small grocery store. A little wagon yard was built, a meat market, a pool hall, and a new barber shop were established. The little boxlike schoolhouse made of twelve-inch boards with knotholes which the older, tobacco-chewing boys, endowed with a spirit of daring and a sure aim, felt had been placed there by Divine Providence, was torn down and a new one of two rooms erected at the western edge of town. Ben Hawkins continued for years to operate his blacksmith shop at the same old stand, with Old Man Chivers, who sang hymns to the accompaniment of his ringing anvil, as his chief competitor. Several new residences were erected where the businessmen lived with their families and a few settlers removed to town in the winter in order to send their children to school.

Life in Navajoe was still varied and colorful and was not without its frontier characteristics, but gradually changes were creeping in. Cowhands and ranchmen were less in evidence, and most of the men who came in to "do a little trading" or merely for the social stimulus derived from "going to town" were homesteaders or their grown-up sons. More farming was carried on in the surrounding country and a little more sophistication became apparent. Men remained largely in the majority in the community and an attractive young woman still had plenty of suitors, but not to the extent apparent in earlier years, when the appearance of a new girl in town or anywhere near it was an event of major importance.

In the late nineties, Navajoe was struck by a mining boom which brought in a considerable number of new people, most of them entirely unlike any of the earlier inhabitants of the town. The Navajo Mountains are the most southwestern group of the Wichitas, which extend east some forty miles or nearly to Fort Sill. For many years old-timers had solemnly asserted that "thar's gold in them thar hills." There were legends of lost Spanish mines, and it was even declared that the Indians knew where vast stores of gold could be found, a rumor which gained credence by the average Indian's tendency to make sport of the white man.

About 1896 there appeared in the little town a lean, bewhiskered individual about forty years old named Edson L. Hewes. He came from Nevada, where he had been a prospector and could see a color of gold in any pan of dirt, regardless of its source, that he decided to wash out. Hewes was a remittance man, receiving every week a money order for two dollars from the New Orleans post office, since he had once lived in that city and apparently still had relatives there. He had studied law and had been a journalist and apparently a good many other things, but for years he had followed the open road more or less as a hobo. He had marched on Washington from Nevada with that state's contingent of Coxey's army and was an ardent champion of democracy and the underdog and the bitter foe of the "interests" and of all aristocrats. He had dreams of writing a book called *The Wandering American,* but apparently could never get around to it. Hewes was certain that there were rich deposits of gold in the Wichitas, so he staked some claims in the Navajo Mountains, found a worthless young fellow as partner, and fitted up a shallow cave among the giant rocks of his favorite claim as a dwelling place. He and his partner worked diligently at panning the mountain dirt, carried their groceries on their backs from the

Navajoe stores, and, while dining on cheese and crackers, talked of the great wealth to be theirs in the near future!

Other so-called miners came in, some with wives and a troop of ragged children. More were single men, most of them old, and virtually all shabby and unkempt and without money, property, or ambition to work at anything except digging for gold. They included such men as Lige Williams, Robert Rayel, the Petersons, father and son, and a number of others.

Some of these told colorful tales of their profitable mining experiences in the past. One asserted that in a remote canyon of the Rocky Mountains he had once turned over a rock with a crowbar and found thirty-three thousand dollars in gold nuggets beneath it. One such experience would doubtless keep the average man busy turning over rocks for the rest of his life! Another shabby, long-whiskered old man who, now that the saloon had been closed, spent most of his scanty, occasional funds at the drug store for Peruna at a dollar a bottle was alleged to have once sold a mining claim in Colorado for two hundred thousand dollars. What he had done with the money no one knew, but someone was heard to remark that it probably went for two hundred thousand bottles of Peruna!

The Navajo Mountains not offering sufficient field for their activities, the miners began to cross the river and operate in the rough mountains on the Indian reservation along the headwaters of Otter Creek. Here they staked mining claims, built little shacks, and, regardless of the fact that United States law prohibited such occupation of Indian lands, eventually secured the establishment of a post office. It was called Wildman in honor of a prosperous citizen of one of the nearby Greer County towns who had given some aid and encouragement to mining ventures. Since the miners frequently shifted the center of their activities the post office was placed on wheels and so resembled a field kitchen or the cook shack of a threshing crew. It followed its patrons about over a considerable area, and in consequence, the mail carrier coming out from Navajoe two or three times a week always started without knowing his exact destination. In the early summer of 1901 a troop of cavalry was sent out from Fort

Sill to destroy the miners' shacks and escort their owners to the reservation line where they were left with a warning not to return.

The mining boom collapsed and was succeeded by something of much greater importance—the opening of the Kiowa-Comanche Indian lands to white settlement. This occurred late in the summer of 1901 by a lottery. All persons desirous of securing a homestead in that region were required to register their names either at Fort Sill or El Reno. Cards bearing their names were then placed in great hollow wheels, thoroughly mixed and drawn out, and the 160-acre tracts, to the number of 13,000, were selected by the lucky registrants in the order that their names were drawn.

Virtually every young man about Navajoe who was twenty-one or more years of age hastened to Fort Sill to register, since there was no longer any government land of value left unclaimed in Greer County. They were accompanied by many older men who had come into the Navajoe community too late to secure land there. It seemed that the opening of these Kiowa-Comanche lands to settlement should have greatly aided the growth and prosperity of Navajoe, located so close to their border, by rounding out the town's trade territory and bringing in much new business.

As a matter of fact it was the beginning of the end. Not a few of the citizens of the town or the surrounding country secured land in the newly opened region, to which they promptly removed. Far more important, the settlement of this large territory brought in railroads and the establishment of new and prosperous towns. Even before registration for lands began, the Rock Island Railway Company was constructing a line south through Lawton, and trains reached that city early in the autumn of 1901. The Blackwell, Enid, and Southwestern was also building a line south to Vernon on which were located Hobart, Snyder, and Frederick. Soon after the construction of these railroads, the Frisco extended a branch from Oklahoma City southwest to Quanah, Texas, on which its officials laid out a town called Headrick only seven or eight miles southeast of Navajoe. This marked the end of the little town which had flourished for more than fifteen years. Every business establishment was promptly removed to Headrick. The smaller buildings, whether residences or shops and stores, were jacked up, placed on wheels and hauled to the new town. Larger ones were wrecked and the lumber either transferred to Headrick to be used in building there or sold to some settler for the construction of a farmhouse or barn. The church and schoolhouse, both growing old and dilapidated, were torn down and a new school building erected on the road half a mile west. The town site was acquired by a farmer who plowed and planted the land in cotton and kafir corn and Navajoe was no more. Even the new school did not remain long. The consolidated school movement was sweeping the country so the district was merged with four or five others, and a new, modern building called Friendship Consolidated School was erected a few miles away. Only the little cemetery on its low, sandy hill and the bits of broken glass and china occasionally turned up by the farmer's plow remain today as mute reminders of the thriving little town which was for so many years the commercial and social center of a large region.

Navajoe was never a large town as size is thought of in Oklahoma now, but for many years it was the largest and most important one which a traveler would pass near in a journey north over the Western Cattle Trail from Vernon, Texas, to Woodward, a distance of some two hundred miles. Moreover, it was the trading center for the people of an area far larger than is the so-called trade territory of almost any Oklahoma town today with a population of upwards of twenty thousand.

Importance, however, does not depend entirely upon size. Except for the fact that it was located near the border of the Kiowa-Comanche reservation and in consequence had much trade from these Indians as well as that of the ranchmen who leased their lands, Navajoe was typical of hundreds of other little prairie towns of its time, not alone in western Oklahoma but throughout the length and breadth of a great region extending north to the Canadian border. Therein lies the justification for telling its story.

Yet, in some respects, Navajoe was unique. Not so much because of the picturesque and colorful character of many of its inhabitants, for every town has its interesting and colorful individuals, but because Navajoe, like Peter Pan, never grew up. Always it was young, lusty, and vigorous with hopes and dreams for a future that were never to be realized. Like the gay young soldier cut down by the enemy's bullet, the little town never knew either the comforts and responsibilities of middle life or the pains and infirmities of old age. Some other towns secured a railroad, a county seat, and industrial or commercial enterprises which caused them to grow to the stature of thriving little cities with paved streets, water works, chambers of commerce, and civic clubs. Others less fortunate found their trade and population drained away to some local metropolis by improved roads and automobiles, leaving them only as decadent, sleepy little villages where a few elderly people still cling to a spot hallowed by memories and live in a past now gone forever. Navajoe met neither of these fates. In the full vigor of youth it simply vanished from the earth.

Few strangers ever visit the site of Old Navajoe now. Once in a great while an automobile, perhaps bearing the license tag of another state, will stop at the little grass-grown cemetery and a gray-haired man alight to spend a few hours cutting weeds or planting some rose bushes about the grave of one who nurtured and cared for him in his childhood of more than half a century ago. Sometimes he may linger at his task until the sun has gone down in a radiant glory of crimson and gold and twilight begins to wrap the wide prairie in an ever darkening mantle. Then as he returns to his car and pauses for a moment to watch the first stars peep over the dark bulk of the Navajo Mountains he may almost imagine that he can hear the ring of ghostly spurs as some lean, brown cowhand rides in to visit his old familiar haunts where these pioneer people lived and loved, and dreamed of the future in the ruddy dawn of western Oklahoma's history.

Index

Index